ACADEMIC LIBRARY OUTREACH

Beyond the Campus Walls

EDITED BY NANCY COURTNEY

D1500445

A Member of the Greenwood Publishing Group

Westport, Connecticut • London

Library of Congress Cataloging-in-Publication Data

Academic library outreach: beyond the campus walls / edited by Nancy Courtney.

    p. cm.

    Includes bibliographical references and index.

    ISBN 978-1-59158-725-5 (alk. paper)

    1. Library outreach programs—United States—Case studies. 2. Academic libraries—Off-campus services—United States—Case studies. 3. Libraries and community—United States—Case studies. I. Courtney, Nancy.

    Z711.7A25   2009

    021.20973–dc22   2008031206

British Library Cataloguing in Publication Data is available.

Library of Congress Catalog Card Number: 2008031206
ISBN: 978-1-59158-725-5

First published in 2009

Libraries Unlimited, 88 Post Road West, Westport, CT 06881
A Member of the Greenwood Publishing Group, Inc.
www.lu.com

Printed in the United States of America

The paper used in this book complies with the Permanent Paper Standard issued by the National Information Standards Organization (Z39.48–1984).

10 9 8 7 6 5 4 3 2 1

CONTENTS

1

BREAKING OUT OF OUR SHELL: EXPANDING THE DEFINITION OF OUTREACH IN ACADEMIC LIBRARIES

Nancy Courtney

Outreach is in the eyes of the beholder. Librarians seem to have difficulty agreeing on a definition of outreach, but, like good art, they know it when they see (or create) it. Many would agree that it means reaching out to those outside the library, but opinions differ on specifically to whom. Some would say to the community or to our users or to our clientele. Despite the assertions of many writers of articles describing outreach efforts, most academic librarians assume that outreach is meant for their own campus communities, specifically faculty and students. In fact, outreach is frequently defined more as a form of public relations (again with the "public" limited to the campus) or general raising of awareness of library resources and services. In this context, the library is certain of whom it wants to reach, and the questions are ones of methodology (brochures, newsletters, librarian office hours, chat reference, etc.) and measures of success (usually more use of services—higher gate counts, reference transactions, bibliographic instruction classes, etc.). In their study of academic library outreach position announcements, Boff, Singer, and Stearns (2006, 139) identified three broad categories of outreach positions: distance education, multicultural services, and what they called "specialized outreach" or "outreach to unique communities that require specialized collections or services." The first two categories were aimed at services to a clientele of registered students and faculty and represented the bulk of the sample. The specialized category did include positions whose responsibilities were aimed at external communities but was limited to only twenty position announcements in a thirty-year period.

Once the concept of outreach is limited to external audiences, the question turns to what is being offered. Access to library resources on-site is the most basic service and often is the extent of outreach. Most academic libraries, both public and private, allow unaffiliated users access to their library buildings and, with it, access to print materials and reference service. A somewhat smaller number also give borrowing privileges to varying categories of users, some quite liberal (Courtney 2003). It is unclear to what extent unaffiliated users are given access to electronic resources in libraries as libraries increasingly require user logins on public access machines and have replaced most journals, indexing tools, and many reference tools with electronic equivalents. Remote access to library resources for external users is rare, exemplifying the traditional library bias toward bringing people into the library and an unwillingness or inability to deal with the complexity of licensing issues. Other examples of basic outreach may include extending electronic reference service to external users or opening to the public programming that is already being created for the campus community, such as exhibits and lectures.

Libraries that want to take the next step into outreach usually focus on unique collections or services to targeted populations. Special collections is an area that is well suited to outreach efforts in that the materials are not commonly held and, as individual collections, are more likely to be of interest to an on-campus small group but a larger, perhaps geographically dispersed group of off-campus parties. Services to targeted populations vary with the interests of individual libraries and librarians but often include the local business community and high schools.

WHY DO OUTREACH?

The question of why to do outreach can consist of two parts: why do academic libraries do outreach to external users and why should they? In her overview of the literature on academic library outreach, Tina Schneider (2003, 201) identified three factors that determine libraries' involvement in outreach to the community: "whether a need is expressed from outside the academy, whether they see their mission as an invitation to pursue an action on their own accord, or whether they construct a form of outreach in response to a specific problem or crisis." Most outreach activities seem to fall in the middle category, and, in fact, throughout the literature descriptions of outreach projects point to one, two, or a small group of people whose inspiration initiated the project. Mission is sometimes invoked but almost as an afterthought. Library mission statements are often vague about specifics and seem most often to be trotted out to justify either doing or not doing something that was already trending in a certain direction. How often do we really let our activities flow from the mission? For that matter, how closely are library mission statements tied to that of their colleges or universities?

Kellogg Commission—The Engaged Institution

The idea of outreach seems to have renewed vigor on many university campuses, and now is a good time for libraries to take a closer look at the goals and activities in which the campus is involved. In 1996 the National Association of State Universities and Land-Grant Colleges (NASULGC) formed a commission funded by the W. K. Kellogg Foundation to make recommendations on the future of public universities. A series of reports was produced including one entitled *Returning to Our Roots: The Engaged Institution* (Kellogg Commission 1999). This document sets forth an agenda for public involvement that has had an important impact on many public university campuses. Although aimed at public institutions, the principles articulated within may also be of interest to smaller, private institutions for whom issues of relevance to the community, accountability to trustees and donors, and recruitment of students are also important.

The Commission's report points to a proud history of outreach and service by public universities but also to a growing frustration on the part of the public. Academe is too often seen as unresponsive to community needs, slow, bureaucratic, confusing, too focused on rural rather than urban issues, and inclined to rest on its laurels. At the same time, universities are faced with budget pressures, demands for more accountability and productivity, and financial support that has shifted away from the institution and is given in the form of direct student aid (Kellogg Commission 1999, 20–21). Student demographics have also changed, bringing demands for more flexible scheduling and postprofessional educational opportunities (Kellogg Commission 1999, 29–30).

The commission also promotes the idea of engagement rather than outreach.

By engagement, we refer to institutions that have redesigned their teaching, research, and extension and service functions to become even more sympathetically and productively involved with their communities, however community may be defined. Engagement goes well beyond extension, conventional outreach, and even most conceptions of public service. Inherited concepts emphasize a one-way process in which the university transfers its expertise to key constituents. Embedded in the engagement ideal is a commitment to sharing and reciprocity. By engagement the Commission envisions partnerships, two-way streets defined by mutual respect among the partners for what each brings to the table. An institution that responds to these imperatives can properly be called what the Kellogg Commission has come to think of as an "engaged institution." (Kellogg Commission 1999, 9)

Two key concepts to keep in mind in this definition is that engagement or outreach is not seen just as a service activity but an integral part of the teaching and research mission of the university as well, and that engagement is meant to be a two-way street between the university and its community partners, not just a bestowing of favors upon the public.

The report offers a seven-point test of characteristics of the engaged institution. These are responsiveness, respect for partners, academic neutrality, accessibility, integration (of scholarship with service and teaching missions—does institutional climate foster outreach, service, and engagement?), coordination, and resource partnerships (how is everything paid for?). For academic libraries, accessibility stands out:

Our institutions are confusing to outsiders. We need to find ways to help inexperienced potential partners negotiate this complex structure so that what we have to offer is more readily available. Do we properly publicize our activities and resources? Have we made a concentrated effort to increase community awareness of the resources and programs available from us that might be useful? Above all, can we honestly say that our expertise is equally accessible to all the constituencies of concern within our states and communities, including minority constituents? (Kellogg Commission 1999, 12)

The Commission also addresses the need for the engaged university to deal with issues of institutional climate, such as

- "the role of engagement within the university mission so that it is seen both as a central purpose and as a means of enhancing the student experience;

- the organizational dimensions of engagement so that success does not have to depend on serendipity, individual influence, or a charismatic leader;
- the reward and benefits structure for faculty and staff (and students), and the possibility of incorporating "engagement" into that structure; and
- a variety of tools for financing engagement in the midst of constraints on resources." (Kellogg Commission 1999, 39)

These are all pertinent issues for academic libraries seeking to engage in outreach projects. It is important that outreach is seen as central to the institution's (and by extension the library's) mission, that it is not just the personal project of one or two people within the library who are committed to its success, that it is seen as a part of the librarians' jobs and not just as a service activity, and that funding or the encouragement to seek outside funding for outreach is provided.

THE LIBRARY IN THE ENGAGED INSTITUTION

Libraries should take time to examine the outreach mission on their campuses. Although the mission statement may be broad, other documents may be more specific. On any campus the academic affairs or the provost's office generally has a planning document that outlines goals and strategies. Does this include outreach to the community? Has the college or university president articulated specific goals for outreach? Individual departments or schools may have program review documents that they would be willing to share. If the campus is pushing outreach, the departments will often address this in their own documents. This is a good way to get the library's departmental liaisons involved. Examine these documents for hints of ways in which the library can support the outreach goals and activities of individual faculty or departments. Does the campus have a central outreach office? Who are the faculty members involved in service-learning activities? Is there a campus liaison with the K–12 community? Are there institutional grant programs to fund outreach activities?

Consider the place of outreach in performance evaluations and distinguish between an individual's service activity and creation of or participation in a structured outreach program either based in the library or in collaboration with other campus units. Are librarians encouraged to seek grant funding, and are there support mechanisms in place for proposal writing, budget preparation, and matching funds? Consider how projects are proposed and how the decisions are made to support or not support them. Has the library developed a plan for reviewing proposals?

Investigate the existence of outreach personnel in community organizations, including museums, arts organizations, and the public library. Set up appointments with these people to discuss ways in which you might collaborate. Many funding organizations now stress or require partnerships and collaborations when seeking grants, so other organizations may be happy to hear from you. Like many members of the public, they may associate libraries only with books and not at first see how a library could be a potential partner. Be prepared to make suggestions that go beyond traditional library activities, but it isn't necessary to have a specific project in mind.

Librarians typically have wanted patrons to come into the library to use our rich resources, but today's reality is that users want the convenience of accessing materials where they are. Targeted outreach populations naturally will also want this.

Unfortunately, while the shift to online resources has made accessing materials ever more convenient for our campus communities, licensing restrictions have seemingly made remote access impossible for unaffiliated users and, in some cases where licenses have not been carefully negotiated, for unaffiliated users onsite. This is an area that the library that is serious about engagement needs to address. We need to get beyond saying no. This may mean working directly with providers to be able to offer remote access to limited populations for limited time periods. This may include a single high school class for a particular semester or a group of corporate scientists working with university faculty on a particular research project (where access would be constrained for research purposes only). Certain community professionals partnering with the university on specific projects may be eligible for visiting or temporary faculty status, allowing them affiliated access to resources for a specified period of time. With some effort, creative solutions to remote access can be found.

Libraries can also look beyond access to books and journals to other resources that might be made available. An online institutional repository might be opened up to collect and preserve materials from community populations. This could include archives and collections of community organizations, research created by high school students participating in university-school programs, or journals and other publications produced in the community. So far, institutional repositories have focused on preserving access to completed work, but libraries should consider a more fluid online platform available to offer space for work on collaborative projects or other types of work that will be ongoing.

The Kellogg Commission report also stresses the importance to our own students of our institutions' involvement in engagement. Students who participate in engagement "acquire a sense of citizenship and community responsibility and stewardship; they develop valuable employment skills; and they broaden their horizons and experiences" (p. 30). Libraries should look for opportunities for outreach that involve students directly in project activities. This may include collaborating with faculty teaching service-learning courses or developing service learning taught by librarians. In this way, students are a resource for accomplishing outreach activities and also benefit from them.

CONCLUSION

The chapters in this book present a variety of ways that different academic libraries have pursued outreach projects and the philosophies of service that are behind them. They encompass service to K–12 populations and the general public, information literacy, events and programming, special collections, and medical and law library outreach. But they should not be construed as the last word in outreach. Academic libraries need to look beyond traditional services to develop innovative programs and services that enhance their institutions' abilities as engaged institutions.

REFERENCES

Boff, Colleen, Carol Singer, and Beverly Stearns. "Reaching Out to the Underserved: More Than Thirty Years of Outreach Job Ads." *Journal of Academic Librarianship* 32, no. 2 (March 2006): 137–147.

Courtney, Nancy. "Unaffiliated Users' Access to Academic Libraries: A Survey." *Journal of Academic Librarianship* 29, no. 1 (January-February 2003): 3–7.

Kellogg Commission on the Future of State and Land-Grant Universities. *Returning to Our Roots: The Engaged Institution*. Washington, D.C.: National Association of State Universities and Land-Grant Colleges, Office of Public Affairs, 1999.

Schneider, Tina. "Outreach: Why, How and Who? Academic Libraries and Their Involvement in the Community." *Reference Librarian* 82 (2003): 199–213.

Part 1

K–12 AND INFORMATION LITERACY

2

REACHING FORWARD: THREE HIGH SCHOOL OUTREACH INITIATIVES AT KENT STATE UNIVERSITY

Kenneth J. Burhanna, Julie A. Gedeon, Mary Lee Jensen, and Barbara F. Schloman

In the late 1990s movements to align K–12 education with higher education began to surface around the United States. States like Georgia, Illinois, Oregon, and Maryland embarked on K–16 reform projects (Kirst and Venezia 2004), and educators at all levels began to take up the question of educational alignment. In 2000 the U.S. Department of Education partnered with a number of foundations to create the National Commission on the High School Senior Year. Among the findings of the Commission's preliminary report was that "the K–12 system is poorly aligned and has not established reliable lines of communication with postsecondary education and the world of work" (2001, 31). At the same time, universities and colleges started to establish first-year experience programs to help college students succeed and persist.

At Kent State University (KSU), librarians began to ask questions such as, "What do our students know when they arrive on campus?" and "How have they been prepared for college-level research?" Previously informal encounters with high school teachers who requested visits to the KSU Library began to take on more serious tones, as librarians discussed these concerns with their K–12 colleagues. Surprisingly, they found that high school teachers and library media specialists were asking similar questions: "What should we be teaching our students about college research?" and "How can we measure their information literacy skills?"

A desire to respond more effectively to these questions and concerns, as well as a long-standing interest in improving student information literacy skills, led Libraries and Media Services at KSU to become a founding partner in the Institute for Library and Information Literacy Education (ILILE) in 2003. ILILE was established through federal grants from the Institute of Museum and Library Services (IMLS) and the U.S. Department of Education to provide local, regional, and national leadership to aid collaboration among K–12 teachers and school library media specialists who are concerned with advancing library and information literacy in the K–12 school curriculum. KSU librarians focused their work with ILILE in two areas: (1) information literacy instruction outreach to high schools and (2) the evaluation of the information literacy skills of K–12 students.

KSU librarians led early discussions and collaborations through ILILE to begin to build connections between high school and university educators. Academic librarians, high school teachers, and school library media specialists throughout Ohio were contacted and invited to several meetings. During initial discussions, these educators established two working groups: one to discover and map the organization, information literacy standards, and collaborative structures within Ohio's secondary education system and another to design and create shareable tools, lessons, and learning objects aimed at easing the high school to college transition of students. From these early efforts, KSU librarians developed three initiatives that seek to reach forward and collaborate with educators and students to improve college preparation and aid information literacy instruction at the high school level. These three initiatives, which will be presented and discussed in this chapter, are as follows:

1. Informed Transitions—The KSU Libraries' outreach program to high schools, which provides college transition experiences to approximately 450 local high school students a year.
2. Transitioning to College: Helping You Succeed—A Web-based set of tools and resources designed to aid high school educators in preparing students for using academic libraries. A key feature of the site is a set of five streaming videos that depict first-year students learning about academic libraries and transitioning to college.
3. TRAILS: Tool for Real-Time Assessment of Information Literacy Skills—A freely available, standards-based online knowledge assessment targeting a variety of information literacy skills appropriate to high school students.

INFORMED TRANSITIONS: OUTREACH PROGRAM TO HIGH SCHOOLS

KSU librarians, using knowledge gained through their ILILE grant work, developed a library outreach program for local high schools during the 2004–2005 academic year. KSU librarians had been informally working with high schools for a number of years, but now they wanted to formalize these collaborations, committing time and resources. The hire of a first-year experience (FYE) librarian in the summer of 2004 secured the needed staff resources, and with the help of ILILE, they were able to create an instructional classroom devoted to visits by high school students. The outreach program, named *Informed Transitions* and coordinated by the FYE librarian, offers a standing invitation to local high schools to plan instructional visits to the Main Library at KSU. The program's mission is to ease student transition to college, with special emphasis on library experiences. Its specific objectives are to:

• Instruct students in information literacy skills helpful for college preparation and a successful transition from high school to college.

- Promote in students positive attitudes toward academic libraries.
- Help students succeed in the near-term on their high school assignments.
- Create collaborations between high school librarians and teachers and academic librarians.
- Promote higher education in general and an interest in KSU specifically.

These objectives also summarize the main benefits of outreach programming to high schools. High school educators benefit from access to additional resources to help them complete their lessons and ultimately better equip their students for success after high school. High school students benefit from information literacy instruction and an introduction to academic libraries, making them more likely to feel comfortable and have success using the services and resources of academic libraries in the future. Academic librarians and high school educators also benefit from their collaboration, each gaining insight into the work and challenges of the other, each improving their approaches and instruction with their own students. The academic library and the university also benefit. The program connects the library and university to its surrounding communities, helps prepare potential new students, and introduces prospective students to the university in a novel and engaging way.

Program Description

KSU librarians first needed to develop program guidelines and policies to guide their work, and they also needed a mechanism for making this information available. They created a program website (www.library.kent.edu/highschool) to meet these purposes. The website provides an overview of the program, including the objectives mentioned above. It offers scheduling guidelines, which identify ideal group sizes, dates within the KSU academic calendar during which visits are preferred, chaperone requirements, and the preferred lead time on scheduling visits. The website also sets instructional expectations for visits. The program prefers to provide instruction that supports the high school research assignments of students, creating an important point of need that bridges high school work with that of the college student. In the absence of a high school assignment, KSU librarians provide a college transition assignment, usually tailored to needs identified through discussions with teachers and media specialists. These assignments typically focus on the differences between school and academic libraries, introducing students to the multiple service points of academic libraries, the Library of Congress Classification System, periodical organization and access, and basic database searching. Because the KSU Libraries' collections often include books that high school students cannot easily access through other libraries, high school borrowing policies and procedures were developed and offered through the website.

Collaboration: How the Program Works

Founded on discussions, ideas, and approaches shared between library media specialists and academic librarians through the initial work of ILILE, Informed Transitions continues to build on these and create new collaborations. High schools participate in Informed Transitions by requesting a library visit by email or telephone. The FYE librarian responds to these requests, working with teachers and media specialists to plan and schedule a visit that fits their needs. During this planning phase, special focus is given to the research assignment students will be working on during their visit. If possible, the FYE librarian obtains a copy of the assignment, or if an assignment doesn't exist, instructional expectations and needs are discussed. Borrowing privileges, if the high school decides to use that service, are also given special attention at this point because it takes time to gather patron information and set up accounts. After these matters have been resolved, the FYE librarian and the high school agree on a date and set a tentative itinerary for the visit. The typical high school visit proceeds as follows:

9:00 A.M. High school group arrives. A librarian meets them in the library lobby and gives a brief library tour.

9:20 Students settle into classroom and receive information literacy instruction.

10:00 Students work independently on their assignment on classroom computers. Librarian moves about the room, providing point-of-need assistance and instruction. As needed, students leave the classroom to access resources within the library building.

1:00 P.M. High school group leaves library, often stopping to have lunch or visit other sites on campus.

Marketing the Program

KSU librarians took the approach of marketing Informed Transitions heavily in its first year with hopes of seeding the program, making marketing less of a need as the program matured. They marketed the program by using a variety of methods. A descriptive flyer was created to lead people to the website. An initial direct mailing was sent to local library media specialists, providing them with an introductory letter and a copy of the flyer. In support of this mailing, follow-up calls were placed. The FYE librarian visited interested high schools and spoke with teachers and media specialists. The FYE librarian also presented the program at the meetings of local media specialist user groups. In addition, several local teachers and media specialists were invited to an open house for the new high school instructional classroom.

Program Results

This approach to marketing proved successful. By the beginning of the program's second year, KSU librarians had begun to think their efforts had worked too well, as their schedule of high school visits had begun to exceed their expectations. Table 2.1 shows participation statistics for Informed Transitions since the program's inception. Although budget issues in local school districts have caused numbers to drop off slightly during the last two years, the program remains popular. In the past year four new high schools have visited through the program.

Beyond the numbers, what results can be found to support the program's objectives? Have the benefits of Informed Transitions been realized or do they remain purely perceived benefits? These are the questions that KSU librarians struggle with when reviewing the program. Anecdotal evidence can be cited. KSU librarians have encountered current KSU students who previously visited while in high school and indicated that they found their experiences helpful. High school educators have lauded the program

Table 2.1
Participation Statistics for Informed Transitions

Academic Year	Participating Schools	Group Visits	Number of Students	Library Tours	Instruction Sessions
2004–2005	8	17	507	17	14
2005–2006	10	19	547	19	16
2006–2007	8	17	453	13	10
2007–2008	9	13	388	11	10
Totals	*19	66	1895	60	50

*Schools are counted only once over the four years.

for both its immediate impact on students and its work in preparing them for college. The following quote from Joann Chess, an English teacher at Southeast High School in Ravenna, Ohio, nicely summarizes the support of high school educators:

I want to thank you for all your help. I think this year was the best—the program seems to get better and better each year, and your staff has been such a great source of knowledge and aid. Our students certainly got so much more than just material for their paper; in addition, they now are not so intimidated entering a university library.

Although formal assessment of the program has been elusive because it is difficult to evaluate students under age 18 not associated with the university, KSU librarians remain confident that Informed Transitions is doing good work. They can personally attest to the benefits enjoyed through the program's collaborations. Having direct experience with college-bound students and their teachers, they feel better prepared to approach and educate these students as they arrive on campus—no longer as high school students, but as college students.

TRANSITIONING TO COLLEGE: HELPING YOU SUCCEED

Transitioning to College (www.transitioning2college.org) is a project designed to prepare students to do academic research while at the same time reducing their anxiety about being able to do college-level work. Transitioning to College (T2C) was purposefully designed to focus on the needs of both high school and college students, and the dual nature of the site was a direct result of the working group discussions sponsored by ILILE. During these discussions, librarians and educators in secondary and higher education realized how much they had in common—while at the same time learning about differences in their respective professional arenas.

At a basic level, many academic librarians were unaware of the efforts being undertaken by school library media specialists to promote information literacy in their schools. It was also a surprise to learn that school librarians fought similar battles with classroom faculty over how and when information-seeking skills should be included in coursework. The important role of state content standards in K–12 curriculum planning and the strong emphasis on accountability was also eye-opening for academic librarians. On other fronts, librarians also became more aware of the existence of each other's state and local professional associations.

The strongest message conveyed during these working group discussions was that school library media specialists were dedicated to improving students' information literacy skills and were eager to learn what they could do better. School library media specialists asked questions such as, "What citation style should we be teaching in high school?" College librarians' answer: "It depends on the discipline." Minor differences in how resources were labeled also figured in the discussion. For example, academic librarians in Ohio referred to databases by their individual names (e.g., Academic Search Complete), whereas school librarians referred to them by the name of the database provider (EBSCOhost). This small bit of information underscored how students transitioning to college were expected to learn a new vocabulary and how each sector approached information literacy instruction in a slightly different way.

From these modest discussions, a plan was formulated to create a resource that could highlight some of the differences between high school and college libraries and that could be used by students in the transitioning process. One model already existed in Ohio. This was the Pathways to Academic Libraries (PALS) project developed by Colleen Boff who, at the time, was the FYE librarian at Bowling Green State University. Colleen had produced instructional videos focused on defining the features of an academic library as well as providing instruction on how best to do research. Although the overall content of the videos was still relevant, the group decided that references to the Jerome Library at Bowling Green might restrict their use by those outside that university and that it would be beneficial to update or create new videos that would be more generic in orientation.

The overall goal of the project was to create a resource that would help reduce student anxiety about college-level research and that would introduce some of the features of college libraries. By providing content in a Web-based environment, the information could be used by librarians and students without geographic restriction and without requiring that students physically visit an academic library.

Creating and Testing the Video Modules

A Library Services and Technology Act (LSTA) minigrant provided funding for the creation of new videos in summer 2005. Librarians from four different Ohio colleges and two high schools collaborated in the overall planning and script creation. The production and editing of the videos took place on the KSU campus, using student actors from the Theatre and Dance program.

During the development phase, the decision was made to reduce the presence of librarians in the videos, creating content that was more student centered. It should be noted that the scripts were purposefully created to be generic in nature, with no direct references to KSU. The videos feature two first-year students, Emily and Jason, who are being mentored by Brian, a college junior and avid library user. The titles of the five videos are:

- Welcome to Academic Libraries (highlights service points of academic libraries)
- Talking to Databases (steps the viewer takes through the creation of an effective search strategy in a database)

- Tips for Research Success (cautions students about overreliance on the Web and provides suggestions for doing effective academic research)
- Getting Help When You Need It (encourages students to take advantage of faculty office hours, tutoring, and study groups)
- College: What to Expect (Emily and Jason answer questions from prospective college students)

The videos were scripted, shot, and edited over a three-month period using Teleproductions staff at KSU. Simultaneously, the outline of a website that would point to the videos was created. The original plan was to have the videos streamed from a server, making them more readily accessible. However, testing by high school librarians soon revealed that there were problems in viewing the videos away from the Kent campus.

The streaming videos were mounted on a server requiring a specific version of Quicktime. Although theoretically updating the version of Quicktime was seen as a relatively easy process, safeguards in most high school computer labs prevented the installation of software upgrades. Transmission of the videos also tended to be slow in some schools where the network infrastructure was older. During this early period, feedback and testing provided by school library media specialists were extremely important. Ultimately, several versions of the videos were provided: Quicktime, Flash, and RealPlayer. CD and DVD versions were also made available to those requesting this medium.

Website Resources

Once the videos were created and able to link from a website, it was decided to expand the project to include supplementary material that could be used in a classroom or workshop setting. For example, the video "Tips for Research Success" is accompanied by additional "tip sheets" on writing papers, avoiding plagiarism, using college libraries to do research, the usefulness of reference books, and links to citation sites.

A glossary of frequently used academic terms on the site and several other components are a direct result of conversations with school librarians who identified information that might be most useful to students. A library school student, who served as a graduate assistant to the project and was also a former teacher, provided guidance in terms of structuring the lesson plans so that they would follow a format familiar to school librarians and teachers.

Although the site has a look and feel designed to be attractive to students (including caricatures of the student actors), it is not the type of resource that students would naturally use on their own. In other words, it is of most value to educators as a tool to be used in a classroom instruction session devoted to college preparation or research. The handouts can be copied and distributed to students and permission is provided to adapt resources as appropriate (with proper credit given to the T2C website). The T2C materials can also be incorporated into high school outreach programs such as Informed Transitions.

Feedback

Transitioning to College has been promoted to Ohio librarians and teachers through mailings sponsored by ILILE and through presentations at the annual conference of the Ohio Educational Library Media Association (OELMA) as well as the Academic Library Association of Ohio (ALAO). Nationally, a 2006 presentation at LOEX of the West and a poster session at the 2007 national conference of the Association of College and Research Libraries (ACRL) also highlighted the project, as well as the other initiatives described in this chapter.

Positive feedback received through a comment section on the T2C website indicates that the resources are being used equally by high school and college librarians, fulfilling one of the key missions of the project. A workshop targeted at school library media specialists will extend the collaborative nature of the project. Input will be solicited as to how the site is currently being incorporated into instruction with college-bound students and how it can be improved.

TRAILS: TOOL FOR REAL-TIME ASSESSMENT OF INFORMATION LITERACY SKILLS

TRAILS (www.trails9.org) is a freely available, Web-based tool for assessing the information literacy skills of students, including those in grades nine through twelve. The tool consists of several assessments with multiple-choice items that are based on both the State of Ohio Academic Content Standards and the American Association of School Librarians' (AASL) *Information Power* standards. The TRAILS project is housed at KSU and was created by KSU librarians. An ILILE-funded initiative, TRAILS is also an outgrowth of Project SAILS (Standardized Assessment of Information Literacy Skills), an international assessment based on Association of College and Research Libraries (ACRL) *Information Literacy Standards for Higher Education* aimed at undergraduate students, which was also created at KSU. As of spring 2008, more than 4,100 users have registered with TRAILS. During the 2006–2007 school year assessments were administered to more than 32,500 students. More information about TRAILS can be found on its website.

Development through Collaboration

From the outset, TRAILS has been a collaborative project between school librarians, teachers, and academic librarians. The genesis of TRAILS can be found within the original working group discussions of ILILE, when school library media specialists lamented the lack of affordable, easy to administer assessment tools for information literacy. During the initial development phase, school library media specialists were contracted to write standards-based objectives and items. Volunteer library media specialists to pilot the first assessments with ninth grade students were recruited through the electronic mailing lists of ILILE, INFOhio (the state K–12 information network), and OELMA. In addition to analyzing the response data, the TRAILS team sought feedback from practitioners about the developing content and format of the assessments.

Following a preview of TRAILS at the fall 2004 OELMA meeting, the system went live in January 2005. After this first use during a school term by schools around the country, response data were analyzed to identify items needing revision. Users were also invited to complete an online survey to gather their experiences and comments. These comments again influenced the development of both the content and format of TRAILS. Reporting was improved to make results easier to understand quickly. In addition to the two general assessments, which cover all information literacy areas, new ten-item assessments were assembled for each of five specific category areas:

1. Developing a topic
2. Identifying potential sources
3. Developing, using, and revising search strategies
4. Evaluating sources and information
5. Recognizing how to use information responsibly, ethically, and legally.

Ongoing Communication with Users

TRAILS now has users in all fifty states and more than thirty countries. After each school year, users are asked to respond to a survey about the assessments, items, reports, and interface. This feedback, in addition to extensive item and test analysis, is used to determine refinements and enhancements.

A TRAILS user community has been established through several vehicles. TRAILS account holders are subscribed to a forum through which they can receive updates, share experiences, and post questions. One active user created a Wiki (http://ilfortrails9.wikispaces.com/) to allow practitioners to share other resources related to information literacy.

Collaboration in Promoting TRAILS

Word-of-mouth promotion of TRAILS within the school library community has been an important means of creating awareness for the tool. We also know that numerous school library media specialists have made presentations to their local and regional groups and have established cooperative assessment and instruction plans. Information on TRAILS also appears on a number of blogs managed by library media specialists. INFOhio has published links to TRAILS on its website and information in its various publications.

School library media specialist organizations have been generous in including members of the TRAILS team in their conference programs. This has included statewide and national opportunities for joint presentations by a project member and a library media specialist who has been an early adopter of TRAILS. Numerous regional and district meetings within Ohio have connected TRAILS team members with library media specialists who have participated in KSU's other K–12 outreach initiatives.

Support Enabling Collaboration

Although TRAILS could not have been developed without the support it received through ILILE, ongoing institutional support from the KSU Libraries have made further developments and project support possible. This has included hosting of the TRAILS website and maintaining the hardware to run the assessments. Importantly, two academic librarians are able to work on TRAILS as part of their regular duties and to consult with other academic librarians as needed.

Benefits

TRAILS provides school librarians and teachers with a standardized, valid, reliable tool for assessing information literacy. They can use their results to target their instructional efforts, to create opportunities to work together, and to provide information to administrators about student needs. Because they have been involved in the development and refinement of TRAILS, better buy-in from practitioners is expected to result in increased use.

By reviewing TRAILS data academic librarians can have a better understanding of high school students' general information literacy skills and what they are able to do when they begin postsecondary education. This provides a check on our assumptions about incoming students' knowledge. Students who have been introduced to basic information literacy skills may make a more seamless transition between high school and postsecondary work, and academic librarians can build on this foundation. Faculty also benefit when students are better prepared for college. Students with strong information literacy skills can do better research and analysis and produce better writing, which can potentially result in more enriching classroom experiences.

Academic librarians and high school educators both benefit from crossing professional boundaries and making connections with new colleagues. Although content and audience may differ slightly, librarians in academic and K–12 settings can share best practices and teaching strategies. These connections have enabled the TRAILS team to identify and consult with outstanding practitioners in the field. Librarians working on the TRAILS project have a greater appreciation for the need for information literacy instruction to occur along the entire K–20 continuum and that partnerships with school librarians provide an important bridge for that work.

RECOMMENDATIONS FOR COLLABORATION

KSU librarians, through their extensive collaborative work with library media specialists on the initiatives discussed in this chapter, have gained numerous insights and learned a number of lessons about working with K–12 colleagues. Academic librarians considering their own outreach programming may want to consider the following recommendations.

Reach Out to Local School Library Media Specialists

Contact local schools and start a dialogue. Consider starting with the local high schools that feed the most students to your institution. KSU librarians learned a great deal by informally talking with school librarians. You may be surprised to find that academic and school librarians face many similar challenges. For example, academic and school librarians both depend on collaboration with classroom faculty to access and instruct students. Above all, evaluate how willing and able your K–12 counterparts are to collaborate. KSU librarians found that, for the most part, school librarians are ready and eager to work together for the benefit of their students.

Learn about Information Literacy at the High School Level

If you are not familiar, find out what role information literacy plays in academic content standards in your state. In Ohio information literacy benchmarks appear at the K–2 and continue through to the 9–12 level. Take a look also at the AASL's *Information Power*. It outlines a set of information literacy standards very similar to the ACRL standards.

Seek Administrative Support

Talk with your library's administrators about your ideas for outreach. KSU librarians enjoy a high level of top-down support for their work that facilitates outreach efforts, especially related to workload issues. But do your homework before having these discussions. Develop a rationale that addresses the benefits such programming can offer to your library, institution, and future students. Learn about other outreach programs on your campus and investigate how you can build on these initiatives.

Connect to Already Existing Resources

Many helpful and freely available resources already exist, which can aid your collaborative work. This chapter points out two resources, T2C and TRAILS, that are readily available to be used at your library and shared with local high schools. Many other good resources are available, such as the College Board's Web page on College Success (www.collegeboard.com/student/plan/college-success/index.html). This and many other resources can be found on the "Additional Resources" page on the T2C website.

Connect with Professional Associations

Just like academic librarians, school librarians have strong professional associations. Association meetings are a great place to meet and collaborate with school librarians. Explore what organizations exist in your state and in your region. Remember too that school librarians often meet in smaller user groups within counties or school districts.

Be Sensitive to Budgetary Constraints

This applies to both the budgetary resources of your library and to those of schools. All three of the KSU projects had the support of ILILE and other grants. Much of their work would not have been possible without this level of support. Does this mean that additional funding is necessary for outreach? Not necessarily, but academic librarians would be prudent to give considerable thought to needed resources. With thoughtful review, academic librarians can determine what level of commitment they can make. School educators also have challenges with their budgetary resources. Recognize that collaboration may be limited or not possible due to the lack of funds and resources that some school districts may be experiencing. KSU's Informed Transitions program has recently seen the sizes of visiting groups increase because high schools have been forced to fill buses with multiple classes to make best use of their only opportunity for a field trip. We are aware too that the financial constraints result in the elimination of field trips for other schools.

It is clear, as we move forward, that communication with school educators and the preparation of their students for college remain important issues for higher education. Many universities have conducted campuswide reviews of outreach efforts to the K–12 system in their regions because they see strong ties between student preparedness and student success in college. Keep in mind that while this chapter has largely focused on outreach to the high school level of education, the entire spectrum of K–12 is of concern and may benefit from outreach efforts. For example, the TRAILS project has just released assessments targeting the sixth grade level. Most importantly, academic librarians can play important roles in these efforts, whether working with their library's programs or in providing leadership for campuswide initiatives, and best of all, they do not have to start from scratch. Many model programs and resources like the ones discussed in this chapter are available as useful and freely available starting points.

REFERENCES

Kirst, M. W. and A. Venezia. *From High School to College: Improving Opportunities for Success in Postsecondary Education.* San Francisco, CA: Jossey-Bass, 2004.

National Commission on the High School Senior Year. *The Lost Opportunity of the Senior Year: Finding a Better Way (Preliminary report).* Washington, D.C.: National Commission on the High School Senior Year, 2001. (ERIC Document Reproduction Service No. ED 453 604).

ADDITIONAL READINGS

American Association of School Librarians. *Information Power: Building Partnerships for Learning.* Chicago: American Library Association, 1998.

Association of College and Research Libraries. *Information Literacy Competency Standards for Higher Education: Standards, Performance Indicators, and Outcomes.* Chicago: ACRL, 2000.

Boff, C. *Pathways to Academic Libraries.* 2006. http://www.bgsu.edu/colleges/library/infosrv/lue/pal/.

Burhanna, K. J. "Instructional Outreach to High Schools: Should You Be Doing It?" *Communication in Information Literacy* 1, no. 2 (Fall 2007): 74–88.

Institute for Library and Information Literacy Education (2008). http://www.ilile.org/.

Schloman, B. F. and J. A. Gedeon. "Creating TRAILS: Tool for Real-Time Assessment of Information Literacy Skills." *Knowledge Quest* 35, no. 5 (May/June 2007): 44–47.

3

K–16 OUTREACH: CREATING CONNECTIONS THAT MATTER

Ellysa Stern Cahoy and Lesley Moyo

INTRODUCTION

A number of trends in higher education are driving a renewed outreach agenda in the twenty-first century. In addition to reaching out to prospective students, universities and colleges have always exemplified their social and civic roles through community outreach and engagement for the last forty to fifty years. However, the renewed urgency with which outreach is being used as a strategic effort in many academic institutions can be attributed to the increasing competitiveness of higher education, the pressure for more accountability of academic institutions to their communities, and the search for productive alliances and collaborative partnerships in fulfilling societal missions and goals. In an educational environment in which over half of the population of students in urban areas do not graduate from high school, collaboration throughout all levels of education is desperately needed (Swanson 2008).

K–16 (K–12 and undergraduate education) collaboration is an educational initiative that has grown as a result of the renewed higher education outreach efforts of the last ten to fifteen years. It is a collaborative effort among K–16 educators and the community to ensure that students have the academic preparation and support that they need to succeed in college. Collaborating to better understand and develop students' information literacy skills is integral to impacting student academic success. Academic libraries are actively participating in this outreach model, increasingly reaching out and partnering with school and public librarians to improve and support students' information literacy skills across the K–16 spectrum.

This chapter highlights existing K–16 initiatives and programs, illustrating new collaborative opportunities for librarians at all levels of education. The existing literature on K–16 collaboration and the benefits of collaboration and networking to build strong communities of engaged learners will be shared. K–16 outreach provides lasting education partnerships with impact—designed to better understand information literacy in education and help students achieve academic success.

LITERATURE REVIEW

The Need for K–16 Collaboration

The goals of most K–16 collaborative efforts are to facilitate seamless transition of students from high school to college through better integration of educational standards and curriculum alignment. Many academic institutions have embarked on initiatives that seek to enhance the achievement of students from kindergarten through their completion of undergraduate education. Gathering Momentum (2002), a report based on the proceedings of the Learning Connection Conference held in Kansas City, Missouri, June 27–28, 2001, is one of the best documents that make a case for the need and value of K–16 collaboration, as well as documenting national progress in this area. The report highlights the interdependence of the K–12 and higher education systems and suggests five perspectives from which K–16 collaboration can be examined: educational equity, governance, standards, teacher preparation, and community building. Larson and Novak (2002) also provide an overview of K–16 initiatives in Minnesota and various other states. They summarize K–16 program issues and suggest how these might be addressed.

Outreach in Academic Libraries

Outreach is increasingly becoming a strategic priority in academic libraries. Schneider (2003) discusses three factors that are often the impetus for academic libraries' outreach to their communities, that is, "whether a need is expressed from outside the academy, whether they see their mission as an invitation to pursue an action on their own accord, or whether they construct a form of outreach in response to a specific problem or crisis." In each of these situations, the nature and scope of the outreach depends on the library's mission and available resources. According to Malanchuk (2005), "Academic librarians already have a keen awareness of the cultural and educational needs of the academic community … Because of their obvious public service orientation, academic librarians are especially well qualified to participate in community outreach programs such as literacy programs for children and youth" thus contributing to the mission of supporting the goals of their institutions beyond the traditional campuses.

K–16 Outreach in Academic Libraries

K–16 outreach is a growing trend in academic libraries because of the need and pressure to align educational standards between K–12 and higher education. Visser (2006) reports that, from her survey of special collections departments' outreach programs to K–12 in ARL (Association of Research Libraries) libraries, over half of the respondents in surveyed libraries collaborate with K–12, and many of those not currently doing so are planning to do so. K–16 collaborative efforts in most academic libraries have focused on information literacy, that is, alignment of the Association of College and Research Libraries (ACRL) *Information Literacy Competency Standards for Higher Education*, with the American Association of School Librarians (AASL) *Standards for the 21st Century Learner.*

The AASL/ACRL Task Force on the Educational Role of Libraries *Blueprint for Collaboration* (2000) recognizes that there is a shared responsibility among academic and school librarians for information literacy and makes recommendations for specific areas and models of collaboration, including examples of collaboration and grant opportunities. Nichols, Spang, Adamany, and Padron (2006) emphasize not only the shared information literacy goals of AASL and ACRL but also the need for instruction librarians in colleges and K–12 educators to be viewed as equal stakeholders in the outreach and collaboration. Specific areas and models of collaboration are reflected in the literature, among them, joint programming, sharing of instructional resources, etc. For example, Seymour (2007) outlines a collaborative model for sharing of library assessment tools and instructional models across K–20.

Manuel (2005) provides one of the best examples of the benefits of K–16 collaboration for information literacy. She details the National History Day program by mapping the learner outcomes of the program to the National Standards for History, Historical Thinking Standards for Grades 5–12, to the AASL and ACRL information literacy standards, clearly showing the correlations between information literacy and history standards. Islam and Murno's (2006) research not only exemplifies the need for collaboration between academic librarians and school librarians but also identifies an information literacy skills gap between the information literacy skills addressed by secondary School Library Media Specialists and academic instruction librarians in colleges, mapping the ACRL information Literacy Competency Standards for Higher Education and the AASL/AECT Information Literacy Standards for Student Learning. To close this knowledge gap, Islam and Murno suggest devising a system of progressive information literacy instruction across the K–16 curriculum based on close collaboration between K–12 and the higher education sector. Carr and Rockman (2003) compare the ACRL and AASL standards and highlight the similarities of the overall information literacy goals of the two standards. Cahoy (2002) also addresses the two sets of information literacy standards from the perspective of high school student preparedness for college. *Knowledge Quest, Journal of the American Association of School Librarians*, published two issues devoted to K–16 information literacy in 2002 and 2004 detailing a wide range of perspective and initiatives related to this subject area and its applicability and importance in school librarianship (American Association of School Librarians, 2002, 2004).

Success Stories in K–16 Outreach in Academic Libraries

There are numerous success stories of K–16 collaboration. To mention a few, Martorana et al. (2001) and Nichols et al. (2006) both present case study accounts of successful K–16 collaborative models and programs, detailing the process and outcomes of the programs. Gresham and Van Tassel (1999) approach K–16 outreach by expanding the academic learning community to college-bound high school students. LeClercq (1986) outlines the study that led to the development of a collaborative model by the University of Tennessee at Knoxville's library to address the inadequacy of research resources in high schools. Through this model, the University of Tennessee library provided local high school students access to research resources that were necessary for their research but unavailable in their high schools. A similar grant-funded project was developed at George Washington University (Nutefall 2001).

STRATEGIES FOR IMPLEMENTING K–16 COLLABORATION

Connecting K–12 and College Information Literacy Standards

Two sets of ALA information literacy standards currently exist: the ACRL *Information Literacy Competency Standards for Higher Education* (2000) and the newly released (October 2007) AASL *Standards for the 21ˢᵗ Century Learner*. The new AASL standards succeed the *Information Literacy Standards for Students Learning*, published within *Information Power: Building Partnerships for Learning* (1998). Related to these standards (but not produced by an ALA-affiliated organization) is ISTE's (International Society for Technology in Education) updated *NETS-S, National Educational Technology Standards for Students* (ISTE 2008). The ISTE-NETS-S standards identify information literacy as a critical thinking skill, which impacts students' effective use of technology for research, content creation, and more. These standards offer a platform for collaboration with information technology in the K–16 environment and a vision for partnerships between IT and librarians in academic libraries.

Each set of ALA information literacy standards communicates a slightly different vision of what information literacy is and how it can be achieved by every student. The AASL and ACRL standards each use a different structure. The ACRL Information Literacy standards focus primarily on cognitive aspects of information literacy; the AASL standards incorporate "dispositions"—positive, affective behaviors students display during each stage of the research process (Cahoy 2002). Even so, the vision and general goals of each set of standards are similar, rendering the standards separate but complementary. The ACRL document states that it should be viewed as a continuum of the AASL standards.

Contained within the AASL/ACRL *Blueprint for Collaboration* (2000) is a call for the creation of a "seamless continuation" of AASL and ACRL information literacy standards. Having one set of information literacy standards spanning all educational levels would impel school and academic librarians to collaborate and consider curriculum together.

Analyzing State and Local Standards for Embedded K–12 Information-Seeking Skills

For school librarians, state standards can mandate the scope and sequence of information literacy within the curriculum. Academic librarians can also analyze state standards to understand further the extent of information literacy education in a specific state and gain a greater picture of incoming area college students' information literacy skills. In Pennsylvania, the Pennsylvania State System of Assessment (PSSA) Assessment Anchors (2004) provide the core standards for measurement of students' academic achievement. The Assessment Anchors describe which state standards are measured by the PSSA and define grade-appropriate expectations for each grade level and content area. The PSSAs also clarify "eligible content" for each grade level.

The Pittsburgh Public Schools recently integrated information literacy skills into the scope and sequence of the public schools curriculum. Using the existing school district curriculum as a guide, area school and academic librarians worked together to identify relevant information literacy standards and outcomes in each grade. The resulting document, *Information Literacy for Lifelong Learning* (2007), shows the progression of information literacy skills from kindergarten to twelfth grade, providing academic librarians with a "roadmap" for planning, as well as a general sense of incoming college students' abilities and information literacy-related accomplishments.

There are broad strategies that can be used to help understand the scope and sequence of K–12 information literacy instruction. Librarians must identify anchors or standards that are a natural fit for information literacy skills and behaviors; track the adoption of information literacy related standards or anchors; and tie curriculum, instruction, and assessment to the standards or anchors. Mapping existing information literacy standards to state standards can provide school librarians with secure footing in curriculum planning and help academic librarians understand their state's educational scope. The edstandards.org website provides access to the computers, library, and information literacy standards for many U.S. states. (Hill 2007)

Strategies for Collaboration

Nationally and at the state level, opportunities for K–16 collaboration abound. A partnership between school and academic librarians is essential to advance K–16 information literacy. In 1998 a joint committee, the AASL/ACRL Task Force on the Educational Role of Libraries, was formed to study the library's central role in student learning and the possibilities for educational collaboration. The AASL/ACRL *Blueprint for Collaboration* (2000) states, "The associations share the goals of fostering lifelong learning and ensuring that students at all educational levels are prepared to meet the challenges of the twenty-first century. ... The Task Force recognizes that there is a shared responsibility among academic and school librarians for information literacy." Since then, the AASL/ACRL Interdivisional Committee on Information Literacy has continued this initiative, nationally fostering discussion on shared information literacy issues and initiatives for K–12 and academic librarians.

One of the oldest existing K–16 library-related initiatives, the Rochester Regional Library Council (RRLC), was the recipient of a 2000 Library Services and Technology Act (LSTA) grant to raise awareness of information literacy within school, academic, and public libraries. As part of the grant, RRLC developed a variety of K–16 supporting materials, including an analysis of the AASL and ACRL information literacy standards and guidelines for working relationships between school, public, and academic librarians. Although these documents are (sadly) only available now via the Internet Archive, the RRLC has continued to develop K–16 programmatic materials. The Core Library Skills 9–14+ outline the sequential information literacy skills to be used as a guideline for library instruction (RRLC 2007).

ILILE, the Institute for Library and Information Literacy Education, is an Institute of Museum and Library Services (IMLS)-funded project focusing on local, state, and national advocacy for fostering K–16 partnerships between school, academic, and public librarians. ILILE provides grant funding for K–16 projects, academic content standards checklists, a toolkit to assist parents in advocating for information literacy and school libraries, and TRAILS, an information literacy assessment tool based on sixth and ninth grade information literacy standards. ILILE also supports a wide variety of information literacy initiatives, including Correlation to Standards, a project for Ohio librarians that connects collections with specific Ohio educational standards (ILILE 2008).

LILi: LifeLong Information Literacy is a California collaborative (initiated by UCLA) focused on investigating statewide information literacy standards and practices throughout public, school, academic, and special libraries. In 2006 LILi conducted a survey of information literacy instruction in California libraries. The survey's preliminary findings indicated a need for sequenced, articulated information literacy standards and instruction throughout the state (LILI, 2008).

Community Partnerships That Impact and Increase Students' Academic Success

On the local level, K–16 partnerships can also help embed information literacy skills sequentially into the curriculum. Community Librarians Outreach and Education (CLOC), an Athens, Georgia-based collective of school, academic, and public librarians, provides periodic workshops and resources to area librarians. The group also has worked on a continuum of K–12 and college information literacy skills that provide consistency for information literacy programming, expectations, and assessment across all grade levels in the state (CLOC 2008).

Established in 2004, the Central Pennsylvania K–16 Information Literacy Network connects area librarians in support of information literacy collaboration and discussion. In addition to yearly workshops, the Network features a comprehensive website and email discussion list that serves as a forum for sharing ideas between different types of libraries. Workshop topics have included "Will Your Students Be Ready for College? Connecting K–12 and College Information Literacy Standards," "Teacher Education and Information Literacy: What Do Our Teachers Know?", and "Where Do We All Fit In: Aligning the PSSA Assessment Anchors with K–16 Information Literacy Standards" (Central Pennsylvania K–16 Information Literacy Network 2008). A report on the Central Pennsylvania K–16 Information Literacy Network (Campbell 2006) contained this insight from a participating school librarian:

"The workshops present a valuable opportunity for face-to-face discussions of issues and to learn how other librarians are dealing with them," Christiana Schell, librarian at the State College Area High School South Building, said. "Through network activities, I hope to get a better understanding of where our students are lacking and what we can do to best help them at the ninth- and 10th-grade level. Knowing that, we can better prepare them for the next step, 11th and 12th grades, and from there to college and lifelong learning."

Strategies for Beginning the K–16 Discussion in Your Community

K–16 collaboration is born of a shared interest in furthering students' information literacy skills. Local and statewide collaboration between librarians from school, public, academic, and special libraries can foster discussion on student learning outcomes, information literacy standards, and assessment. Groups can map and discuss state and national information literacy standards and establish advocacy networks to assist in promoting and furthering community-based information literacy initiatives. At its greatest, local K–16 collaboration can be a springboard to articulating information literacy throughout the curriculum and within statewide standards. At all levels of collaboration, it is an avenue for librarians to connect, share, and learn from one another.

Resources for Connecting and Collaborating

State or locally based professional associations can provide a wonderful springboard for connecting informally with librarians in public, school, and academic libraries. Attending local meetings will bring opportunities for networking and discussions with other librarians in the community and may lead to collaborative projects. The American Library Association (2008) provides a listing of state and regional ALA-affiliated chapters.

CLOC and the Central Pennsylvania K–16 Information Literacy Network are examples of two university-based K–16 groups. Each was started as a professional development program by academic librarians interested in forging ties with area school, public, and other academic librarians. The Network receives outreach funding from the Penn State University Libraries for workshop programs, speaker fees, and refreshments. Penn State librarians develop and organize the yearly workshops, based on feedback and suggestions from Network members. There is no cost for area librarians to attend any of the Network's programs. The Network also provides a valuable outreach outlet to the Penn State Libraries, providing a consistent vehicle for reaching out to the local library community.

Informal feedback from Network participants indicate that there are never enough affordable program opportunities for school and public librarians. Holding local workshops can provide a valuable outlet for librarians to connect and absorb new ideas, while also providing needed continuing professional education credits to participating K–12 librarians. As one librarian at a recent Central Pennsylvania K–16 Network workshop explained: "I was struck by the fact my library is experiencing the same challenges as an academic library in Pittsburgh, a high school or elementary library or a large public library in State College. We all have different size buildings and staff and yet we are so similar in many ways. It was an opportunity to have a fresh perspective on an old problem. Thank you for providing this workshop" (Central Pennsylvania K–16 Workshop Assessment 2008).

Even an electronic discussion list, wiki, or blog can help area librarians connect and learn more about the pedagogy, practices, and challenges of other librarians in the community. As long as an outlet exists to encourage idea sharing and collaboration among area librarians, relationships will form in support of building students' information literacy skills.

CONCLUSION

The need for a seamless and supportive education that facilitates students' success has been the major impetus for K–16 outreach and collaboration. There are many different models that have been adopted in these collaborative efforts that are growing nationally, each reflecting the specific area of focus and goals for the collaboration. Academic libraries have been active players in this K–16 movement, particularly in the area of information literacy. The need not only to align ACRL and AASL information literacy standards but to also create fruitful connections among the stakeholders has been central to most academic library outreach efforts in this area. Among the benefits reported in the literature and by members of the Central Pennsylvania K–16 Network is a shared and wider view of the continuum of information literacy skills needed for students to succeed as lifelong learners.

REFERENCES

AASL/ACRL Task Force on the Educational Role of Libraries. *ACRL/AASL Blueprint for Collaboration.* 2000. http://www.ala.org/ala/acrl/acrlpubs/whitepapers/acrlaaslblueprint. cfm (accessed May 30, 2008).

American Association of School Librarians. *ALA/AASL Standards for the 21st-Century Learner.* 2007. http://www.ala.org/ala/aasl/aaslproftools/learningstandards/standards. cfm (accessed May 30, 2008).

American Association of School Librarians. "One Step Beyond: From High School to College." *Knowledge Quest: Journal of the American Association of School Librarians* 30, no. 4 (2002):1–60.

American Association of School Librarians. "Information Literacy K–20." *Knowledge Quest: Journal of the American Association of School Librarians* 32, no. 4 (2004):1–56.

American Association of School Librarians and Association for Educational Technology and Communications. *Information Literacy Standards for Student Learning.* 1998. http://www.ala.org/ala/aasl/aaslproftools/informationpower/InformationLiteracy Standards_final.pdf (accessed May 30, 2008).

American Library Association. ALA State and Regional Chapters. http://www.ala.org/ala/ ourassociation/chapters/stateandregional/stateregional.cfm (accessed May 30, 2008).

Association of College & Research Libraries. *Information Literacy Competency Standards for Higher Education.* 2000. http://www.ala.org/ala/acrl/acrlstandards/informationli teracycompetency.cfm (accessed May 29, 2008).

Cahoy, E. S. "Will Your Students Be Ready for College? Connecting K–12 and College Standards for Information Literacy." *Knowledge Quest* 30, no. 4 (2002): 12–15.

Campbell, Bill. *Penn State Live—K–16 Literacy Network Helps Ensure Students Have Information Skills.* 2006. http://live.psu.edu/index.php?sec=vs&story=18362 (accessed May 29, 2008).

Carr, Jo Ann and Ilene F. Rockman. "Information Literacy Collaboration: A Shared Responsibility." *American Libraries* (September 2003): 52–54.

Central Pennsylvania K–16 Information Literacy Network. http://www.libraries.psu.edu/ lls/k-16/index.html (accessed May 29, 2008).

Central Pennsylvania K–16 Information Literacy Network. 2008 Workshop Assessment Results. http://www.libraries.psu.edu/lls/k-16/workshop_2008.htm (accessed August 27, 2008).

CLOC. K–16 Information Literacy Skills Checklist. http://ncohen.myweb.uga.edu/IL college.htm (accessed April 11, 2008).

Gathering Momentum: Building the Learning Connection Between Schools and Colleges. Proceedings from the Learning Connection Conference. Washington, D.C.: Institute for Educational Leadership, 2002.

Gresham, Keith and Debra Van Tassel. "Expanding the Learning Community: An Academic Library Outreach Program to High Schools." *The Reference Librarian* 67/68 (1999): 161–173.

Hill, Charles. *Developing Educational Standards.* 2007. http://edstandards.org/Standards. html (accessed May 30, 2008).

ILILE, Institute for Library and Information Literacy Education. http://ilile.org/ (accessed May 30, 2008).

International Society for Technology in Education. ISTE/NETS for Students 2007. http://www.iste.org/Content/NavigationMenu/NETS/ForStudents/2007Standards/NETS_for_Students_2007.htm (accessed May 29, 2008).

Islam, Ramona L., and Lisa Anne Murno. "From Perceptions to Connections: Informing Information Literacy Program Planning in Academic Libraries through Examination of High School Library Media Center Curricula." *College & Research Libraries* 67, no. 6 (November 2006): 492–514.

Larson, Lisa and Kathy Novak. *States' K–16 Education System*, Information Brief. St. Paul, MN: Minnesota House of Representatives, Research Department, 2002.

LeClercq, Angie. "The Academic Library/High School Library Connection: Needs Assessment and Proposed Model." *Journal of Academic Librarianship* 12, no. 1 (1986): 12–18.

Lifelong Information Literacy (LiLI). http://www.library.ucla.edu/college/lili/index.htm (accessed May 30, 2008).

Malanchuk, I. R. and Marilyn N. Ochoa. "Academic Librarians and Outreach Beyond the College Campus." *The Southeastern Librarian* 53, no. 3 (2005): 23–29.

Manuel, Kate. "National History Day: An Opportunity for K–16 Collaboration." *Reference Services Review* 33, no.4 (2005): 459–486.

Martorana, Janet, Sylvia Curtis, Sherry DeDecker, Sylvelin Edgerton, Carol Gibbens, and Lorna Lueck. "Bridging the Gap: Information Literacy Workshops for High School Teachers." *Research Strategies* 18, no. 2 (2001): 113–120.

Nichols, Janet, Lothar Spang, David Adamany, and Kristy Padron. "Building a Foundation for Collaboration: K–20 Partnerships in Information Literacy." *Resource Sharing and Information Networks* 18, no. 1/2 (2005/2006): 5–12.

Nutefall, Jennifer E. "Information Literacy: Developing Partnerships across Library Types." *Research Strategies* 18 (2001): 311–318.

Pennsylvania State System of Assessment. *Assessment Anchors.* 2004. http://www.pde.state.pa.us/a_and_t/cwp/view.asp?q=103127 (accessed May 30, 2008).

Pittsburgh Public Schools. *Information Literacy for Lifelong Learning.* 2007. http://www.pps.k12.pa.us/143110323123832603/lib/143110323123832603/PPS-Library Services-ScopeAndSequence-Nov2007.pdf (accessed May 29, 2008).

Rochester Regional Library Council. *Core Library and Research Skills Grade 9–14+.* 2007. http://rrlc.entrexp.com/orgmain.asp?orgID=1&storyID=10251 (accessed April 11, 2008).

Schneider, T. "Outreach: Why, How and Who? Academic Libraries and Their Involvement in the Community." *The Reference Librarian* 82 (2003): 199–213.

Seymour, Celene. "Information Technology Assessment: A Foundation for School and Academic Library Collaboration." *Knowledge Quest* 35, no. 5 (May/June 2007): 32–35.

Swanson, Christopher B. *Cities In Crisis: A Special Analytic Report on Higher Education.* Editorial Projects in Education Research Center, 2008. http://www.americaspromise.org/uploadedFiles/AmericasPromiseAlliance/Dropout_Crisis/SWANSONCitiesInCrisis 040108.pdf (accessed May 29, 2008).

Visser, M. "Special Collections at ARL Libraries and K–12 Outreach: Current Trends." *Journal of Academic Librarianship* 32, no. 3 (May 2006): 313–319.

ADDITIONAL READINGS

Boatman, William. "Public Libraries as a Bridge for College–Bound Young Adults." *Reference & User Services Quarterly* 42, no. 3 (Spring 2003): 229–234.

Cahoy, Ellysa Stern. "'Put Some Feeling Into It!' Integrating Affective Competencies into K–20 Information Literacy Standards." *Knowledge Quest* 32, no. 4 (March/April 2004): 25–28.

Carr, J. A. and I. F. Rockman. "Information-Literacy Collaboration: A Shared Responsibility." *American Libraries* 34 (September 2003): 52–54.

Eisenberg, M. B. and R. E. Berkowitz. *Teaching Information Literacy and Technology Skills: The Big 6 in Elementary Schools.* Worthington, OH: Linworth Publishing, 1999.

Ercegovac, Zorana. "Bridging the Knowledge Gap between Secondary and Higher Education." *College and Research Libraries* 64, no. 1 (January 2003): 75–85.

Evans, Beth. "Building Bridges between New York City Public High Schools and a College: The Cooperative Library Project." *Research Strategies* 15 (1997): 89–99.

Fitzgerald, Mary Ann. "Making the Leap from High School to College: Three New Studies about Information Literacy Skills of First-Year College Students." *Knowledge Quest* 32, no. 4 (March/April 2004): 19–24.

Gordon, Carol. "A Room with a View: Looking at School Library Instruction from a Higher Education Perspective." *Knowledge Quest* 30, no. 4 (March/April 2002): 16–21.

Harris, Frances Jacobson. "Information Literacy in School Libraries: It Takes a Community." *Reference and User Services Quarterly* 42, no. 3 (Spring 2003): 215–223.

Hughes-Hassell, S., and A. Wheelock, eds. *The Information-Powered School.* Chicago: American Library Association, 2001.

Nichols, Janet. "Building Bridges: High School and University Partnerships for Information Literacy." *NASSP Bulletin* 83, no. 605 (March 1999): 75–81.

O'Hanlon, N. "Library Skills, Critical Thinking, and the Teacher-Training Curriculum." *College & Research Libraries* 48 (1987): 17–26.

Pearson, Debra and Beth McNeil. "From High School Users College Students Grow." *Knowledge Quest* 30, no. 4 (March/April 2002): 24–28.

4

CULTURAL LESSONS: ACADEMIC OUTREACH ACROSS BORDERS

Thembi Hadebe, Robin Kear, and Paula M. Smith

During the fall of 2006, four academic librarians met at a leadership conference and came together to create a project that embraced globalization, community engagement, and partnering across borders. The end result, while simplistic in concept, would prove complex in its execution and provide cultural lessons for all involved.

GLOBALIZATION OF EDUCATION

It can be argued that the globalization of higher education is nothing new. The process began in the late nineteenth century with the replication of European models in Asia, Africa, Oceania, and elsewhere and was spurred on by early global economic expansion (Forest 2002). These European models themselves began with the specific medieval model born in Paris and Bologna. Even then, students and professors traveled from all over Europe to participate, mingling their cultures and ideas. Although the educational models were cloned across the world, mirroring a common educational culture, cross-cultural understanding of societies was not yet emphasized or explored.

According to Forest, in the United States learning about other countries and cultures became important only after World War II and the onset of the Cold War in the mid-twentieth century (2002). This mirrors the rise of international organizations, such as the United Nations and the World Bank, and the rise of multinational corporations doing business around the globe. All of these changes were facilitated and/or caused by changes in technology, communication modes, market forces, and finance. Therefore, the change in higher education is a reflection and extension of the globalization of various political, social, and economic processes.

This transformation continues into the current twenty-first century higher educational environment. Presently, the "term globalisation [sic] is typically used to describe a trend of institutions, faculty, and students developing an increasingly sophisticated understanding of—and salient relationships with—their counterparts worldwide" (Forest 2002, 435). A specific example of this is the mission statement adopted in 2000 by Fairleigh Dickinson University in New Jersey "to prepare students as global citizens who can function and succeed across cultures and environments in an increasingly interdependent world" (Adams and Sperling 2003, 31).

The impact of the current form of globalization on education is demonstrated by the greater emphasis on studying and teaching abroad and the importance placed on cross-cultural understanding through these exchanges. According to the Institute of International Education (2007), there were 582,984 international students studying in the United States during 2006–2007 and 223,534 U.S. students that studied abroad for academic credit during 2005–2006. The number of American students abroad has increased 360 percent from the 1985–1986 number of just fewer than 50,000. There were also 98,239 international scholars in the United States during 2006–2007.

In higher education, internationalizing the curriculum has become a goal for many campuses, and secondary education increasingly emphasizes multicultural understanding and world cultures. The considerable overlap that exists between each of these constituencies lends itself to areas in which collaborative work can be shaped. To this end, four academic librarians located in the United States and South Africa embarked on a project to connect two urban high schools from their respective countries in a discourse on contemporary societal issues, such as education, violence, and HIV/AIDS. With the use of Web 2.0 technologies, in the form of a blog and a photo-sharing application, these students were able to come together, learn about each other's cultural diversity, and expand their worldview beyond their immediate communities.

FORMATION OF AN INTERNATIONAL LIBRARY OUTREACH PROJECT

The project was conceived and planned during the librarian's attendance at "Thinking Outside the Borders," an international library leadership program. This program was sponsored by the Illinois State Library and the Mortenson Center for International Library Programs at the University of Illinois at Urbana-Champaign and funded by a grant from the United States Institute of Museum and Library Services (IMLS). The program brought together thirty-two librarians from Canada, Latin America, South Africa, and the United States to share and learn lessons in cross-cultural communications, librarianship, and leadership. It was structured to pair each international librarian with an American librarian to identify a project in which they could collaborate after the program. As a result, Thembi Hadebe (University of Pretoria), Robin Kear (University of Pittsburgh), Ina Smith (University of Pretoria), and Paula Smith (Penn State Abington) were matched as pairs, but they chose to work on a project collectively.

The ensuing "blog" project was a short-term goal envisioned as part of a larger project that entailed acquiring resources for the South African high school library. This modern version of a pen pal project was meant to promote cross-cultural learning for the students and to create a forum for global societal issues. In addition to learning about each other's culture, a parallel goal was to provide access to, and teach students about, the use of new technology in a manner that was both engaging and educational. With this in mind, enthusiasm and technology joined these classrooms in Philadelphia, Pennsylvania and Mamelodi, Pretoria to create real-life cultural lessons.

The relationship between the high schools was initiated by Thembi Hadebe and Paula Smith, who had existing connections with the schools. By spring 2007 twenty-five students from Gatang Comprehensive School in Mamelodi, Pretoria, South Africa and twenty-three students from the Philadelphia Northwest High School for Peace and Social Justice in Philadelphia, Pennsylvania, in the United States met on the "Cultural Lessons" blog to exchange ideas, thoughts, and information about their lives and communities and view each other's photos through a Flickr account.

CULTURAL LESSONS I

During the months following the conference we planned the details of the project. Initially, the immediate goal was to create a connection between high school students in Fort Lauderdale, Philadelphia, and Mamelodi; however, the larger objective was to promote diverse perspectives, cross-cultural literacy, and global awareness. The latter objective was particularly important given that the members of each school primarily heralded from relatively insular communities, with little to no experience with the larger global environment except what they may have viewed or read in the media. As one South African student commented:

We all haven't been to America, although we think we know about your lifestyle, but that's probably about the celebrity's news flash we learn about in the media and that's about it. We know nothing about your culture, challenges you come across, and the big difference between our two countries. I would like to have a long relationship with my pen pal in your country, to update each other about the life-threatening problems we face as the youth of today, like STDs, crime, and teenage pregnancy.

By providing these students the opportunity to reach outside of their conventional educational environments, we hoped to create an online forum that would also encourage personal growth and development.

THE SCHOOLS AND THE STUDENTS

Gatang Comprehensive School is located in Mamelodi, East Pretoria, South Africa and consists of 1,700 students and 45 educators. The school's mission is to provide its students, the majority of whom are from poor communities, with an excellent education. Its curriculum contains lessons in three languages, English, Zulu, and Sotho, along with basic sciences, mathematics, business courses, and life orientation.

In the aftermath of apartheid, the Department of Education introduced the National Curriculum Statement (NCS), a revamped set of policies and procedures designed to provide equitable educational opportunities in South Africa. By 2005 the curriculum was revisited and a new learning area, Life Orientation, was added. Its purpose is to teach students life skills useful to them in their daily lives. Although conceptually sound in its focus and need, the educational community has been challenged by its implementation.

The Parkway Northwest High School for Peace and Social Justice in Philadelphia, Pennsylvania, is a small public school (population 350) where students are admitted on the basis of an application process that includes an interview with a faculty committee. The "Peace" School was born out of the idea that an alternative educational environment to the military academy should exist—an alternative that would help students critically think about choosing different responses to conflict and their personal role in making the world a better place. As demonstrated by its name, the school emphasizes conflict resolution and peacemaking skills as an ingrained part of its curriculum and extracurricular activities. However, in contrast to the school's vision and goals, many of the students come from difficult home situations and unsafe communities.

In Fort Lauderdale, Florida, rather than working with a specific high school, the teen group from the Nova Southeastern University (NSU) Alvin Sherman Library, Research, and Information Technology Center was contacted. This library is a joint-use facility serving the residents of Broward County and NSU students, faculty, and staff members. Although most of the library's collections and research resources are academic in nature, it maintains active programming for children, young adults, and adults. Project member Robin Kear, who at that time worked for the NSU library, collaborated with the young adult librarian to recruit the teens. A flyer was created to announce the project, and the young adult librarian offered volunteer credit hours for participation. Despite some initial commitment by the students, none of the teens concretely responded. Consequently, we did not pursue their involvement further.

Nonetheless, the commonalities and differences shared by the remaining groups of students provided fertile ground for a dialogue about social problems and cultural perceptions. After much discussion and input from the respective high schools, we determined that a quick and easy strategy for facilitating the student's communications was to develop a blog. The benefits of using a blog were fourfold: (1) students could learn about blogging as a form of technology and information, (2) students could post profiles and photos, (3) topical conversations could be managed through threaded discussions, and (4) the discussions could be monitored. Once the communications mechanism was decided, the immediate plan was to have students introduce themselves followed by a weekly posting of pertinent topics for their discussion. As beginners to establishing this type of forum and blogging in general, we had no sense of the project's outcome, only our hope-filled anxieties.

SA AND US, BUMPS IN THE ROAD, SUCCESS AND DISAPPOINTMENT!

Although we had begun planning in January 2007, various meetings and permissions were required to get the project off the ground. The first step was to convince school administrators and educators of its merit. In Philadelphia, Paula met with the principal of the "Peace" School, who in turn introduced her to two teachers who might be interested in the project. After email exchanges and a face-to-face meeting, one teacher agreed to have her students involved. Rachel Davis teaches

World History and her students were studying multiculturalism and global ethics. As a part of our project she was willing to include lessons on South Africa, which would also encompass the students researching topics related to contemporary South Africa. These lessons were invaluable for establishing a basis by which the American students could inquire about their South African partner's daily lives.

In Mamelodi, Thembi met with Gatang Comprehensive's principal, who in turn referred her to Mr. Malima, an educator serving on the library committee. This led to Thembi, Mr. Malima, Ms. Tsele, the librarian from the municipality library housed at Gatang, and Mrs. Chauke, the head of the English department, to form a project committee. They met several times with the school, which resulted in twenty-five grade ten learners being able to participate in the project.

As luck would have it, while preparations were being made to begin training the students, the educators embarked on an industrial action. This created a major inconvenience because Thembi could not communicate with anyone at the school as a result. Instead, she relied on students coming to inquire about the progress of the project to tell other students that she needed to meet with them. The resulting meeting turned out to be with twenty-five learners not involved with the project but wanting training and access to the computers. In the end, fifty students were trained on the available technology.

As if having twice the number of students to train wasn't enough, Thembi was beset with a logistical nightmare. The computer lab available to the students was located at the library on the University of Pretoria's Mamelodi campus, but this was complicated by the campus academic semester being in session; consequently, access to the lab required Thembi to engage in very intense scheduling. The students were allowed to use the computer lab once a week and during a specific period. Still, when a time slot became available, Internet access would often be a problem, which limited the students in being able to respond to the blog as well as practice other skills acquired during training.

The other challenge for Thembi was that these students had not used computers before and required training in basic computer skills before they could be trained in electronic mail, blogging, Internet searches, and information strategy. However, after receiving the training from Ina and Thembi, the students became independent in their use of the technologies and were very excited. They spent much of their time at the university computer laboratories. This independence increased their self-esteem and confidence, especially because they were sharing space with older university students. Along with participating on the blog, Gatang students were now equipped with skills to perform information searches for their own academic endeavors. This achievement resulted in several requests from their educators and other schools to train additional learners. Unfortunately, given the limited resources and time, this was not possible.

Although the obstacles encountered by Paula in Philadelphia were nowhere near those in Mamelodi, the most prominent was obtaining parental consent. Because the project's execution was occurring relatively late in the semester, there was not enough time to obtain parental permission for the students' individual participation. Philadelphia's school district has developed strict policies involving Internet access to ensure the safety and privacy of its students. There were concerns about providing personal information to people unknown to the students and their parents as well as the content of the information that the children might divulge without thinking about it. Consequently, neither assigning each student a pen pal nor posting their individual photos to the blog could occur without parental consent. As a solution to this problem, Mrs. Davis, the student's teacher, suggested posting a group photo and assigning one student to post responses for everyone.

Once the blog was set up, coordinating the discussion proved the most difficult. None of us had considered the implications of time zones or the school calendar; as a result the communications among the learners were a bit staggered. The solution for clarifying the difference in time zones was easy; world clocks for Philadelphia and South Africa were simply added to the blog. In contrast, access to the computers was difficult and the students found themselves waiting for responses from each other. By the last week of April, the Parkway students began introducing themselves on the blog. They blogged about their families and communities, favorite colors, and their general likes and dislikes. They wanted to know more about South Africa, the things they held in common, and the differences they shared. Toward the end of the following week, we began to hear from the Gatang students. Similar to the Parkway students they were curious about the personal lives of their American partners.

We never envisioned that introductions might take two weeks of the plan, however. Between access to computers and the standard lesson plans, the initial communications became stretched out. By the end of the third week, we announced discussion topics would begin the following week. As a project team, we had decided that the first question would be about violence. At the time, Philadelphia was experiencing a growing problem with violence in general and youth violence specifically. In South Africa the same problems existed. The students discussed the need for greater security measures, the importance of communications as a means of resolving conflict, and the impact of violence on their communities. Separately, Philadelphia students began to post information they were learning through their research, and the Mamelodi students responded with questions and explanations of their customs. At this stage, the students began to respond to each other through threaded discussions, whereas prior to this, the students were posting single threads and not responding directly to each other. Once they began the threaded discussions, it was obvious the cultural exchange was beginning to work.

Unfortunately, just as the students began to exchange valuable cultural lessons with each other, the Philadelphia students had to exit the project because of existing lesson plans and the academic year coming to a close. The abrupt ending of the project left each party disappointed that more time could not be devoted to its continuance. However, in its first iteration, the Cultural Lessons blog established a foundation for personal experience and classroom lessons to be a bridge for students to connect to each other in a significant way. One student described this partnership as "the highlight of his life and great exposure [to another culture]."

SOUTH AFRICA BOUND! CONNECTING WITH THE GATANG AND UNIVERSITY OF PRETORIA COMMUNITY

One of the highlights of the project was when Paula visited Gatang Comprehensive School during her time in South Africa for the International Federation of Library Associations and Institutions (IFLA) conference in August 2007. Gathered together again with Ina and Thembi, Paula was welcomed by the Deputy-Head Mistress Mrs. Matsebela and Ms. Chauke, the head of the English Department. On their way to meet the students, the project participants formed the guard of honor from the staff room to the school library. They wore T-shirts, contributed by the University of Pretoria's Mamelodi Campus Director, Edwin Smith, that were emblazoned on the back with "Paula's Links" and the students names listed beneath.

The event was a celebration and an opportunity to learn more about each other, discuss the project, and understand some of the ongoing library needs of Gatang. The students planned and facilitated the entire event, from the introductions to the program presentations. During the function, the learners performed a traditional South African song and dance and recited a poem they had written. The gathering also provided the chance for some of the students to voice what they had gained from participating in the project. It was a heartwarming occasion for all and provided closure to what had been an abrupt ending to the project.

The following day a breakfast meeting was held with the Director of the Department of Library Services (University of Pretoria), Mr. Robert Moropa, and this opportunity was used to emphasize the importance of the project. After the breakfast meeting, Paula delivered a presentation about the project and responded to questions from staff members of the University of Pretoria. Further meetings were held with Mrs. Hilda Kriel (Deputy Director: Library Services), Dr. Heila Pienaar (Deputy Director: Library Services), Mrs. Monica Hammes (Assistant Director: Open Scholarship & Quality Assurance), and Mrs. Ujala Satgoor (Faculty Library Leader: Economic & Management Sciences). An important outcome from these meetings was the suggestion that a collaborative model based on our project should be considered as part of our next steps.

CULTURAL LESSONS II AND SERVICE LEARNING

As the fall semester began in 2007, Paula was contacted by the "Peace" School for a meeting with educators and other interested parties to discuss potential South African projects. One of the attendees was Mrs. Davis, the instructor whose class had participated in the Cultural Lessons blog project. Mrs. Davis has a long history with service-learning activities, which essentially opened the door for expanding our project from a cultural dialogue to engaging the students in a learning activity that could benefit one or both communities. By the end of the meeting, a decision was made to establish an afterschool international club with a service-learning mission. The service-learning project would encompass not only establishing a second iteration of the Cultural Lessons blog but would also encompass the larger project initially envisioned by the original group of librarians, which was to assist Gatang Comprehensive School in the development of their library. The project included students from both high schools, a student advisor from Penn State Abington, and faculty advisors from Parkway Northwest, Penn State Abington, University of Pretoria, and Gatang Comprehensive.

At the time of this writing, five students have joined the international club at Parkway Northwest, and twenty-three students are participating from Gatang. The students have established a fundraising campaign to purchase books for the Gatang library, alternately entitled "Change 4 Change" or "The Power of Change." Each group will collect pocket change from their fellow students, school administrators, and teachers for the project. They also will make presentations to their schools and community to gain support for their fundraising efforts. The students will also create PowerPoint presentations about their communities that will be linked to the blog and used to inform each other about their lives as well as used for their fundraising presentations. Cultural Lessons II is up and running, and the students are in the midst of introductions and their first discussion topic—teenage pregnancy. In parallel with these efforts the advisors are researching grant and donor opportunities that would enable the U.S. students to visit their South African counterparts.

ACADEMIC LIBRARY OUTREACH

Placing this project into the greater realm of library outreach is difficult. The population for the project is a high school, the librarians are academic, the location is international, and the format is untraditional. The more factors included the narrower the field becomes. If library outreach is "bringing services out to where they are needed," as Marcia Trotta is quoted in Williams and Walters (2003, 21), this project truly brings services to the far reaches of the world and transcends borders and cultures.

Much of the published literature surrounding academic library outreach focuses on outreach to the internal university or college community. These traditional efforts have included students, staff, faculty, and sometimes alumni. This constituency is the most obvious and natural choice for any academic library to pursue, considering outreach is often designed to publicize programs and services to the general campus community (Withers 2006) or to enhance library services to diverse populations on campus (Walter 2005). Other standard practices of outreach include developing relationships with faculty and academic departments to discern their collection needs and publicize available, relevant resources.

Only recently have academic librarians begun writing about and performing outreach outside of these traditional communities. The nontraditional outreach approach has included local community groups, local secondary student populations, and communicating to the general community the breadth and depth of the collection, and individual borrowing privileges. For instance, an academic librarian may perform outreach to the local business community to publicize its government document collection. Academic library outreach also encompasses distance library services to individuals outside of the campus communities such as those studying at other distant educational institutions (Dugan 1997). The literature suggests various technology trends have been used to conduct outreach, including websites, online tutorials (Williams and Walters 2003), and now blogs, RSS feeds, and other social software.

Academic library outreach to local high school communities is a logical extension of the work of academic librarians but is not widely researched or reported. The high school group is conceivably the future attendees of the outreach institution. Visser (2006) researched the outreach of special collections staff at the Association of Research Libraries (ARL) to the local K–12 population. She surveyed 115 ARL Special Collections Departments (with a 70 percent response rate) and found that over half of the respondents worked with K–12 populations in some way (Visser

2006). Bailey, Teel, and Walker (2006) of East Carolina University reached out to local school educators but not directly to the students. There is little research about academic librarians reaching out to high school populations and, admittedly, it often falls outside of their traditional duties and responsibilities, as our project did. Academic library outreach for K–12 populations can take the form of a library research session conducted by reference or instruction librarians for those that come to campus through university summer programs or something similar.

International outreach among libraries and between communities is currently a markedly small and narrow niche within the topic of academic outreach. Although a formal outreach component does not exist in the IFLA, librarians across specialties (e.g., academic, public, and special) and countries work together on various project committees, which can potentially produce individual outreach initiatives. Another example is the International Association of Music Libraries that connects music librarians from all over the world with each other and helps to formalize outreach work to each other (Hellen 2007). Other library associations also may bring international librarians together but not necessarily their populations. With this in mind, the trend to internationalize education curriculums and existing international academic connections of many universities and colleges suggests that expanded opportunities for academic librarians to participate in international outreach projects will experience future growth.

CREATING AN INTERNATIONAL LIBRARY OUTREACH PROJECT

Projects like this one stem from a passion for international librarianship and a passion for community engagement. They require collective effort, understanding, and commitment. Our group found that it was hard work, particularly when navigating the policies and procedures of the local high school educational systems. Even with extensive email communication, unforeseen problems occurred, often out of our control or foresight. Sometimes the problems came from our own lives; for example, after the blog Robin took a new job and moved to a new city, and her level of commitment waned. Still the disparities in time, effort, and culture proved surmountable and the project progressed.

There are many issues to consider when planning an international academic library outreach project. What specific need will be addressed or problem solved by the project? What are the benefits of the project? What resources (i.e., financial, time, and people) are available for the project's success? How does distance impact the overall goal? How will language barriers and cultural missteps be handled? What methods of communication are available (i.e., Skype, email, or texting)? What methods of documentation will you use (i.e., blogs, wikis, or Microsoft Word)? How tech savvy are the participants and should training be built into the plan? These are just a few but important aspects that can have an impact on the overall project.

Our experience suggests that the following ideas may be helpful in designing an international academic outreach project:

- Formalize a commitment: Who will be responsible for what? How long will the project exist? A memorandum of understanding can be created. Identify roles and responsibilities early in the process.

- Connect with the targeted constituency: To whom will the project reach out? What connections already exist that can be built upon? Who needs to be kept in the loop? What permissions are needed? Perform a needs analysis that includes the targeted constituency. Identify potential stakeholders.

- Share leadership: Who is responsible for what? How do you build in active participation by all parties? These projects are often outside of daily job duties, sharing leadership responsibilities can help move the project along. In addition, the community receiving the benefits of the project must co-own the project direction.

- Be conscious of your project commitment: What other commitments may impinge on your participation? How much time can you realistically commit to the success of the project? What talents or skills do you bring to the project? Be willing to participate, remain committed to the vision of the project, and keep others aware of your work and personal situation. Understand that contextually the project may have greater or lesser meaning for the other participants of the project than it does for you.

- Be aware of emerging technologies for project support: Social software collaborative technologies, commonly called Web 2.0, can make international projects like these possible and easier than ever. These new and emerging technologies also offer new and creative ways to connect around the world.

- Embody flexibility and patience: Be willing to take a step back and wait when things are not moving as fast as you would like. There may be roadblocks that occur within or outside the project group.

- Build in assessment: It is important to build and offer some kind of mechanism for feedback from the participants. This could be during the project to refocus efforts or after the project for another iteration or continuation.

- Be aware of the potential for cultural miscommunications: Language barriers and cultural missteps are inherent products of the process. Emails are often exchanged to facilitate the project and misinterpretations can occur.

- Nonetheless: communicate, communicate, and communicate!

Making international library connections can be easier than one might think. Organizations, such as the American Library Association (ALA) International Relations Office and ALA's International Relations Round Table (IRRT), have a mission to promote international librarianship. Within these groups are committees dedicated to facilitating sister library connections, promoting international library understanding among various geographical regions, providing information on international exchanges, and various other aspects of international librarianship. The IFLA, Special Library Association (SLA), and Chartered Institute of Library and Information Professionals (CILIP) of the United Kingdom also have various committees and activities designed to bring together librarians around the world. Becoming aware of these groups can facilitate connections and create ideas and sparks for projects.

LESSONS LEARNED

The lessons learned from this small project outdistance the original goals. Although we were concerned with the students gaining cultural lessons from their foreign partners, we never imagined the impact the project would have on each of our lives. In various ways, this project was an experiment in bridging a digital, cultural, and academic divide.

The influence of technology on this period in our history is unmatched. Never before has access to information and each other been so prevalent. Among the myriad of tools and toys available to educate and entertain are also products that shape our identity and culture. For many of the students involved in this project, the Cultural Lessons blogs might be their only access to another culture beyond what they see on popular media and the Internet. Yet comments made by some of the students indicate that this experience may be motivation to learn more about the world they live in and seek other opportunities for exposure to different cultures.

As academic librarians with interests in global issues and education, we know the benefits of studying abroad. However, "data from the Institute of International Education and the U.S. Department of Education show study abroad participation rates have remained stagnant for African-American, Hispanic, and Native American students ... for example, only 3.4 percent of study abroad participants are African-American" (Redden 2007). Perhaps providing early exposure to other world cultures in which students are personally invested, as this project has, will help reduce concerns students from urban environments have about exploring other countries.

The benefits and lessons from this project, however, are not only from the possibilities of cultural exposure. They also exist in the dialogue between the learners. Having topical discussions on societal issues permitted the students to understand their similarities rather than emphasizing their differences. They learned that they each have pride and concern about the state of their communities and want to change things for the better. Overall, the project assisted them in understanding cultural diversity and exposed them to other perspectives on societal problems.

Although we consider this project to be innovative in its simplicity and definitely expandable across disciplines and age groups, its success lies in the participants not its structure. While the librarians fretted and worried about the details, the learners, under difficult circumstances, committed to the process and delivered. They kept the project interesting and the librarians motivated. Yet missing from the process was the feedback loop that helps any project to improve on its implementation. As we move forward to the next iteration of the Cultural Lessons blog, we will take these lessons, omissions, and benefits and build on their foundation to try to provide a richer and broader cultural experience.

REFERENCES

Adams, J. M. and M. B. Sperling. "Ubiquitous Distributed Learning and Global Citizenship." *Presidency* 6, no. 1 (2003): 30–36.

Bailey, A. R., L. M. Teel, and H. J. Walker. "Designing an Academic Outreach Program through Partnerships with Public Schools." *E-JASL: Electronic Journal of Academic and Special Librarianship* 7, no. 1 (2006). http://southernlibrarianship.icaap.org/content/v07n01/bailey_a01.htm (accessed March 31, 2008).

Dugan, R. E. "Distance Education: Provider and Victim Libraries." *Journal of Academic Librarianship* 23, no. 4 (1997): 315–318.

Forest, J. J. F. "Globalisation, Universities and Professors." *Cambridge Review of International Affairs* 15, no. 3 (2002): 435–450.

Hellen, R. "Music: the International Language. IAML: The International Association of Music Libraries, Archives and Documentation Centres." *Focus on International Library and Information Work* 38, no. 2 (2007): 44–48.

Institute of International Education. *Open Doors: Report on International Educational Exchange.* New York: Institute of International Education, 2007.

Redden, E. "Study Abroad Isn't Just for White Students." *Inside Higher Ed.* June 22, 2007. http://www.insidehighered.com/news/2007/06/11/diversity (accessed March 29, 2008).

Visser, M. "Special Collections at ARL libraries and K-12 Outreach: Current Trends." *Journal of Academic Librarianship* 32, no. 3 (2006): 313–319.

Walter, S. "Moving Beyond Collections: Academic Library Outreach to Multicultural Student Centers." *Reference Services Review* 33, no. 4 (2005): 438–458.

Williams, C. R. and T. O. Walters. "Reference and Instruction Services Go Virtual as a Form of Outreach: Case Studies from Academic Libraries." *Information Outlook* 7, no. 8, (2003): 20–27.

Withers, R. "Getting the Word Out: Publicizing Library Programs and Services to the Community." *College and Undergraduate Libraries* 12, no. 1/2 (2006): 35–45.

5

—————

REACHING OUT TO FUTURE USERS: K–12 OUTREACH AT KANSAS STATE LIBRARIES

Tara L. Coleman and Jenny E. McCraw

INTRODUCTION

Academic libraries have historically engaged in outreach within their own scholarly communities—to faculty, students, departments, and organizations on their campuses. Working with these groups remains a key function of college and university libraries, but it is increasingly important that we, as academic librarians, seek opportunities for partnerships with institutions and groups engaged in learning beyond the boundaries of our own campuses.

Miranda Bennett (2007), in an article exploring the intersections between the Association of College and Research Libraries (ACRL) strategic plan and the 2006 report "A Test of Leadership," commonly known as the Spellings report, outlines several areas of opportunity for academic librarians. One such area is K–12 education. Bennett refers to "the need for members of the higher education community to work together with K–12 educators to ensure that students are well prepared for the challenges of postsecondary life and aware of the opportunities available to them." Bennett suggests that librarians at college and university libraries can meet this need by "creating outreach programs to the K–12 community" (Bennett 2007, 371). She recommends working with K–12 teachers and library media specialists (LMS), hosting high school groups for instruction and introducing them to the world of academic libraries and developing outreach initiatives to increase overall community awareness of higher education.

Bennett's words are likely to resonate with the many academic librarians already committed to working with students from local communities. As coordinators of K–12 outreach at Kansas State University (K-State) Libraries, we strive to meet the needs of the high school students that feature so prominently in Bennett's argument, while also seeking opportunities to introduce younger students to our resources. This chapter outlines our comprehensive K–12 outreach program, covering its history and place within our mission and vision, and also provides tips for starting or developing such a program in your library.

LITERATURE REVIEW

A review of the literature indicates that academic librarians have long been interested and engaged in outreach to K–12 communities. Many of these librarians are employed by public universities similar to K-State, which is a land grant institution. As such, these libraries have a clear charge to serve their local communities in addition to the academic community. The University of Nebraska, for instance, established a program for high school users in the late 1980s and has maintained a structured relationship with area high school groups since. Their program, which is housed in the circulation department and focuses on providing access to physical materials, is closely tied to the university's land grant status. The authors write that the University Libraries "take this land-grant mission seriously, serving as a state-wide resource and making the research collection available throughout the state to Nebraska citizens" (Pearson and McNeil 2002, 24). Librarians from private schools, including prominent institutions like Yale University, have also been active in K–12 outreach, even without the same mission to serve users beyond their academic communities (Young 2007).

Although the emphasis varies from institution to institution, the following reasons for working with K–12 students in an academic library setting are frequently mentioned:

- decreasing the anxiety experienced by students by providing them with a basic introduction to academic libraries before they enter the university environment
- marketing the university to prospective students
- introducing key information literacy concepts earlier in the educational process, both indirectly, by working with LMS, and directly, by providing instruction to students
- supplementing resources available at school and public libraries
- exposing younger students to the higher education environment, which relates closely to the marketing function of this outreach (Burhanna and Jensen 2006; Jackson and Hansen 2006; Kunda 2007; Pearson and McNeil 2002).

Much of the literature refers specifically to working with high school students, but the same goals also apply to younger groups who might visit an academic library. Several authors speak to the importance of outreach to elementary and middle school students in addition to high school visitors, focusing in some cases on unique opportunities to collaborate with K–12 educators and LMS, such as National History Day (Manuel 2005). Sue Kunda speaks more broadly of the benefits of working with a wide range of students, writing, "There is a growing acceptance of a seamless K–16 educational system, compelling educators who rarely dealt with one another in the past to work together now and in the future" (Kunda 2007, 25). Her words relate closely to Bennett's, challenging librarians to expand the scope of our educational services beyond our own students, faculty, and staff, to include students as young as five. Working with students before they even reach high school can instill information literacy concepts early in life, ideally contributing to future academic success. Timothy G. Young from Yale University's Beinecke Rare Book and Manuscript Library writes in support of outreach, particularly to younger children. He advocates working with these children to introduce the research library early in their lives. This exposure to the research library ultimately decreases library anxiety and "demystifies the institution by placing it in context of what libraries, in general, do" (Young 2007, 235).

The literature also refers to the rewards of working with K–12 users beyond the larger goals mentioned above. As Kunda writes, "The enthusiasm of younger students is a welcome relief from the oftentimes blasé attitude of college students" (Kunda 2007, 25). The unique rewards of working with K–12 students, as well as the larger goals outlined in the literature, have shaped and inspired our program at K-State Libraries.

K–12 OUTREACH AND OUR MISSION

As a land grant institution, K-State has a strong tradition of outreach to the citizens of the state of Kansas. K-State's current mission, adopted in 1991, includes "enriching the lives of the citizens of Kansas by extending to them opportunities to engage in lifelong learning and to benefit from the results of research" (Kansas State University 1991). K-State Libraries, though an integral part of the University community, had little formal involvement in many of these enrichment activities before the early 2000s.

Since then, K-State Libraries have become increasingly committed to outreach, particularly to the K–12 community, which supports the University's mission by providing unique learning opportunities to K–12 students. K–12 outreach also supports the libraries' new strategic plan, which explicitly refers to the K–12 community as a user group. The plan indicates a strong commitment to outreach, with one of its goals reading, "We will strengthen our outreach activities to ensure users know how the Libraries can and do serve them" (K-State Libraries 2006).

The feeder schools for K-State vary from well-funded suburban schools to rural and urban schools with smaller and sometimes underfunded libraries. K-State also has a small but significant contingent of students who were home schooled and thus relied on the resources available at their local public libraries. Some of these libraries, both school and public, still maintain card catalogs, and many have limited print and online resources. As a result, many undergraduates who attend K-State begin their university careers with little or no exposure to the information resources available to them through libraries. K-State Libraries offer services to K–12 students to uphold the mission of our university and libraries—giving back to the local community by teaching information literacy skills, by promoting lifelong learning, and by welcoming students to the K-State community with the hope that they will consider us when they select an institution of higher learning.

HISTORY OF LIBRARY INSTRUCTION AT K-STATE LIBRARIES

In the 1970s and early 1980s, K-State Libraries had an instruction librarian whose position focused primarily on providing basic research skills classes. In the mid-1980s these classes were incorporated into large introductory courses for undergraduates, such as Public Speaking and Expository Writing. At that time, the position was converted to a reference position. This left the libraries without a formal instruction program, with the bulk of student instruction being provided by subject librarians.

The expansion of our K–12 outreach program occurred in conjunction with the formal establishment of the Library Instruction Unit. Beginning in the late 1990s, K-State Libraries experienced a growing demand for library instruction for general education courses on campus. At that time, there was no official librarian or program in place to meet these needs. Responding to the increasing number of requests, the libraries created the Patron Instruction Team in 2001. This team was small, with just five staff members, only one of whom was a full-time librarian, and none of whom were solely devoted to instruction. The unit concentrated on offering basic drop-in instruction classes and supplemented those with a variety of online tutorials and modules. With all the work required to get the program off the ground and to meet the needs of campus users, the small unit was unable to provide formal outreach to K–12 groups. It was decided that the libraries would offer services to high school groups, although the staff typically only had time to do brief tours of our main library, Hale, and basic instruction on the use of reference resources and online databases.

In 2004 the Libraries hired a resident librarian whose responsibilities were primarily instruction-related. With the help of this resident, the Patron Instruction Team was able to expand its services to the K–12 community. In 2005 an instruction coordinator was hired, and the Library Instruction Unit was created to meet the rising information literacy needs of students on campus. A new resident librarian took responsibility for K–12 tours and instruction, increasing the visibility of these services in our local community and beyond.

CURRENT PROGRAM

Since 2001, when the Patron Instruction Team was formed and the Libraries began to offer more formalized tours and instruction for K–12 groups, the demand for these services has increased markedly.

Year	Number of K–12 Students
2001	69
2002	60
2003	0/No data
2004	0/No data
2005	228
2006	366
2007	479

Prior to 2005 we offered tours and basic instruction for high school (and some middle school) groups, but we did not advertise our services widely. Once we began advertising on our website and on email lists, we saw a sharp increase in demand.

Particularly for those schools in surrounding counties, K-State Libraries are an unparalleled resource, and teachers and LMS express appreciation for the opportunity for their students to make use of our print materials and electronic resources. Although Kansas does offer statewide access to a group of databases to anyone with a Kansas Library Card, the wider range of scholarly article databases available at K-State Libraries can be a major asset to students looking to supplement their research. Even those visitors who do not come to the Libraries for research benefit from an introduction to a large academic library, and younger students particularly find our main library, with five floors, 200 computers, and nearly two million volumes, an exciting place to visit.

We currently provide two basic types of services to our K–12 users: instruction for older groups and story time activities for younger groups. All groups also receive a basic tour of Hale Library, which is especially important for older students who might be exploring the building on their own to find materials.

STARTING A K–12 OUTREACH PROGRAM AT YOUR LIBRARY

If you are interested in starting a program like ours at your own library, there are a number of things to consider as you begin to make your plans. Perhaps the most important question to answer is who will be responsible for the program. Although we have assumed coordinator roles for this program in our own library, K–12 outreach is not an official part of our job descriptions. In your institution you may consider taking a different approach and formally associating this responsibility with a position or positions. You do not want K–12 outreach responsibilities to be passed around each time staffing and job duties change because the service could easily fall through the cracks.

Another critical question to ask is where K–12 outreach best fits in your organizational structure. A primary advantage of the service having a clear home unit or department is that it will be easier for your colleagues and your users to identify you. Our K–12 program lives in the Library Instruction Unit, although the contact person responsibilities have changed hands several times. The literature on K–12 outreach indicates that academic libraries have chosen to centralize their outreach programs in a variety of departmental areas, including circulation and other public services areas (Burhanna and Jensen 2006; Pearson and McNeil 2002). Other good homes for this program may be through a community service or outreach librarian.

There are a number of other things to consider as you develop your program. Do you have

- space for students to work and keep their belongings?
- time to work with them?
- money—will librarians be paid extra or will this be added to "duties as assigned"?
- buy-in from your administration and colleagues?
- an environment appropriate for the age group?
- enough physical resources, such as computers, copiers, and classrooms, to share with people not affiliated with your institution?
- the facilities to keep their presence from distracting or annoying your primary users and to keep your primary users from intimidating or distracting visitors?

We offer services to students from kindergarten through twelfth grade, but that range may not be appropriate for your library. If your library is small, if resources are scarce, or if your collections are especially valuable, you may prefer to limit access to older children who may be more responsible and better able to comport themselves. Also keep in mind that, in working with large groups, it may be hard to keep younger students quiet. If noise is a concern, keep age in mind.

We welcome students from all over Kansas. If you live in a more densely populated area or simply need to set parameters for your program, you may wish to focus your outreach to specific school districts. Your admissions office can usually advise you on the primary feeder schools for your institution.

PROMOTING YOUR PROGRAM

Once you have made the decision and received approval to start your program, you will need to get the word out so that local K–12 groups know what services you have available. Here are a few simple ways to promote your new program:

- Advertise on your library and university websites.
- Contact the schools and home school groups directly.
- Announce the service on email lists.
- Provide your local public librarians with information about the service.

One of the easiest ways to get the word out about your program is to make sure that there is information on your library website. If people do not see explicit text that tells them they are welcome on your campus and in your library, they may assume that they are not. In addition, it is important to make sure that campus and library staff members know that this service is available so that they do not unknowingly turn people away. As noted earlier, we have had success providing information on our library website, including our direct contact information and a form that teachers and LMS can easily submit in advance of a visit (http://www.lib.k-state.edu/depts/libinst/highschool.html). We also collaborate with New Student Services at our university, because they frequently field requests for campus tours as field trips for K–12 students. Along with the bug zoo and the campus dairy bar, Hale Library is a popular spot (http://consider.k-state.edu/grouptours).

It is also a good idea to contact schools directly. This can be done by sending out brochures to principals, teachers, and LMS, posting information in newsletters, and sending out emails via an email list. With knowledge of the program, teachers can plan ahead and work a visit into their course planning. When you are sending out information, do not forget private schools and home schoolers. These two groups may not have the same information resources that a public school does and might particularly appreciate the invitation.

Last but not least, let other libraries know. Teachers, librarians, and parents use libraries too and may not know that the local college or university library allows people not affiliated with the school in their library.

When your program has been approved and advertised, the next step is to get volunteers. Even if you think you can do it all on your own, it is a good idea to ask your colleagues if they are interested in helping out. This will help ease the burden when you get a large class of precocious elementary students or a group of high schoolers with lots of questions. You may have colleagues who have experience—professional or personal—and can share techniques on how to work with these students. It can also foster a sense of community among people in your organization who are committed to working with potential future users. In addition, working with K–12 groups can be fun! Even if you do not like working with them full time, it can be refreshing to work with people who are enthusiastic about your resources, the size of your building, or just being on a college campus.

ORGANIZING AND PLANNING K–12 VISITS

When planning a visit, there are some vital bits of information that you will need from the teacher or LMS requesting the tour or instruction:

- Phone or email contact
- Number of students and adults
- Information needs and type of assignment

It is a good idea to confirm the visit one week in advance and to ask if any changes have been made to the assignment. Keep in mind that teachers have busy schedules and may be difficult to get in touch with. If possible, do not save any key communication for the last minute.

For some, grades five through seven (ten to thirteen years old) may not seem that different from one another but, in our experience, this is a time of transition for students during which they trade in Disney Channel and dolls/action figures for Facebook.com and iPods. It can be difficult to decide what is appropriate for what age. For that reason, we divide our activities into tours/story time and tours/instruction.

Tours

Tours are provided for all K–12 groups, though the length and focus may vary. Giving tours is a great way to introduce information literacy and critical thinking skills into the visit. The American Association of School Librarians and Association for Educational Communications and Technology (1998) published "Information Literacy Standards for Student Learning," which might inspire you to develop activities or questions that integrate information literacy concepts into the tour. The standards focus on developing the potential of students to be independent learners and to pursue knowledge of all kinds.

At K-State Libraries we try to keep these guidelines in mind while also considering what kinds of questions might keep students of different ages engaged and interested during the tour. Questions that have worked well for us include:

- How many books are in the library? Why do you think we have so many books? Should we get more? Why should/n't we get more?
- This is the science section. What are some types of sciences? What are some types of jobs that involved science? Why do we need science?

The most popular parts of the tour in Hale Library are the compact shelving, our murals, the DOW Chemical Multicultural Resource Center, and Special Collections/Archives.

- Compact shelving questions include: Why do we have moving shelves? Can they hurt you? Can they crush your teacher?
- Murals—The "We Are The Dream" Mural, depicting the minority experience in the United States, was created, painted, and partially funded by KSU students in the late 1970s. Four murals representing K-State's original colleges hang in our Great Room. Questions include: Who is in the pictures? What are they doing? Why are they doing it? Why was a mural painted about it?
- DOW Chemical Multicultural Resource Center questions include: Do you know what culture is? Can you give us an example of something unique from your culture?
- Special Collections/Archives—Our archivist and special collections staff select materials that will interest younger students, including items that they can touch. Questions include: How old is this? Why is it important? Why do we keep this?

Story Time

For younger children, generally those in first through sixth grades, we often choose to provide a library tour paired with a story time activity. We do this for several reasons. Students at this age generally have shorter attention spans and plenty of energy. It may be in the best interests of the students and the library users to keep the little ones on the move. Another reason we prefer to keep the activities limited to a tour and/or story time is that we may not have any materials that are appropriate for their reading level. Even if your library has a juvenile literature collection like ours does, it may not have enough nonfiction to support their research project.

Before your first tour, it is important to decide on the "rules" of your library. One of those rules may be what you wish to be called. In academia, we often address each other by our first names, but many younger students are used to calling people Mrs., Miss, Ms., Mr., so that is an appropriate way to introduce yourself. If this is more formal than you are comfortable with, Ms. Tara or Mr. Dan works fine too. Most likely the teachers and other adults accompanying the students have already asked them to be on their best behavior and told them what to do and not do. You might want to ask the children if they know what the library rules are—they may have been given more rules than you expect. Some obvious rules that we have in our library tours and story times for younger students are that students need to raise their hands, stick with a buddy, and whisper. Some K-State librarians also have rules that children have to tip-toe through the quiet areas, sit on the floor until it is their turn to use the restroom, or cover their mouths as they walk up stairs. Little kids (and even their teachers) may think the rules are silly or funny, but they will go along with it if you do it too. We have found that these rules, while sometimes silly, help to keep the students' attention while keeping noise and disruption to a minimum.

Instruction

More structured instruction activities, such as catalog and database searching demonstrations, are generally reserved for middle and high school students, though we have had gifted classes of fourth to sixth graders request instruction as well. The way you introduce your library to the younger children will probably be the same way you will want to introduce it to the older students. But when more in-depth instruction is involved, more preparation is necessary. If possible, find out what resources the students can access at their library and what type of format (books, microforms, etc.) the teacher would like them to use. Many times, high school students prefer print materials over on-line databases. This may be because they are more familiar with books, or because books have the more general information that they are seeking, or because this is their first time in a large library and they want to take advantage of all the books available. If this is the case with your group of students, make sure the teachers know about circulation privileges for community users in advance so that there are no surprises or disappointments at the end of the day. Being as familiar as possible with the rules at your institution is an asset, so find out the following information before working with a group of students looking to check out books: whether non-university users can check out materials, how much it costs, and how many books can they check out at a time? If teachers are going to check out books for students, let the students know the consequences of damaging or losing materials. If the teacher plans to check out materials for the class, he or she may have already warned them about this, but it does not hurt for them to hear the information twice.

If given enough advance notice about the class and their assignment, it may be helpful to create a handout for the students. We also create online resources pages that outline a combination of resources: those they can access only on campus and those they can access from home, school, or a local public library.

Because many college students do not understand that databases and ejournals, while online, are not free, high school students are not likely to understand either. You may need to explain this to them. Remind them that because things are subscription based they will not be able to save the URL and access the article from home. They will need to print or save materials before they leave the library. It may be useful to suggest to teachers in advance that students bring flash drives, if possible. We encourage students to save articles or email them as attachments to an email account they can access.

Behavior and Teacher Participation

Needless to say, good teacher-librarian communication is essential to make any visit successful. For this reason, it is vital for both parties to express their expectations clearly before the class arrives at your library. These expectations should include behavior guidelines as well as content and structure of the visit. We would love to tell you that students are always well behaved, but, unfortunately, that is not always the case. Much like working with college students, you may experience students not participating, goofing off, or perhaps even fighting. If you find that things are not going well after the class has arrived, there are a few things you can do. Treat these students the same way you would college students who have gotten out of hand. If students are too loud, ask them to be quiet. If your library does not allow food, ask them to put or throw the food away. If your suggestions are not effective or you do not feel comfortable doing this, ask for support from the teacher. It is always best to let the teacher know how things are going, especially if you think there are problems. Most likely, a few words from their teacher will be the reminder the students need. On rare occasions, you may feel that the teachers or adults with the class are not contributing and you may need to take charge of the situation. If students are misbehaving and teachers are doing little to support you, pull the teacher aside and let them know that you will not be able to help the students if they do not behave in the library.

Regardless of the outcome of the class visit, let the teacher know formally how smoothly you felt the visit went. Because many teachers keep a portfolio of their activities and accomplishments, we like to send thank you notes on official letterhead to both the teachers and their school principals. We thank the class for their visit and comment on our perceptions of its success. We have not yet had to send a note with bad news, and we hope that we will never need to, but this is one way of letting someone in authority know the outcome.

Concerns

Although we would like to say working with K–12 is sunshine and roses, that is not always the case. Because academic libraries are so familiar to us, we can easily forget that our libraries are adult environments and things are not generally geared toward young people. The design of your library is likely to be more open and users will primarily be aged seventeen and older. With that said, here are a few things to keep in mind.

Field trips are an adventure for K–12 students, and as is the case with many adventures, people can actually get lost. Luckily, we have not lost any children, but high school kids have mysteriously "disappeared" in the stacks, and students of all ages are apprehensive about striking out on their own in such a large building. Be sure to point out all the exits and the places to get help before, during, and near the end of your tour or instruction session. Establish a meeting place for them in case someone gets separated. It is also a good idea to let your library staff know in advance that you are working with a school group. If a staff member notices confused children walking around the building, they can be sent your way.

Teachers or parents may prefer that their child not be introduced to certain issues. There may be demonstrations on campus in the free speech zone that cover topics that are new, offensive, or inappropriate for younger people. We have had campus tours and visits coincide with a celebration of National Coming Out Day, with student groups that were handing out condoms, and with abortion protests (complete with graphic images). It is not always possible to anticipate these activities, so it is helpful to let teachers and LMS know that there is a possibility they will witness these events. Teachers should be aware that academic libraries and their resources are aimed at an adult audience before they bring their students. Public Internet access computers are unlikely to have filters. There is always the possibility that K–12 students will accidentally or actively access inappropriate subject matter. Or, like many college students, they may spend a good portion of their time on social networking sites such as Facebook or MySpace. You will want to emphasize that their visit to your library is a special occasion so that they are more likely to take advantage of the visit and stay on task. Your collection may also contain materials not suitable for young eyes. Many academic libraries have Playboy, nude art books, and radical or controversial books and authors. If this is a concern, it is best to let the teachers know so they can steer students away from these materials. We are careful to emphasize this and other issues that may arise on our Web page detailing our K–12 services.

Feedback

Finally, you may want to consider ways in which to receive feedback on your K–12 activities. We have done little to assess our program formally, but we frequently receive thank you letters and emails from teachers and students who have visited Hale Library. More formal assessment could include surveys mailed or emailed to participating schools, students, and teachers or linked from your library website.

CONCLUSION

The literature clearly indicates the advantages of providing K–12 services in academic libraries. Although our program and our activities are unique to K-State, the lessons we have learned can be easily applied in other academic library settings. Looking back to Miranda Bennett's arguments with which we opened this discussion, we have found that working with K–12 groups is a good way to prepare incoming students for the challenging academic world of higher education. We also agree that K–12 outreach can be an excellent promotional tool, and we make every attempt during our work with these students to point out the many services the library provides to the K-State community.

Although we have a solid start with our program, it is still in its early stages and we have plans to experiment with ways to improve our services. For instance, we would like to find effective ways to do more outreach to home-schooled students and their families. We would also like to develop strategies for working with teachers who would like to bring students in for an introduction to our academic environment but who do not choose assignments that fit the scope of our resources. In the future, we hope that our program continues to grow and that we are able to establish lasting partnerships with schools, teachers, and LMS.

REFERENCES

American Association of School Librarians, Association for Educational Communications and Technology. Information Literacy Standards for Student Learning. American Library Association and Association for Educational Communications and Technology, 1998. http://www.acrl.org/aasltemplate.cfm?section=aaslinfolit (accessed April 9, 2008).

Bennett, Miranda. "Charting the Same Future? The ACRL Strategic Plan and the Report of the Commission on the Future of Higher Education." *College & Research Libraries News* 68, no. 6 (June 2007): 370–372, 377.

Burhanna, Kenneth J. and Mary Lee Jensen. "Collaborations for Success: High School to College Transitions." *Reference Services Review* 34, no. 4 (2006): 509–519.

Jackson, Lydia and Julia Hansen. "Creating Collaborative Partnerships: Building the Framework." *Reference Services Review* 34, no. 2 (2006): 575–588.

Kansas State University. "Mission Statement for Kansas State University." 1991. http://www.k-state.edu/provost/planning/mission.html (accessed April 10, 2008).

K-State Libraries. "K-State Libraries Strategic Plan." 2006. http://www.lib.k-state.edu/geninfo/plan/ (accessed April 10, 2008).

Kunda, Sue. "What's a Second Grader Doing in Special Collections? Academic Libraries Reach Out to K–12 Schools." *OLA Quarterly* 13, no. 1 (Spring 2007): 22–25.

Manuel, Kate. "National History Day: An Opportunity for K–16 Collaboration." *Reference Services Review* 33, no. 4 (2005): 459–486.

Pearson, Debra and Beth McNeil. "From High School Users College Students Grow; Providing Academic Library Research Opportunities to High School Students." *Knowledge Quest* 30, no. 4 (March/April 2002): 24–28.

Young, Timothy G. "The Young Visitors: Introducing Children to the Research Library through Exhibition Tours." *College & Research Libraries News* 68, no. 4 (April 2007): 235–238.

6

———◦•◦•◦———

A NEW EXPLORATION IN OUR INTELLECTUAL COMMONWEALTH

Eric P. Garcia

Academic librarians in the twenty-first century are facing profound exponential information growth, the continuing evolution of new information formats, and rapidly developing new technologies. The library community is thus faced with a daunting challenge: promoting library services and ensuring that high school students benefit from the academic community's wealth of knowledge. One way to meet this challenge is by building an effective outreach program that benefits not only high school students but also the university and the community as a whole.

CONTEXT: CALIFORNIA STATE UNIVERSITY NORTHRIDGE (CSUN)

CSUN is a part of the twenty-three-campus CSU system. CSUN's Oviatt Library currently has twenty-five librarians at the rank of faculty. As part of CSU, the Oviatt Library has been committed to fostering information competency and lifelong learning skills within the academic community. In the 1990s CSU created the "Work Group," which defined information competency. The Work Group determined that "the ability to find, evaluate, use, and communicate information in all of its various formats" would become the nucleus of CSU's definition of information competency (Information Competencies Final Report 1995). This definition serves as a guiding principle of the library's outreach program, which reaches across campus and community to make students aware of the library's services and resources.

In 2004 the library established an outreach librarian position. Working with members of the Reference and Instructional Services Department, the Outreach Librarian ensures that the library's mission of promoting information competency reaches across the academic community. The largest component of this goal is an outreach initiative to K–12 students. Occasionally, tours are provided to elementary-level students, a rare occurrence for students in primary education, who traditionally may have received only rudimentary library instruction. Generally, though, the library performs outreach to secondary-level (high school) students.

To reach out to high schools, the library has established an Advance Placement Student Program (APSP), allowing participating high schools a unique opportunity to borrow materials except for certain restricted items that are limited to CSUN faculty, staff, and currently enrolled students; the privilege is extended to only Advanced Placement (AP) students. The library also provides instruction sessions to both general and AP high school classes when teachers or high school librarians arrange a session with the Outreach Librarian.

The opportunity to offer library sessions to high school students, however, is not without its challenges. The Los Angeles Unified School (LAUSD) mandates a pre-approved curriculum that teachers must follow and benchmarks teachers must meet; time constraints therefore become an issue for high school teachers wanting to bring their classes to the Oviatt Library for an instructional session. Even if teachers' schedules allow their classes an opportunity to visit the Library, this one-shot session is more taxing on high school students than on college students.

TRADITIONAL OUTREACH

The term "Outreach" in academic libraries is a broad based and relatively loosely defined term. Literature related to academic library outreach generally focuses on the relationship between libraries and campus students or faculty and on how services enhance the library's ties to the academic community. The library markets itself to faculty through various modes of outreach initiatives, such as library liaisons, special online forms and Web pages, poster sessions at faculty retreats, and special workshops. Marketing services to students, however, is slightly different; specialized class Web pages, resource guides, tutorials, wikis, blogs, podcasting, embedded librarians within course management systems, and library sessions are just a few methods librarians have used to reach out to students.

Academic library outreach can thus take many forms, but the final result is built around a commitment to instruction and to fostering lifelong learning skills. The overall objective is to foster within students the necessary skills to not only navigate through classes but to also apply these skills to professional careers and lifelong learning needs. The concept of reaching across the campus community from an outreach standpoint, then, has much wider effects.

The pedagogy within higher education provides opportunities for collaborative learning, problem solving, lifelong learning skills, and information competency to provide students "greater coherence in what they are learning as well as increased intellectual interaction with faculty members and fellow students" (Gresham and Van Tassel 2000, 16). Compared to elementary and secondary education, academic library activities address a wide range of issues that include an active learning curriculum (Gresham and Van Tassel 2000). Such activities range from active learning, team learning, shared leadership, collective responsibility, and a "broad engagement of parents, community members and community leaders in building and achieving the school's vision" (Wallace, Engel, and Mooney 1997, 181).

In contrast, the current form of providing outreach service to high school students—the one-shot or one-hour session—often falls short. When the model of the one-shot session is applied to college students, there is a certain expectation as to how the librarian deals with a particular audience. Library session materials differ according to the class level with which students are associated; freshmen, for example, are simply provided a general overview and basic understanding of what the library has to offer. These sessions tend to focus on general information-gathering techniques and introductions to databases that provide a breadth of information. As students progress through their educational careers and continue to advance in the curriculum, library lectures become less about general information, and instead become much more focused on research strategies and techniques. Students are thus gradually introduced to databases that provide the depth of information needed for research topics. Although this approach is designed to best serve college students, the cookie-cutter approach to providing library one-shot sessions does not work with high school students.

When arrangements are made for a library session by a high school media librarian or teacher, the Outreach Librarian first performs an evaluation of the incoming class. This fact-finding mission helps to provide a general foundation for the class's visit. Once the class has arrived at the library, librarians will ask the class some general questions, such as:

- What are the some differences between a high school library and an academic library?
- How big is your school library?
- How would you behave in a library?
- If you do not want to come to the library to use the databases, where can you go to use them for free?
- What can you look at in the library?

These questions are designed to get the students thinking about the new setting in which they find themselves and to open them up to a librarian they have never met. Prior to the high school students sitting in the computer lab, the computers are locked down so students are prevented from checking email or surfing the Web during instructional sessions and will only see what the librarian wants them to see. As introductions to the library and discussions of the research topic are reviewed, the librarian will proceed to show the students how to access the library. Because high school students tend not to visit the library's homepage on a daily basis, generally the introduction to the library's homepage is started from a website with which students are familiar, such as YouTube or MySpace. The students are taught how to search for books in the online catalog, how to find a book in the library, the difference between Dewey Decimal and Library of Congress call numbers, and how to search for articles. Students are also introduced to similar databases within the Los Angeles Public Library (LAPL) system. Once the session has concluded, the computers are unlocked and students can begin their research. Because most high school classes generally are not AP, students will only have the opportunity to photocopy materials or to find articles within a databases and forward the content to themselves.

These one-shot sessions do have drawbacks, such as coverage of materials within a short amount of time (generally thirty minutes), students' inability to check out materials, and large class sizes requiring more than just the services of the dedicated Outreach Librarian. Another major issue with high school visits is that not every high school student is exposed to a library information session; typically, only one or two English classes visit the library, and these classes tend to be from just one teacher. As the students move on from one grade to the next, the likelihood of the student returning to the library is diminished because the students typically will not have the same teacher. As a result, tracking the success rate of the outreach program becomes problematic.

The Oviatt Library, like many other academic libraries, values the relationships it has established with traditional high schools; the challenge becomes on how to find ways to ensure that information competency and literacy are indeed being adequately addressed by the outreach program. This issue might best be examined by exploring the relationship between the Oviatt Library and the Northridge Academy High School.

NORTHRIDGE ACADEMY HIGH SCHOOL

In March of 2002 CSUN entered into a joint lease agreement with the LAUSD to develop an LAUSD high school on property owned by CSUN. This educational partnership was designed with the express purpose of creating "a model academic environment for high school students with a career interest in teaching, arts and media, and health services, as well as to improve performance in basic subjects, facilitate school to career transitions, and enhance student's preparation for higher education" (Shared Use Agreement 2002, 1). What followed was the creation of New Valley High School, which eventually renamed itself Northridge Academy High School (NAHS).

NAHS is truly unique compared with other LAUSD high schools. NAHS developed a coordinated research curriculum for ninth to twelfth grades, involving appropriate grade-level research projects designed to motivate students to think critically when performing research within English classes. Every year, starting in the ninth grade, students visit the library for a library session provided by the Outreach Librarian and reinforced by the NAHS Media Librarian and NAHS teachers. All students at NAHS are extended borrowing privileges of up to three items from the collection, plus renewal of items after two weeks. These features are superior to the APSP program geared for AP students at other high schools. In addition, students can check out materials even if they are unrelated to their English class assignments.

NAHS's research curriculum development is continually evolving. During the 2004–2005 school year, NAHS opened its doors to ninth and tenth graders, and some classes began informal visits to the library. During the 2005–2006 school year, most of the ninth grade classes had visited the library for a mythology research project. Although the visits to the library continued to increase, NAHS refined and improved its coordinated research curriculum. During the 2006–2007 school year, for the first time, all ninth and tenth graders visited the library. At that time, and continuing to this day, all ninth graders were required to research mythology, and all tenth graders were required to research genocide/gendercide. During the 2005–2006 school year, both grade levels were reintroduced to the same introductory instruction. In addition, all ninth graders came back to the library for a second time and received instruction on using selected databases. Within the 2007–2008 school year, all students within the ninth to eleventh grades either have visited or will be visiting the library. As a result, the tenth and eleventh grade students will be the first to build on previously taught skills because they were introduced to the research curriculum as ninth and tenth grade students.

At each grade level, students are introduced to a particular topic; the complexity level increases as students progress from one grade level to the next (ninth grade: Mythology Research Project; tenth grade: Genocide/Gendercide Research Project; eleventh grade: Civil Rights Research Project; twelfth grade: TBA). At each step of the way, students are not just asked to provide a review, regurgitation, or a summation of the topic but to also think critically about the information they are digesting and to analyze the research they have found.

SYNERGY: NAHS LIBRARY AND OVIATT LIBRARY

One institution alone cannot be responsible for achieving the goal of motivating students to think critically; the expression "It takes a village" is an apt description of the NAHS-Oviatt relationship. In a joint partnership, the NAHS Library and the Oviatt Library work together to introduce students to their respective libraries and resources. Ninth grade students must research Greek and Roman mythology in their English classes; at the end of this project, students are required to pick a Greek or Roman god, goddess, hero, heroine, myth, or monster, and then select another culture (e.g., the Maya, Norse, Mongolian, Chinese, Egyptian, Japanese, or Hindu) and write a two- to four-page research paper comparing one of the other culture's myths with the Greek or Roman one that they have selected. The papers must be written in MLA format, double spaced, and in twelve-point Times New Roman font.

To begin the research project, students are introduced to the library at two different points. An in-class visit by the Library Media Teacher (LMT) occurs first; she or he provides an overview to students on how to search for materials within the NAHS Library. Second, students will physically visit the NAHS library and check out the mythology books they need to complete the first part of their assignment. To complete the second part of the assignment (researching a mythology beyond the Greeks and Romans), the high school students will visit the library to check out materials related to the mythology of other cultures or civilizations. Although the NAHS Library does have a healthy collection, it does not have the depth of the 1.3 million items and more than 150 databases compared to the library of the university.

The introduction to the library does not begin when the high school students sit in the library lecture room, but before students even step foot into the library. Because the NAHS is on CSUN property, students take a ten-minute walk from their classroom to the library and are shown how to get to the library from their high school. While on route, they are shown key markers, legends, and book drop locations that are easily accessible. Once the students enter into the library, they are greeted by the Outreach Librarian in the lobby and given a two-minute general overview of where the Circulation and Information Desks are located and what services they provide. The students are then escorted to a designated lab to begin their library session.

Entering into the lab, students take seats at any available computer terminal; generally, every student is ensured of having his or her own personal workstation. The Outreach Librarian then proceeds to give a brief description of his or her role and how he or she can be contacted. The homepage of the NAHS is displayed on the overhead projector and on all the computers within the lab. Prior to the students entering the lab, the computer stations are enabled with the NetSupport School Pro software program, an educational technology tool that allows the instructor to view a student's workstation to see how he or she is performing. If a student raises a question about a research issue, the instructor has the ability to display the information on the main projector or on all additional workstations. The instructor can also display on all the student PC screens in real time what is being displayed on the instructor's computer screen. Although this technology serves as a teaching tool, it can also be used to prevent students from accessing the Internet while a library session is occurring, which is especially necessary when working with high school students.

All grade levels are instructed on how to navigate from the NAHS homepage to the Oviatt Library homepage. The introduction to the Oviatt website is applied to all NAHS classes, but the dissemination of information is applied differently at each grade level.

The ninth grade students, for example, are introduced to topics such as "Search the Library Catalog," "MLA Style Examples," and "Library Hours." As part of catalog search instructions, students are introduced to basic keyword searching, such as "Aztec and Mythology"; one particular mythology is used as an example to get students to start thinking in a broader context. Asking the class, for example, if anyone is going to examine Vedic mythology usually yields three or more students who have selected this culture. A new search, focusing on "Vedic and Mythology," is performed, and the students are asked to look at one of the results, *Vedic Mythology* by Arthur Anthony MacDonell. They are then asked, "What is a broader or another term for Vedic?" The students will scan the MacDonell record and shout out "Hindu," because they see "Mythology, Hindu" as a subject heading. Four to five examples are used to explain this type of keyword searching. In addition to Boolean Logic, truncation is explained as well. With every example, students are asked, "Where is the item located within the library?" This question is important, because although most of the books are on the second and third floors, students may come across an item with an obscure location (i.e., "TCC" = Teacher Curriculum Center or "Stored" = in the ASRS or Automated Storage Retrieval System). Students are also introduced to the differences between Dewey Decimal and Library of Congress call numbers because the topic of the session that typically stops students in their tracks is a discussion of Library of Congress call numbers. With every sample record displayed, a review of how to locate the item using the LC classification system is discussed. After the final example, prior to allowing students to begin their research, two handouts, each in different colors, are disseminated to the class. The first handout describes simplified versions of MLA citations; the second handout is a worksheet on which students will record information about the example shown on the overhead. The project requires students to review necessary information and create citations. To motivate students working with research materials, it helps if there is an incentive; English teachers thus apply a point value to make sure students are thinking about what they are writing. Once the students have completed the worksheets, they are collected and the computers are unlocked so students may begin their information search.

The goals for the tenth grade students are designed to build on skills introduced in the ninth grade. Students will also learn Web-searching strategies, keyword usage, and website evaluation techniques, as well as how to navigate and use an electronic database effectively. The tenth graders are given a lesson on how to use and navigate Google, involving reading an article from the Internet, identifying keywords, and applying the words for a future search in Google or in a subscription database. By using Google's advanced search and applying selected keywords, students will thus be able to produce a better search than they would generate from just using the basic search interface. As students navigate within Google, they are introduced to Web page evaluation and are shown examples of untrustworthy websites.

Learning goals for the tenth graders are thus broken down into two sections: New Skills and Reinforced Skills. Students are introduced to subscription databases, such as Academic Search Elite by EBSCOHost and General OneFile by Thomson Gale. While both databases provide a wide breadth of information, ease of use, and a user-friendly interface, General OneFile can be accessed via Los Angeles Public Library's (LAPL) subscription. Although students are encouraged to visit the library and access the databases, they are restricted from accessing the databases from off campus. Students are shown how to access LAPL subscription databases by using a LAPL card, which is the main reason General OneFile is demonstrated. Students are also introduced to how some databases (e.g., Academic Search Elite) allow for sorting results in different ways, such as by data, title, or relevance. Because of Academic Search Elite's document email function and MLA citation format, it is the preferred choice for demonstrating to high school students. Students are also taught the differences between a magazine and an academic (scholarly) journal. As students progress from one grade level to the next, they will continue to build on what they have learned in previous sessions at the library.

EXTENDING THE LEARNING SESSION: BEYOND THE LIBRARY

Learning can be defined as receiving instruction or acquiring knowledge through a process that changes behavior or adds to new abilities or responses. The end result is developmental growth (Oxford English Dictionary Online 2008). There is no question that students differ enormously in their individual learning styles. These various patterns are impacted by "prior knowledge and skills, cognitive abilities, and personality variables" (Kiguwa 2007). Tutorials were thus created to help address the different issues that arise when working with various learning styles.

Online tutorials (i.e., video or step-by-step screenshots) originally were designed for students with disabilities. It soon became apparent, however, that all students would benefit from such reference tools. Although video tutorials tend to consist of an audio (voice narration) and visual component, adding captions extends the video tutorials' versatility. The step-by-step screenshot tutorial provides an extra source students can use if they prefer a nonvideo tutorial. An advantage of the screenshot is that it allows students to gain confidence as they proceed through the step-by-step instructions; if the video tutorial goes too fast, or if there are visual issues, the step-by-step tutorial can be magnified if needed, without much distortion. The visual elements of screenshots and videos are much easier to follow than nonvisual materials. The visual material also helps learners build their confidence by providing immediate visual feedback and anchor points to return to if students become lost. Step-by-step screenshots also reduce cognitive work load by showing what will happen next (Van der Meij 1996).

While tutorials help to reinforce what has been covered in a library session, Web pages also provide students with additional research assistance and general information. Such guides may provide examples of basic keywords students can use and searching techniques for navigating the OPAC at the Oviatt Library. A simple Boolean diagram was added to explain how the word "AND" narrows down search results, as well as an illustration of how students can find a book about MLA at the Oviatt Library or at the NAHS Library. Finally, the Web page provides general information regarding student privileges, lets parents/guardians know how to contact the library, and explains the costs of overdue fines. In addition to having the contents available on the Internet, hard copies of the Web pages were created for students, thus increasing the probability of students having the knowledge to access the information they need.

IMPLICATIONS

Fostering information literacy and lifelong learning skills are just a few of the services an academic library targets primarily to its own student body. Outreaching to high school students with the same focus, however, offers additional long-term benefits to the high school, university, and community.

Information literacy is not an ideal goal for a one-shot session offered to a high school class; instead, the process of reinforcing information over time is more beneficial to high school students. The sessions provided to high school students are not intended to cover as much material as humanly possible within a particular time frame; instead, sessions are deliberately structured to ensure that small bits of information are dispensed over time, thus allowing the student to absorb the material adequately. As students are introduced to the academic experience, the process of engaging students to think critically about research will in turn lead students also to think critically about the world around them. Such student engagement will allow teachers to raise expectations in their classrooms and thus may help the high school to achieve higher test scores.

Now in its fourth year, Northridge Academy High School was established under an agreement by LAUSD and CSUN to "create a model academic environment for high school students" (Shared Use Agreement 2002, 1). The relationship between NAHS and the Oviatt Library is strengthened by the opportunity to work together to improve information literacy skills among high school students and by fostering communications between high school students and academic librarians. As the viewpoint of high school students evolves from the preconceived notion that the university is beyond the scope of their high school, the university instead becomes part of their community, and they begin to incorporate it into their daily life. The subsequent benefit of the outreach program, then, is establishing an image of the library, and, to a greater extent, the university community itself, that will resonate with high school students as they make critical decisions about selecting colleges/universities to attend after completing their high school educations.

For over 222 years, the crusade against the darkness of ignorance has been fought gallantly by American educators. In a letter to a dear friend, Thomas Jefferson eloquently appealed for the passage of his bill, "More General Diffusion of Knowledge":

Preach, my dear Sir, a crusade against ignorance; establish and improve the law for educating the common people. Let our countrymen know ... that the tax which will be paid ... is not more than the thousandth part of what will be paid to kings, priests, and nobles, who will rise up among us if we leave the people in ignorance. (Gilreath 1999, 118–119)

CONCLUSION: TWEAKING AS WE GO

The Oviatt Library's outreach program and its relationship with the NAHS present opportunities that elude other university/high school relationships. By building stronger relationships with high school students, the library opens worlds beyond that of just the high school diploma. In the near future, to ensure that the outreach program succeeds, a program assessment will be implemented. Such an assessment will provide the necessary data to ensure that both sides are benefiting from the outreach experience. Although the No Child Left Behind Act requires K–12 educators to demonstrate accountability, in 2005 the Commission on the Future of Higher Education (also known as the Spellings Commission) charged that the "overwhelming majority of both college and high school faculty and administrators are unaware of the standards and assessments being used by their counterparts in other sectors" (A Test of Leadership 2006).

By assessing the outreach program, modifications can be made, additional support can be justified, and the program's success can be judged by the administration on both sides. In contrast to traditional schools where students can enroll at any grade level, NAHS only enrolls students during the first year of the ninth grade, and no students are added during any other grade level or allowed to reenter if withdrawn. As a result, the number of students at NAHS may decrease over a four-year period, but the information gathered from tracking student progress over this four-year period will be much more accurate, because every student from the ninth to twelfth grades will have participated in a library session.

In an environment in which libraries are "no longer closed universes of preselected, appropriated educational resources [but] instead portals to the world of information," addressing the challenges of information literacy cannot be placed on the shoulders of just one group of educators (Farmer 2008, 14). There is too much work to do and very little time to tackle all the issues individually. By meeting the issues head-on and collaboratively, our chances for success are increased. Some educators have indicated that twelfth grade is a "vast wasteland"; however, CSUN and Oviatt Library, by working with the NAHS, view high school students at all grade levels as future citizens of untapped potential (A Test of Leadership 2006).

"Finis origine pendet" simply means "the end depends upon the beginning." To this end, colleges and universities must be involved actively in a student's life, long before he or she is confronted with the question of what to do after high school. As educators, we have a moral responsibility to encourage and guide students as they navigate their academic journey; while their private dreams are their North Star, we must endeavor to be their compass.

REFERENCES

A Test of Leadership, Charting the Future of U.S. Higher Education. A report of the Commission appointed by Secretary of Education Margaret Spellings (September 2006). http://www.ed.gov/about/bdscomm/list/hiedfuture/index.html (accessed December 21, 2007).

Farmer, L. *Information Literacy Assessment in K–12 Setting.* Lanham, MD: Scarecrow Press, 2008.

Gilreath, J. *Thomas Jefferson and the Education of a Citizen.* Washington: Library of Congress, 1999.

Gresham, K. and D. Van Tassel. "Expanding the Learning Community: An Academic Library Outreach Program to High Schools." In W. Arant and P. A. Mosley, eds. *Library Outreach, Partnerships, and Distance Education: Reference Librarians at the Gateway,* pp. 161–173. New York: Haworth Information Press, 2000.

Information Competencies Final Report. Report by the Commission on Learning on Resources and Instructional Technology, Commission on Learning Resources and Instructional Technology Work Group on Information Competence CLRIT Task 6.1. 1995. http://www.calstate.edu/AcadSen/Records/Reports/ic.shtml (accessed January 18, 2008).

Kiguwa, P. S. "Teaching and Learning: Addressing the Gap through Learning Styles. *South African Journal of Psychology* 37, no. 2 (2007): 354–360.

Oxford English Dictionary Online (2008). (accessed February 12, 2008).

Shared Use Agreement: Between Los Angeles Unified School District and California State University Northridge (2002).

Van Der Meij, H. "A Closer Look At Visual Manuals." *Journal of Technical Writing and Communication* 26, no. 4 (1996): 371–383.

Wallace, R. C., D. Engel, and J. E. Mooney. *The Learning School: A Guide to Vision-Based Leadership.* Thousand Oaks, CA: Corwin Press, 1997.

Part 2

PUBLIC LIBRARIES

7

COLLABORATING WITH YOUR LOCAL PUBLIC LIBRARY

Starr Hoffman, Annie Downey, and Suzanne Sears

In 2006 the University of North Texas (UNT) Libraries began a more conscious effort to collaborate with the local Denton Public Library. This effort developed into three distinct programs: a seamless service for delivery of government information, a cooperative one-book one-community program, and public library workshops led by UNT librarians. These efforts keep all of the libraries in town strong because we share resources and knowledge and present a unified front to our citizenry. This chapter focuses on the dynamics of these three distinct programs and identifies the pros and cons of this collaboration. It also includes the procedures and timeline for establishing this partnership and identifies some of the key decision makers to include in the planning process.

SEAMLESS SERVICE FOR GOVERNMENT INFORMATION

The UNT Libraries have been a federal depository library since 1948 and a state depository since 1963. Depository libraries are mandated by law to receive government information and provide permanent, free public access to that information. The Federal Depository Library Program was formed by Congress over 140 years ago to ensure that our government's information was accessible to the public. This is imperative not only because of the value of this information that is made available at no cost but also because our government must be kept accountable to its people to uphold the democratic ideals on which it was formed.

However, sometimes it is difficult to ensure and encourage this kind of public access to government information. Like UNT, many depository libraries are also academic libraries, which can create obstacles to public access. The first obstacle is visitor parking, which can be difficult on university campuses. At UNT, all visitors must obtain a visitor parking permit for their vehicle and must then locate appropriate visitor parking spots. The parking office and visitor parking spaces are often difficult to locate for those unfamiliar with the campus. Members of the general public may feel too intimidated to use the campus library or may not realize that they are allowed to use it even if they have no affiliation with the university. In addition, some universities are dealing with security issues that arise from nonstudent access to their general library collections.

In August 2007 the UNT Libraries began to seek alternatives for facilitating public access to the depository collection. Our Government Documents Department generated the idea to provide a "seamless service" for our depository items in cooperation with the Denton Public Libraries (DPL), because the public library is not a depository. The goal we had in mind was that a customer should be able to use a service desk at the public library to gain access to the UNT depository collection. Through discussion among our department staff, we determined that this service would deliver materials from the UNT collection to the public library by a variety of means: fax, email, or by courier delivery. Patrons may call the UNT Libraries Government Documents Department directly or request material from the service desk at any of the three public library branches. If a patron requests information from the public library branch, then a public librarian contacts the UNT Government Documents Department on the patron's behalf.

After receiving an information request, the documents staff searches for the appropriate material and determines the best method of delivery to the patron. If the item is less than twenty-five pages it is scanned into a PDF file and emailed directly to the patron. (Because the majority of government documents are in the public domain, copyright is not an issue.) If the patron does not have an email account, the scanned document is emailed or faxed to the branch library of his or her choice. The majority of these requests may be filled within moments of receiving the initial call, so that the information is delivered to the patron while they are still standing at the public library reference desk. If the document is too long to scan in an efficient and timely manner, or is not a standard size, then it is delivered to the branch library specified by the patron. First, the document is checked out to the public library's account, and then a documents staff member delivers the item to the branch library. The patron is then allowed to use the document at that branch; the item is specified as in-library use only. When the patron is finished with the material, the branch library staff contacts the Government Documents Department to let them know the item is ready to be picked up and returned to the UNT collection. If the item is noncirculating, every attempt is made to scan the appropriate information from the document even if it exceeds twenty-five pages.

PLANNING FOR THE SERVICE

To transform the idea of this "seamless service" into reality, the Government Documents Department consulted several key players. First, the idea was thoroughly discussed in the department to develop the plan fully and allow staff input. Once the staff was behind the idea, the department head met with the administration of the UNT Libraries and presented the idea to the dean and assistant dean. Her presentation included information on how the new service would help fulfill

the depository guidelines for public access, particularly in light of the current difficulties that some of the public experiences accessing the collection. In addition, she
mentioned the potential benefit of this service to distance learner students, a growing population at many colleges and universities, and at UNT specifically. A full 29
percent of UNT's student body now takes online courses, and to support those students, the library must provide materials online whenever possible. Finally, the
department head demonstrated how this service fulfills the UNT Libraries' mission
to "acquire, preserve, provide access to, and disseminate recorded knowledge in all
its forms" and also its stipulation that this access "will be provided increasingly
through electronic networks and consortial arrangements." The presentation convinced the administration that this would be a beneficial service, and the initial
investigation into the cost and procedures of such a service was approved.

Next, the documents department head contacted Eva Poole, director of DPL, to
see if the public library was interested in this collaboration. She and her staff
responded enthusiastically to this possibility and discussion began. A draft set of
guidelines were developed and sent to the DPL director and senior-level managers
for review. This document underwent revision and review between DPL and UNT
administrators.

Various issues had to be considered when forming policies for this new service.
Some of the concerns were as follows:

- How should noncirculating items be handled?
- How will materials be delivered from UNT to the public library branches?
- What is the expected turn-around time when requests are received from the public library?
- How will the service operate when the UNT Libraries are closed or have shortened hours (due to the academic calendar)?
- How many items can be scanned at one time?
- Are there limits on the number of pages to be scanned for one patron?
- What level of research can be performed by the UNT Libraries staff?
- What kind of training will the DPL staff receive?
- What kind of publicity will be generated for the service and who is responsible for it?
- How will lost items be dealt with?
- Will patrons be required to have valid public library cards to use the service?
- How will the DPL library staff know when to call the UNT Documents Department?

These issues continue to be addressed as the planning documents and the service itself
are revised. Each issue is considered from the standpoint of both the UNT Libraries
and DPL. However, the focus during this entire process is that the ultimate goal is
better service for the patron. Each decision is made by first considering how to best
serve the patron and next how best to use the resources of both UNT and DPL. The
initial passion for this service, as revealed in the enthusiastic responses by the documents staff and the administration of both libraries, is grounded in its purpose of providing better access for all patrons.

The planning period also brought up the issue of what this service would cost
the UNT Libraries. After some initial conversation with the public library, it was
determined that the cost of in-person delivery would likely be minimal. These

deliveries are to be performed primarily during hours that staff leave the UNT Libraries, dropping off items on their way home and thus entailing little extra time or expense in that delivery. The major piece of equipment that was purchased was an all-in-one scanner/fax/copy machine. Although there are already scanners and fax machines in the library building, most are not accessible after 6:00 P.M. In addition, on nights and weekends only one person staffs the documents department and must remain on duty at the third floor reference desk. During this time, the staff is unable to leave the reference desk or the department to scan and email items. Thus, it was deemed that the purchase of a scanner/fax/copier for the Government Documents Department was warranted. Purchase of this equipment was the majority of the cost outlay for the service.

Thus far, preparing the procedural guidelines and getting approval of them from both libraries' administration has been the most time-consuming part of setting up the service. Our hope is that the service will increase awareness and usage of the documents collection and reference service at the UNT Libraries. The public library also benefits by expanding their ability to answer government-related reference questions without collecting more materials or taking up shelf space. And of course the primary purpose for the service is that the public benefits by being able to have quick access to this valuable information without having to travel to an unfamiliar library or obtain a visitor parking permit. We want the public to see their local libraries as cooperative gateways to access so that they are encouraged to make use of our resources and our services.

Future plans are to extend the service to the surrounding public library systems and initial discussions have begun with the Decatur Public Library. They are very interested in not only the "seamless service" possibilities but also in the public and staff workshops mentioned later in this chapter. This service was envisioned by the UNT Libraries Government Documents Department, but, ultimately, it was made possible by the existing communication and collaboration between UNT and DPL that had begun a year earlier during the One-Book, One-Community project called Denton Reads.

COOPERATIVE ONE-BOOK, ONE-COMMUNITY

Denton Reads is a collaborative effort between the libraries of two public universities, the public school district, and the public libraries. It is a month-long program with activities and events for all age groups and designed to attract people of differing interests. Planning for Denton Reads begins a year in advance, and every committee has at least one employee from each library system to ensure that all of the libraries' constituencies are being served.

This work has opened up lines of communication between the libraries that did not previously exist. We know more about one another's specialties, expertise, and collections. We can now easily and with confidence refer patrons to the other libraries when necessary. For example, the public libraries know to send patrons to us when they need help with in-depth business research, and we know to direct many reader's advisory questions to them.

Denton Reads began in November 2006 when Melody Kelly, assistant dean of the UNT Libraries, and Eva Poole, director of DPL, decided the time was ripe for the two library systems, along with their colleagues in town, to begin collaboration on a citywide reading program. Melody and Eva put together a team of two librarians to work on the project and began contacting Texas Woman's University (TWU) Library and the Denton Independent School District (DISD) Libraries to ask for their collaboration as well.

After a small team was established, we set up some basic guidelines for the program that have guided us throughout all phases of planning. First, we strive to reach out to all members of the community regardless of age, race, religion, class, etc. Second, all events are free. This enables broad community participation and fulfills our libraries' missions to provide public services at no cost. Third, it is an equal partnership of all of the libraries and each will be fairly represented. And finally, our overall goal for all programs and events is to promote a love of reading.

The initial team that met to begin discussions on the project chose an environmental theme for the first year because the Denton community has a strong interest in environmental issues. We believed that this theme would guarantee support for the inaugural program from many in the community and its semi-controversial nature would allow for good discussion and dialogue to open up. We chose April for the first program because Earth Day is April 22, Texas often has perfect weather that time of year, and it is before the university semesters and the K–12 school year begin to wrap up. We chose our first book, *The Legacy of Luna* by Julia Butterfly Hill, based on the theme, our timeline, budget, because the author is a great public speaker, and most importantly because it is a book that is compelling for readers from high school age to senior citizens.

The preliminary planning stage brought to light several issues that have proven to be the central challenges at every stage of the process. One of the most important strategies in planning such a program is making sure that there are representatives from each library system at every meeting where crucial decisions are made. We planned our April date and set everything in motion along that timeline before the representative from the DISD Libraries was able to join us and enlighten us that April is when Texas schools do their annual testing. Not only did this severely limit the amount of time the school librarians were able to dedicate to the program, it also had a negative effect on participation from the teachers and K–12 students. Future Denton Reads will be held in October when we have the same weather benefits and hit a similar window of time in the university semesters but will not conflict with public school testing.

A second challenge we have confronted over and over is that of understanding the audience. We are trying to create a program that will appeal to a very wide audience that includes all ages, socioeconomic backgrounds, races, religious beliefs, education levels, etc. We all have areas of the audience that we know very well, and it is imperative that all of these varied interest and ability levels are taken into account. This is not always easy and has pointed to the necessity of offering a wide variety of events and compromising on the book and theme selection.

One of the reasons we chose to do a month-long program rather than just focusing on the author event is so that we can offer many different programs aimed at the different audiences. The final author event targets everyone and brings the whole community together. The major events we planned for 2007 were a children's festival, a film festival, a xeriscaping program, and many book clubs. The children's festival was for young children and their parents and included several environmentally themed games, activities, and special story times. This festival had a number of booths sponsored by community groups and schools, many of which were educational. The film festival was held at a local movie tavern and was open to the whole community, but it had special interest for college students. The films included *An Inconvenient Truth* and *Who Killed the Electric Car?* We were able to keep the film festival free by contracting with the theater and guaranteeing to bring in a certain number of people who would presumably buy food and drinks. Additional related films were also shown for free at each library location throughout the month of April, many of which were oriented toward family audiences. The xeriscaping program was also open to the whole community, but it had special appeal to older citizens. Finally, we offered both intensive three-week book clubs and one-time book discussion groups at every library at several times. We also offered book clubs at a local coffee shop, a natural foods café, and the local Barnes and Noble.

When it comes to choosing the book and theme, again all of the libraries must have input. The different libraries have users that often have vastly different interests. We are in the middle of planning our second Denton Reads program and have selected *Ender's Game* by Orson Scott Card. This book selection is very different from the 2007 selection, particularly in that it is fiction rather than nonfiction. This was designed specifically so we can pull in community members we may have missed the previous year. In some ways it is probably a bit more appealing to the public library and school library constituents than to the university users. But the previous year's program was a little more appealing to the university faculty and students. Our hope is to select books and themes with wide appeal each year but also to reach a balance from year to year.

Establishing the basic guidelines at the outset has helped us keep on task and provided the guidance necessary when challenges pop up. Working together with librarians from several different libraries with different responsibilities and schedules can be difficult, but it is also tremendously rewarding. As one committee member said: "The author event and the film festival and everything else were nice and all, but what I have enjoyed most about Denton Reads is getting to know all of the other librarians and finding out what they do. Our jobs are so different and we all know such different things; it has been really fun and good for our work [at our own libraries]." This sums up the experience for most of us who have worked on Denton Reads. The lines of communication between the libraries that this program has opened up are remarkable. We actually know one another by name and face now and know who to refer patrons to when one of the other libraries and or librarians could be more helpful. Not only are we offering community members the chance to have memorable experiences with books, libraries, and each other, we are also creating fantastic experiences for ourselves.

PUBLIC WORKSHOPS

In an effort to reach out for the greater good of the community, UNT librarians are also providing a variety of programming for both public library patrons and public library staff. The contacts made from the Denton Reads campaign have been instrumental in opening the lines of communication between the staff of the two libraries regarding collaboration on programming. Individual discussions among the DPL and UNT staff have led to many opportunities to partner on public programming.

The UNT Government Documents Department has made a concentrated effort to provide informational sessions several times a year at the DPL branch libraries for the general public. This service is part of the overall guidelines for depository libraries to participate in marketing and outreach of the collection. Public workshops on genealogical resources in the documents collection, military history resources for a Veteran's Day program, and government information on the Web and censorship issues related to that information have been presented by UNT staff. These workshops were publicized by both the UNT libraries and the DPL. UNT librarians have also presented during DPL's dedicated training times for their reference staff. These training sessions have included topics such as accessing government information sources on the Internet.

In addition, the UNT Libraries host daylong summer workshops for area high school students. The 2007 workshop was titled "Enemies of History: Murdering the Past" and was hosted by the UNT Libraries' Archives and Rare Books Department. On June 16 high school students from area districts spent the day learning how to preserve collections and items that they might have in their own homes. After a quick welcome, the students watched a short film, which consisted of clips from movies showing examples of how not to treat books and other library materials. After the students introduced themselves, a series of fun preservation presentations followed on stamps, comic books, money, and clothing—wedding dresses, specifically. In the afternoon the students learned how to do an oral history interview and practiced on Dr. Fred Karr, who answered their questions about his memories of the day John F. Kennedy was assassinated, and one of the other students who recounted memories of 9/11. The last sessions of the day included a presentation in the Digital Projects Lab on the Portal to Texas History and digitizing photos. Finally, we returned to the Rare Book Room for a segment on preserving books, followed by a question and answer period. Each student went home with a goody bag that included library promotional materials, cotton gloves to use when handling photos and delicate items, and various other samples of preservation supplies.

A previous workshop was titled "Community in World War II," also hosted by the Archives and Rare Books Department. Fifteen students from the Dallas/Fort Worth area spent a day learning all about community in World War II. They received a timeline glimpse of the war through a tour of the artifacts in the Rare Book Room, making their own posters for a cause, learning about the uses of film and cinematography in propaganda, finding out about German and American soldiers' uniforms and lives from UNT student reenactors, seeing the role of artwork in our comprehension of the lives of Germans prior to the war, and reading real letters to and from an American soldier. At the end of the day, each student was asked to imagine themselves as a person in the war and to write a V-mail letter to someone as that person. Each of these workshops successfully engaged area students and enabled UNT to reach out to a larger community.

The success of these programs has led to discussion of other possible collaborative programs such as information for small businesses and consumer protection programs. In addition, UNT is working with DPL on the 2009 American Library

Association-sponsored exhibit Benjamin Franklin: In Search of a Better World. Several faculty members from UNT are presenting programs in support of the exhibit. In addition, the Documents Department is providing the public library with pocket U.S. Constitutions to hand out. These Constitutions will be branded with the UNT Libraries logo and the Documents Department contact information. The cost of the Constitutions is being absorbed by the marketing budget for the Documents Department. These booklets will not only provide the public with ready access to one of our nation's most important documents, but we also hope it will familiarize them with the UNT Documents Department.

PROS AND CONS OF COLLABORATING WITH THE PUBLIC LIBRARY

Before embarking on a similar cooperative effort between your local public and academic libraries, it is imperative that you consider the pros and cons of such a collaboration. Many of the pros are quite obvious, such as your library gaining a stronger place in the community. Individuals who normally would feel intimidated by the idea of using a university library will become familiar with the staff and services available. Holding events and services with the public library will enhance your own library's profile.

You may find that this increased familiarity encourages more members of the public to travel to your academic library location. The increased traffic at the reference desk could potentially have great impact. Although it's certainly preferable that the public is encouraged to make greater use of your materials and service, a heavy increase may result in the need for additional staff or additional reference desk hours, thus incurring significant cost.

The public library also benefits from free programming on topics of general interest to their patrons. They receive skilled reference assistance with difficult government information questions and also receive training on those questions. They increase their accessibility to government information without the cost of additional materials, cataloging time, or shelf space.

While the "seamless service" may increase the use of library materials and resources, thus increasing usage statistics, this may also increase some costs for the academic library. In addition to the purchase of the necessary equipment, there is staff time involved in scanning and emailing materials, as well as costs associated with the delivery of the materials in person if scanning is not a viable option. The cost of replacing lost items is also a possible issue for the academic library. There also may be policy considerations, which is a good reason to bring your administration in on the plan as soon as possible.

You should also consider whether such a collaboration is supported by your university and library's mission. Being able to show this connection is essential to obtain support from the various administrators. If this collaboration is not supported in the library mission, this may be an issue for further consideration because your depository library status ought to be reflected in the library's overall mission. Consider which key players in your administration would be instrumental in identifying possible ways to expand the library's mission to better reflect its depository status.

It is our hope that through the collaborative documents reference service, the Denton Reads events, and the collaborative workshops, Denton residents will come to think of the UNT Libraries not as an academic library but as another avenue for information. Even the merely visible signs of this collaboration—a UNT logo on a Constitution handed out at the public library, or a flier advertising a collaborative event—will help foster this sense that the various local libraries are not completely separate entities but cooperative partners whose ultimate goal is to provide the Denton community with valuable information and excellent service.

8

GROWING GRASSROOTS COLLABORATION BETWEEN ACADEMIC AND PUBLIC LIBRARIES

Stephanie M. Mathson, Robin M. Sabo, and Joyce Salisbury

Most of the literature on partnerships between academic and public libraries focuses on joint-use, shared facilities. Little has been written about collaborations between physically separate but geographically close public and academic libraries. Mount Pleasant, Michigan, is home to both the Central Michigan University (CMU) Libraries and the Veterans' Memorial Library (VML) branch of the Chippewa River District Library (CRDL) system. During the past few years, staff members at these libraries have embarked on several joint ventures, including National Library Week celebrations, community reading programs, and a large cataloging project.

HISTORY OF THE RELATIONSHIP BETWEEN THE TWO LIBRARIES

Professional relationships are frequently responsible for the development of partnerships between libraries, and that proved to be the case for CMU and CRDL. Ruth Helwig, systems librarian and education bibliographer at CMU's Charles V. Park Library, is also vice president of the CRDL Board of Trustees and has served on the Board since 2000. Her involvement began as a "Friend of the Library" for the CRDL when Helwig and another "Friend" proved instrumental in hiring a new library director, Lise Mitchell, in 1999. That action established an ongoing professional relationship between Helwig and Mitchell.

In 2004 staff members at the Park Library approached employees at the VML about collaborating on National Library Week activities. The Mid-Michigan Reads partnership and the joint cataloging project followed. Helwig points out that the public library has also worked with other local libraries such as the Saginaw Chippewa Tribal Library and the Mount Pleasant High School Library in collaborative cataloging projects (one of which resulted in the creation of the IC More Shared Catalog).

Although some of the previous joint activities have been discontinued because of low public attendance, Helwig thinks that the sharing of knowledge and best practices between the academic and public libraries has been valuable. She credits the success of the partnership to having "willing, enthusiastic, pleasant people on both sides who value collaboration and what we can learn from one another" and states in conclusion, "We are all part of the community. What can we do to make the community better?" (Helwig, interview).

EXAMPLES OF ACADEMIC AND PUBLIC LIBRARY COLLABORATIONS

Since the 1980s the cost of new technologies has driven many cooperative arrangements (Maxwell 1992). For example, sharing the cost and development of Online Public Access Catalogs (OPACs) is one area where public and academic libraries have partnered. Keene State College Library and the Keene Public Library in New Hampshire (Halverson and Plotas 2006), Lower Columbia College and Longview Public Library in Washington State (Baker 1988), and Franklin University and Columbus (Ohio) Metropolitan Library (Maxwell 1992) are three examples where public and academic libraries cooperated in merging their OPACs. These partnerships demonstrate how geographically close public and academic libraries can work together to achieve mutually beneficial goals.

Jointly applying for grant funding represents another opportunity for collaboration. The OPAC merger project between Franklin University and the Columbus Metropolitan Library was funded by a grant from the Columbus Foundation along with matching gifts from local corporations (Maxwell 1992). The integrated computerized library system between Lower Columbia College and Longview Public Library was funded by a Library Services and Construction Act Title II grant of $112,000 awarded by the Washington State Library Commission (Baker 1988). A National Library of Medicine grant provided monies to the Health Sciences Library System at the University of Pittsburgh to partner with the Allegheny County Library Association in training public librarians (Wessel, Wozar, and Epstein 2003).

Mutually beneficial library programming and instruction initiatives, literacy efforts, and staff training programs have resulted from public/academic library cooperation. In Alabama, public and academic librarians worked together to conceive, plan, and implement *Mobile's Book: Share the Experience*, a citywide reading project (Bahr and Bolton 2002). Newport News Public Library System and Brickell Medical Sciences Library of Eastern Virginia Medical School partnered to present a series of classes to senior citizens about health information on the Internet. This collaboration grew out of a previous partnership during which librarians from the Brickell Medical Sciences Library provided free training to 1,000 public librarians on accessing health information (Smith, Knight, and Jones 2005). Another example of a collaborative training venture is the University of Pittsburgh Health Sciences Library's provision of health-related reference training to public librarians in sixteen western Pennsylvania counties (Wessel, Wozar, and Epstein 2003). Creating bibliographies and joint advertising of library programs are yet other instances of collaborations (Halverson and Plotas 2006).

While an in-depth discussion of shared resources through consortia is beyond the scope of this chapter, studying several examples of joint-use shared-facility libraries is instructive.

Because of demand for additional information on joint-use partnerships, the American Library Association (2007) published a bibliography of articles, books, and websites on this topic. A joint-use library is defined as "a library in which two or more distinct library services providers, usually a school and a public library, serve their client groups in the same building, based on an agreement that specifies the relationship between the providers" (Bundy 2003, 1).

Joint use includes "shared space and co-location" and these arrangements are becoming increasingly popular (Todaro 2005/2006, 142). Although only 2 percent of public libraries in the United States are joint-use facilities, internationally joint-use libraries have gained greater acceptance. International statistics for joint-use public libraries show Sweden at 40 percent, Australia at 9 percent, and Canada at 8 percent (Bundy 2003).

Two well-known joint-use libraries in the United States are the South Regional/ Broward Community College Library in Broward County Florida and the Dr. Martin Luther King Library in San Jose, California. Broward County and Broward Community College opened Florida's first combined public/academic library in 1983 (Passalacqua 1999). The resulting South Regional/Broward Community College Library found that the joint-use model worked particularly well for outreach, programming, and marketing. The public librarians and the community college librarians work together to purchase materials and provide bibliographic instruction. A decade later, a second joint-use facility, also in partnership with the Broward County Library, opened on Broward Community College's North campus (Gnage 1995), and in 2007 a new "green" building opened that houses the original South Regional/Broward Community College Library (Broward County Library 2007). The Dr. Martin Luther King Library opened in 2004, resulting from a collaborative effort between San Jose State University and the San Jose Public Library (Brevik and McDermand 2004). In this case, both libraries needed more space and technological infrastructure. The resulting eight-story, 3,600-seat library was *Library Journal's* 2004 Library of the Year (Berry 2004). Public and academic library staff members were integrated, and a tiered reference service was implemented. Basic questions are answered on the first floor by librarians and staff, while research librarians and collections are located on the upper floors (Albanese 2003).

BENEFITS OF ACADEMIC AND PUBLIC LIBRARY PARTNERSHIPS

Lindenfeld (1984) points out that public libraries and community college libraries have several commonalities supporting cooperative ventures. Both types of libraries are generally open to the public and encourage lifelong learning. In addition, most community colleges and some public libraries support remedial programs. When discussing the benefits of joint-use public/academic libraries, Patricia Breivik, previously dean at the San Jose State University Libraries stated, "We start with children in preschool story hours and take them ... through all of their formal schooling to when they are senior citizens" (Albanese 2003).

In addition to sharing automated systems, collections, and facilities, planners of successful public/academic library collaborations frequently report reaping unanticipated benefits. Todaro (2005/2006) compiled a comprehensive list of benefits to libraries involved in successful partnerships. Most importantly, establishing successful relationships between two libraries can lead to the development of future collaborations. Specific examples cited in the literature include:

- Improved Relationships—Increased collegiality between library staff members is cited as one of the benefits to cost sharing and development of a joint OPAC between the Keene State College Library and the Keene Public Library (Halverson and Plotas 2006). In addition, improved "town-gown" relationships were a positive outcome of this continuing collaboration.

- Synergies in Staff Expertise—When health sciences librarians from Brickell Medical Sciences library and public librarians from Newport News Public Library team taught classes to help seniors find health information on the Internet, they reported, "Librarians at both systems gained a deeper understanding of the continued need to provide the public with health resource location training, the need to promote collections and services, and how to successfully achieve these goals through teamwork" (Smith, Knight, and Jones 2005, 26).

- Higher Visibility—The director of the Franklin University Library reported that developing a joint OPAC with Columbus Metropolitan Library resulted in increased visibility of the University's name on the Web (Maxwell 1992). In addition, partnerships help to recruit new students and faculty (Berry 2004). In discussing Broward Community College/North Regional Library, a joint-use facility, Gnage (1995, 13) points out that "What some may view as a liability—bringing those noisy children into an academic library—has become one of the strongest positives. Children and parents whose first encounter with Broward Community College (BCC) is a child's story time, find they like BCC, are comfortable on campus, and later become students."

- Establishing Successful Partnerships—Beneficial collaborations must provide benefits to all partners. Starting with smaller, informal projects gives the respective libraries a chance to see if the organizations are a "good fit" (Todaro 2005). Prior to their joint-use agreement, Broward County Community College Library and the Broward County Public Library had a long history of working together, which staff members credited as helping with the success of the joint-use venture (Passalacqua 1999).

NATIONAL LIBRARY WEEK ACTIVITIES

The authors' interest in collaborative efforts between different kinds of libraries grew out of chance. In 2003 the CMU Libraries began commemorating National Library Week (NLW) with a wide range of activities. Though NLW is routinely celebrated in public libraries, less attention is given to it in academic institutions. Why did the CMU Libraries, therefore, decide to launch NLW festivities? The library building actually played a large part in the matter. In January 2002 the Charles V. Park Library building (home to the University Library, Clarke Historical Library, and Off-Campus Library Services) reopened its doors to the university community after a two-and-a-half year, fifty million dollar renovation. The new and improved library building with its thirty-three miles of compact shelving, airy and modern design, dozens of study rooms, and Wi-Fi access was an immediate hit with students, staff, faculty, and the public. However, as with other celebrated things, the excitement about the new facility died down after awhile.

In early 2003 Anne Marie Casey, the associate dean of libraries, thought that it would be a great idea to hold special events during NLW to generate renewed interest in the Library place, so a committee was established to plan activities for NLW that spring. Though one activity conducted during the inaugural celebration of NLW was not well received (patrons did not appreciate hourly public address announcements of Park Library fun facts!), the campus community's overall interest in the events proved to be an impetus to attempt another NLW commemoration in 2004.

In January 2004 a new team of volunteers assembled to start planning activities. An important addition was a partnership with the CRDL, which had been conducting NLW activities for some time. Both library organizations were careful to plan individual major events at times that did not conflict with those offered in the other institution (Casey 2004). Publicity for NLW activities was a joint undertaking via bookmarks and flyers listing all the happenings at each library during the week, as well as contact information for both the CRDL and Park Library. In both 2005 and 2006 staff members in each library set up displays in the other library to advertise the activities and contests that were being offered at both venues. This gave the patrons of each institution the opportunity to learn more about the resources and community events offered by the other.

The one major activity on which librarians from both the university and public library collaborated was a "Stump the Librarian" contest. During NLW in 2004, 2005, and 2006, a Web page hosted on the CMU Libraries website invited all interested parties to submit (via e-mail) difficult questions for librarians to answer—or attempt to answer. The one rule for contestants was that their questions had to be of the sort that could be answered by using library resources. In other words, librarians would not attempt to read minds and guess what contestants' favorite colors are!

For librarians to respond to the questions in a timely manner, an email list was created, so that as questions were submitted, they were sent directly to all of the librarians involved in this activity. It became a friendly contest among the public and academic librarians to answer those hard questions first! In the three years that the librarians collaborated on "Stump the Librarian," only a handful of people managed to truly mystify the information professionals!

MID-MICHIGAN READS PROGRAMS

Out of the NLW collaboration grew other notable joint activities between the CMU Libraries and CRDL. During the summer of 2005 Pamela Grudzien, head of technical services in the CMU Libraries, had a casual conversation with CRDL Director Lise Mitchell about community reading programs. Both women agreed that it would be a great idea to try the idea in the Mount Pleasant area. Mitchell later contacted Grudzien via email, and the two got the ball rolling.

The project committee consisted of Grudzien, Mitchell, a librarian at Mid-Michigan Community College (in Mount Pleasant), the director of the Pere Marquette District Library in Clare (a town about fifteen miles north of Mount Pleasant), and the director of the Harrison Public Library (a small town about twenty-five miles north of Mount Pleasant). The members discussed a list of book titles that had met with success in other community reading programs around the country. According to Grudzien, "There was a lot of conversation about the differences among the mid-Michigan communities involved—Harrison, Clare, and Mount Pleasant—a lot about 'town and gown' and 'town and country'" (P. Grudzien, personal communication). The group ultimately settled on Ray Bradbury's classic, *Fahrenheit 451,* because it could borrow programmatic ideas that had met success in other communities. The committee members also believed that the subject of the book would appeal to people of all ages in the communities sponsoring the program.

Each person on the committee had many tasks to complete during the planning process for the 2006 Mid-Michigan Reads Program. Activities included a screening of the film, *Fahrenheit 451,* in an old-fashioned movie house in Mount Pleasant; numerous discussion group meetings over coffee at various locations throughout the three communities involved; and a visit by Bradbury biographer, Sam Weller, who arranged an evening call to Mr. Bradbury (who was at home in southern California) and gave the audience members opportunities to ask the famous writer questions about his works. According to Grudzien, all of these activities constituted "a small scale program ... because we were testing the interest/involvement of the entire area. And it was a lot of work for five people (on the committee)" (P. Grudzien, personal communication).

Once the Community Reading program concluded in April 2006, the committee members agreed that the first go of it had been successful. For the next program, however, they wanted more community involvement in selecting the title.

The initial five-person group became a group of eight for the 2007 Mid-Michigan Reads project. The CRDL had several representatives, including three individuals from the Mount Pleasant branch (VML). Committee members invited the public to nominate books by submitting ballots, and many community leaders from all of the participating towns were asked to help choose a title. From the nominations the large advisory committee discussed and narrowed down the candidates and eventually selected Barbara Ehrenreich's *Nickel and Dimed: On Not Getting by in America.* Once the title was chosen, however, the collaborative planning and coordination of programs and activities evaporated. According to Grudzien, "Two VML librarians planned and organized programs and advertising for CRDL. They reported their plans to the rest of the planning committee, but there was no inclusion or joint planning" (P. Grudzien, personal communication). Minimal involvement of other committee members resulted partly from restrictions on their time and partly because their enthusiasm had waned.

During the first year of the program, time, money, and public relations all posed challenges. Planning began in November for a March project, so a great deal of work was compressed into a few weeks. The Friends of the CMU Libraries contributed a generous amount of money to support the program, and grants were obtained from the state of Michigan and the Michigan Council for the Humanities. All of the various supporters had to be recognized on the program posters and flyers. Obtaining permission to use the organizations' logos and then receiving appropriate files of the logos themselves proved problematic. By the end of the project, CMU accounting regulations required detailed records to show how all of the funds were expended. Because of these accounting issues, the university's financial support for the second Mid-Michigan Reads project (2007) was limited to the purchase of print and audio books.

JOINT CATALOGING PROJECT

Previous collaborative efforts came to fruition during the summer of 2007 when ten staff members from Mount Pleasant area public libraries assisted staff at the CMU Libraries in a massive retroactive conversion of children's literature and non-fiction resources in CMU's Instructional Materials Center (IMC). Teacher Education programs are among the strongest at CMU, which was founded as Central Michigan Normal School and Business Institute in 1892, and IMC resources are an integral part of these programs. The resources are also of interest to area teachers, home schoolers, and the general public for use with their children. Lise Mitchell, the director of the CRDL, volunteered to have her staff members assist CMU librarians with the project. CRDL is a member of the IC More Shared Catalog system, which has six participating library systems. (IC stands for Isabella and Clare counties, which are home to the majority of those six library systems.) Staff members from CRDL, Pere Marquette District Library in Clare, the Coleman Area Library, and the Surrey Township Library participated in this project. "The goal of the IC More Shared Catalog is to increase the opportunities for all residents of the community, including the under-served, to access and borrow materials. We achieve this goal by sharing a common database of bibliographic records but still have individual websites to best meet the needs of our users. By sharing this database we maximize resources not only in lending and borrowing materials but in staff time in maintaining the database" (CRDL website n.d.).

Mitchell volunteered staff time for the CMU project because she wanted to make the IMC resources available to CRDL's patrons through MeLCat. MeLCat is a consortium of Michigan libraries, a growing union catalog for the state, through which patrons can borrow books from any library in the consortium and have them delivered in a timely manner to their home library. As part of MeLCat, the IMC books would be accessible beyond the confines of the university to patrons throughout the state of Michigan and would also become part of the WorldCat database. An extra university impetus for the conversion was the fact that the IMC collection will be physically relocated to the Park Library in December 2008.

Prior to this project, many of the IMC materials were cataloged and searchable only in the IMC's system, so they were less accessible to the university community at large. Books added to the IMC collection before the early 1990s, purchased for the IMC through College of Education funds by the IMC librarian or obtained by the librarian at conferences, were not in the University Libraries' OPAC. Beginning in the early 1990s IMC materials purchased by Park Library librarians and processed by Park's Technical Services Department were cataloged as part of the University Libraries' system, even though the materials were housed in the IMC. These books had barcodes and records for them could be searched in the Libraries' OPAC.

The purpose of the retroactive conversion was to ensure that all books in the IMC had records in the University Libraries' OPAC. Incorporating records for IMC resources into the Libraries' OPAC had been an ongoing project since 2002, but by necessity this had not been a high priority. As time permitted, one staff member and one student from the Park Library would visit the IMC and write down the titles, authors, and ISBNs of books to search. After returning to the Park Library, the employees searched OCLC WorldCat using the Z39.50 protocol and downloaded records using information gathered at the IMC. No barcodes were entered and no holdings were attached to the OCLC results. This was a time-consuming method of conversion, which left room for error. Over the five-year period from 2002 to 2007, 2,121 records were completed and added to the University Libraries' OPAC.

During the retroactive conversion project during the summer of 2007, catalogers searched the University Libraries' OPAC to determine whether or not each book was in the catalog. If it was, the cataloger verified the accuracy of the record against the item in hand, checked to make sure the barcode number matched the number in the OPAC, and verified that a record existed in WorldCat documenting CMU's ownership of the book. If all of these characteristics were correct, the record was complete, and the cataloger moved on to the next item. When a book was not located in the OPAC, a record was imported from OCLC, a barcode was added to the book, and the record was entered into the OPAC.

During the summer conversion project, through the cooperation of employees from area public libraries and a concerted effort by CMU staff, 9,421 records were added to or verified and updated in the OPAC. Of that number, 1,191 were new records added to the OPAC—more than half the total number of records entered during the previous five-year period. To make this intensive project possible, a bank of seven computers was set up in the IMC. At least two, and often more, staff members from various libraries were scheduled to work continually throughout the business day over a six-week period. In addition to ten staff members from the public libraries scheduled for shifts throughout the work week, at least one CMU staff member spent significant portions of the work week on the project while another one or two worked approximately half of the work week at the IMC. Other CMU staff members periodically worked throughout the summer on the conversion.

Prior to the beginning of the project, meetings were held with staff members from both the CMU Libraries and CRDL to streamline the process. Mitchell, who had completed similar retroactive conversions as part of the IC More Shared Catalog system, was part of this collaborative effort to develop a system to perform the task in an orderly manner. The process was complex, but the organizers tried to make it as quick and easy as possible. Although all the staff members were familiar with copy cataloging, some training was required to familiarize them with the system. The preparation and training paid off. The contributions of the public libraries' staff members were invaluable in the intensive push during the summer to enter the lion's share of records for the IMC's fiction collection. In total, the public library employees completed approximately 24 percent of the records that were verified, updated, and/or added to the libraries' OPAC that summer. CMU staff members continued to work on the project throughout the academic year of 2007–2008. Some "clean-up" of records will be required once the IMC collection is moved to the Park Library in December 2008.

Another benefit to the public libraries who participated in the project, according to Mitchell, was "the exposure to a different automation system." The project gave them a chance to see how Innovative Interfaces, Inc. (III) and OCLC work. "Our cataloging module handles bib and item records very differently." She also was in favor of the project because she believes there is not enough "cross interaction between public and academic libraries" (L. Mitchell, personal communication).

At the end of the summer, to celebrate the completion of a large portion of the project, Anne Marie Casey, associate dean of the CMU Libraries, hosted a luncheon for the staff from all of the libraries involved to thank them for their efforts in this endeavor. The concerted effort, collaboration between public and academic library staff members, ensured that the entire collection will be properly cataloged and available to the entire CMU community as well as patrons throughout the state shortly after the start of the university's winter 2009 semester.

CONCLUSION

The variety of projects that have come to fruition because of the cooperation of staff members in the CMU Libraries and the CRDL illustrates that the sky is the limit for such ventures. Whether celebrating NLW, administering community reading programs, or completing retrospective cataloging projects, there are a tremendous number of possibilities for interlibrary cooperation that push past the traditional borders of an academic library's walls as well as an entire university campus.

As a result of collaborating with staff members of the CRDL over the past few years, the authors have developed a list of tips to offer other academic and public institutions about working together, starting with planning ahead for joint meetings and learning how to play to each type of library's strengths. In addition, make sure to ask for volunteers from each institution to work on each collaborative project. Do not assume that every employee will be excited about the opportunity to meet new people and learn new procedures or practices. Review the following section for more general guidelines on interlibrary collaboration.

TIPS FOR PLANNING

Community Reading Programs

1. Establish an agreement about how committee members will share the workload and follow it.
2. Discuss money and budget right away and make sure to inform everyone involved about any regulations or strings attached to the funding.
3. Choose a fun book with community input.
4. Advertise, advertise, advertise!

Joint National Library Week Activities

1. Communicate often and include some face-to-face interaction (i.e., group meetings at one library or the other).

2. Identify and concentrate on a few high visibility opportunities.

3. Repeat only those activities that have been well received in the past, and drop activities that were not popular.

Other Joint Projects

1. Start small! Get a feel for how people will work together by collaborating on a smaller project before moving onto larger ones.

2. Discuss mutually beneficial goals at the outset.

3. Focus on building synergies based on the strengths of the respective libraries.

ACKNOWLEDGMENTS

The authors thank Pamela Grudzien (Head of Technical Services at CMU), Ruth Helwig (Systems Librarian and Education Bibliographer at CMU), Lise Mitchell (Director, CRDL), and Amie Pifer (Manager/Technical Services at CMU) for their assistance.

REFERENCES

Albanese, Andrew. "Joint San Jose Library Opens." *Library Journal* 128, no. 14 (2003): 17.

American Library Association. "Joint-Use Libraries: A Bibliography." August 2007. ALA Library Fact Sheet Number 20. http://www.ala.org/ala/alalibrary/libraryfactsheet/alalibraryfactsheet20.cfm (accessed March 4, 2008).

Bahr, Alice Harrison and Nancy Bolton. "Share the Experience: Academic Library, Public Library and Community Partnerships." *The Southeastern Librarian* 50, no. 2 (2002):26–32.

Baker, Robert K. "Expanding Small College LRC Services through Creative Partnerships." *Community & Junior College Libraries* 61, no. 1 (1988): 89–93.

Berry, John N. "The San Jose Model." *Library Journal* 129, no. 11 (2004): 34–37.

Brevik, Patricia Senn and Robert McDermand. "Campus Partnerships Building on Success: A Look at San Jose State University." *College and Research Library News* 65, no. 4 (2004): 210–215.

Broward County Library. "Grand Opening Ceremony." 2007. http://www.broward.org/library/grandopening_sr.htm (accessed March 4, 2008).

Bundy, Alan. "Joint-Use Libraries—The Ultimate Form of Cooperation." In *Planning the Modern Public Library Building*, ed. G. B. McCabe and J. R. Kennedy. Westport, CT: Libraries Unlimited, 2003. Also available online at http://www.library.unisa.edu.au/about/papers/jointuse.pdf (accessed March 4, 2008).

Casey, Anne Marie. "National Library Week Activities at CMU." *Michigan Libraries* 70, no. 2 (2004): 6. http://www.mla.lib.mi.us/files/mlibraries/20050304.pdf (accessed 20 March 2008).

Chippewa River District Library. "IC More Shared Catalog." http://youseemore.com/chippewa/about.asp?loc=233 (accessed March 24, 2008).

Gnage, David. "Strategic Considerations to be Used to Evaluate Joint Ventures." Annual International Conference of the League for Innovation in the Community College and the Community College Leadership Program (7th San Francisco, C. July 23–26, 1995). ERIC, ED 385329.

Grudzien, Pamela. Email to Stephanie Mathson, March 5, 2008.

Halverson, Kathleen and Jean Plotas. "Creating and Capitalizing on the Town/Gown Relationship: An Academic Library and a Public Library Form a Community Partnership." *Journal of Academic Librarianship* 32, no. 6 (2006): 624–629.

Helwig, Ruth. Interviewed by Robin Sabo. March 11, 2008. Charles V. Park Library, Central Michigan University.

Lindenfield, Joseph F. "Six Patterns of Community College/Public Library Cooperation." *Community & Junior College Libraries* 24, no. 4 (1984): 33–41.

Maxwell, James E. "A Summary of the Online Public Access Catalog Merger between the Library of the Franklin University and the Columbus Ohio Metropolitan Library and an Analysis of the Intralibrary Loan Relationship." Master's Research Paper, Kent State University, Kent State University, 1992. ERIC, ED 355962.

Mitchell, Lise H. Email to Joyce Salisbury, March 21, 2008.

Passalacqua, Debbie. "Broward Community College." In *The Librarian's Guide to Partnerships*, ed. S. Lynch. Fort Atkinson, Wisconsin: Highsmith Press, 1999.

Smith, Ruth, David Knight, and Dawn Jones. "Improving the Health of Seniors: A Partnership between a Public Library and an Academic Health Sciences Library." *Virginia Libraries* 51, no. 4 (2005): 25–26.

Todaro, Julie Beth. "Community Collaborations at Work and in Practice Today: An A to Z Overview." *Resource Sharing & Information Networks* 18, no. 1/2 (2005/2006): 137–156.

Wessel, Charles B., Jody A. Wozar, and Barbara A. Epstein. "The Role of the Academic Medical Center Library in Training Public Librarians." *Journal of the Medical Library Association* 91, no. 3 (2003): 352–360.

Part 3

SPECIAL COLLECTIONS AND
DIGITAL PROJECTS

9

———◦•◦———

OUTREACH IN SPECIAL COLLECTIONS LIBRARIANSHIP

Florence M. Turcotte

Special Collections librarians in academic libraries have a wide variety of opportunities for outreach activities and innovative partnerships with their constituencies. As part of an academic institution, the primary mission of Special Collections is to serve the needs of faculty and students in reaching their educational and research goals. At the same time, expectations for Special Collections continue to change. We can no longer build collections in a vacuum and assume that researchers will crowd into our reading rooms to use them. Our focus must be in acquiring materials that complement and add depth to our existing collections. We also need to add new materials that help to diversify our collections and, as a consequence, our research population. User-centered collection development and access-oriented public services are the hallmark of the new Special Collections. Focus is newly placed on promoting collections to nontraditional research populations. Local and regional community groups; genealogists; women's groups; and members of ethnic, cultural, and sexual minorities need research materials to advance their work.[1]

This chapter on outreach in Special Collections examines these issues in three sections. The first section focuses on what we promote and why. What are special collections and what are the services we provide? What is the impetus for outreach in the Special Collections environment? What are the target audiences and underlying reasons behind outreach activities? The second section focuses on the methods used in Special Collections outreach: bibliographic instruction, exhibits, public programs, K–12 programs, partnerships with other institutions and community groups, etc. The third section analyzes the impact of technology on the way Special Collections librarians do outreach. Electronic finding aids, Web publishing, online exhibits, digitization projects, and social networking software are all tools for outreach currently in use in the academic library. How these are used in the Special Collections environment is examined.

In this chapter, the term "special collections" is meant to include any or all of the following: the institution's archives, rare books, and other book collections with a state or local interest, and manuscript, personal papers, and other archival collections. The term "Special Collections" refers to the department or administrative unit within an academic library system that houses these materials.

Change will continue to be the norm in academic librarianship in general, and Special Collections are no exception. Special Collections librarians have to respond and adapt to these changes, and outreach is an important aspect of this evolutionary process.

YOUR OUTREACH PROGRAM: IF YOU BUILD IT, THEY WILL COME

The motivating force behind any outreach activity is the *message* we wish to convey. What is the message of Special Collections? First of all, we have our collections and we want people to discover and use them for their research. The second part of the message of Special Collections is the service we provide, from collecting, acquiring, and preserving materials to making them accessible through description, scanning, digitizing, and even loaning. We also want to promote the concept of the intrinsic value of special collections as repositories of material culture and history, and ensure their future by convincing people of the importance of these activities and of the collection and preservation of the materials with which we are charged.

In the modern college and university environment, one of our first responsibilities is to educate each new generation of constituents about the importance of using primary (first-hand) source materials in the research process. With all the electronic databases available to students and the variability of the quality of information available online, the process of discernment often entails the ability to distinguish between primary and secondary sources. You can't always judge this by the age or the format it comes in: some primary source documents are digitized, and some secondary source materials are printed on brittle and crumbling paper. All online data is not created equal, and students need to be taught the skills of recognizing trustworthy sources. Of course, not all special collections materials are primary sources, and not all primary sources are in Special Collections. We need to explain to students why some materials don't circulate and, nowadays, why we can't just put everything up on the Internet.

Why do Special Collections engage in outreach? Of course, when researchers access our collections, we are making good use of our institution's significant investment in acquiring, maintaining, and making them available. Providing services related to our own unique and valuable holdings helps us to fulfill the university's mission. When outside scholars travel to visit our repository and then publish articles and books referencing them, still more researchers are attracted to our collections, and it increases the visibility and prestige of our host institutions. Knowledge and scholarship are augmented, and this furthers the broader goals of higher learning. In addition, increased awareness of our holdings calls attention to those materials that might complement and supplement them and may give rise to more donors and donations and generally more stakeholders for Special Collections.

Who are these stakeholders? Students, faculty, and staff of our institutions, and our own colleagues in the library or archives are our core constituents. In addition, special collections are known for attracting those outside the academy; researchers, community groups, alumni groups, "friends," or other groups of supporters comprise another level of the stakeholder population. Of course, all these layers interact and outreach activities can have an impact on more than one group of stakeholders. These activities help to ensure the future of Special Collections and the historical/cultural record we work so hard to preserve.

HOW DO WE GET THEM THROUGH THE DOOR?

In doing outreach, our goal is to increase the visibility, appeal, and accessibility of our collections. Our materials have value to our users for many different reasons: for research, for personal interest, for fun, and maybe even for profit. In turn, we need support from our constituents for collection maintenance, development, and to ensure a future for special collections. With service to our users being our primary goal, we have to communicate the value of our collections to them. When they realize this value, they in turn will support us in our endeavors.

Special Collections public services are promoted and advertised primarily by website, word of mouth, open houses, and flyers or brochures. The key to attracting patrons is to emphasize a user-centered approach to operations. Unlike the circulating collections, most special collections are kept in a closed stacks environment. Paged collections are frustrating and intimidating for researchers, especially for humanities scholars. Most of them love nothing more than to plop down in front of a shelf of old books and browse to their heart's content. The prohibition of physical browsing creates more than just an aura of mystery and exoticism around special collections; it also just makes them harder to use. Special Collections librarians continually have to demonstrate their openness and willingness to help patrons in every way we can. This doesn't mean eliminating security measures or all the rules we have in place to protect our materials from coffee spills, leaking ink pens, etc. It means stressing a user-centered service orientation with every encounter in the research room and beyond. It means training people to listen, establish eye contact, and use body language to convey attentiveness, respect, and even interest in the researcher's needs. It means working as a team to get people the materials they need in a timely fashion. And most of all, it means following up. Not just assuming they found what they were looking for, but asking; that is, using a pro-active approach to reference services whether face-to-face or via telephone or email.[2]

Connect with Students

Busy students in today's modern academic environment don't have time to wander into Special Collections just to see "what you have." Very few even attend library orientations unless it is a class requirement. Some campus groups here at the University of Florida send freshman students on a "scavenger hunt" to explore various places on campus, and one of these activities is to investigate holdings in the library. Many first stumble upon Special Collections in search of such objects as the 1947 yearbook, or a photo of the construction of the football stadium, etc. This may give them a vague idea of the purpose of the University Archives, but this first encounter is usually superficial.

In the area of curriculum support, the first step for a Special Collections librarian or archivist is to get onto the syllabus! The professor has to be contacted and convinced that the students will benefit from a class session introducing them to special collections. We know that connecting students with primary resource materials yields more original ideas and better research. Convincing an instructor of this may take a serious effort. Professors and teaching assistants are extremely busy and with so much material to cover are often reluctant to surrender precious contact time with their students to have an outsider talk to them about library resources. The librarian may have to try several approaches. Attending faculty and curriculum-planning meetings, setting up meetings with individual faculty members, emailing, and phone calls have all met with success, depending on the subject matter, the climate of the department and the personalities of the parties involved. Successful outcomes are often achieved with the assignment of a term paper or project using special collections materials. Graduate students may need specialized subject-specific bibliographic instruction, with personalized follow-up. Undergraduates need a general orientation, then a time-sensitive short-term research assignment using special collections. Getting directions to Special Collections right on the syllabus is critical to getting students through the door.

An orientation session near the beginning of the semester, either in the classroom or in the Special Collections facility, can be followed up with individual or team consultations by the librarian or archivist to help students do their research and complete their assignments. Often the librarian can be an instructor's best friend, especially if he or she is juggling a busy schedule or trying to get away to attend a conference during the semester. In this case, the librarian can be the one to come to the rescue. Cultivating relationships with graduate students and teaching assistants can be the key to getting onto the syllabus, into the undergraduate classroom, and onto the radar of our most important stakeholders, our students.[3]

Here at the University of Florida, bibliographic instruction activities using special collections take place every semester for classes in nearly all of these academic disciplines: History, Sports History, Museum Studies, Book Arts, Print-making, Cartography and Geography, Literature, Creative Writing, Anthropology and Cultural Studies, and Library Science. Another example related to curriculum is the use of special collections in the production of documentary films in the College of Journalism. One project involved the production of a video with an accompanying online exhibition of materials from Special Collections. Patrons searching the finding aids could then find out about the video, which they could borrow from the circulating collection.

Another success came out of an assignment called *Archive Exercise*, which required students of environmental history to write a five-page paper with footnotes and bibliography. They needed to use manuscript materials from the University of Florida Special and Area Studies Collections, most of them using materials from the P. K. Yonge Library of Florida History. They could, for instance, write a short environmental history of their home county; or about the human relationship with the natural world as recorded in the letters, journal, or diary of an early Florida pioneer; or about the environments that early travel writers of the South encountered. They attended an orientation at the Special Collections library that familiarized them with the primary source materials available. One objective of this assignment was to give the students hands-on experience working with original primary resources as opposed to Internet sources.

History 4944 is an internship class in Special Collections for undergraduate history majors. They receive three credits, and four faculty members from Special Collections give introductory lectures and an orientation program. Then each of the students takes on an arrangement project and a description project. They have to work in the library at least three hours a week throughout the semester and turn in a finding guide and a report of their experience as a final exam. Most of the students enjoy this departure from the traditional class setting, and the archivists can get some help with processing tasks. Some students even end up identifying the archival profession or librarianship as a possible career goal.

Connect with Colleagues

In Special Collections at the University of Florida, we make it a priority to inform our colleagues about our materials and to get referrals from public services staff in the other eight branch libraries on campus. If they don't know about our holdings, then they can't send patrons to use our collections. We hold brown-bag seminars in our conference room and present research to our colleagues. Staff members from other units are usually interested in some aspect of special collections. Strategies for increasing awareness of special collections among other library staff members include:

- In-house training and outreach
- Giving a tour for new employees
- Hosting an open house event
- Hosting an outside lecturer for staff development
- Collaborating with a subject bibliographer and teaching faculty on projects

The best way to get researchers referred to Special Collections is to respond quickly and effectively to colleagues who call on you for assistance with a reference question. If they have a "go-to" person in Special Collections, then their trust is gained, and they will confidently send new patrons to you.[4]

Another aspect of outreach is connecting with colleagues outside your institution. This is usually accomplished by attending meetings and making presentations at conferences, but it can also mean collaborative activities with community and state-wide groups, as well as with other Special Collections librarians who are mutually searching for ways to better publicize special collections and expand and diversify their research populations.

Connect with Outside Researchers

The key to outreach to the off-campus community is having well-organized materials that are accurately described online. A brief, to-the-point description of what you have, how much of it you have, and how to find it is integral to attracting the outside scholar who has very specific needs. Detailed bibliographies, finding aids, and contents lists are only worthwhile if the researcher is first convinced that there might be enough there to merit a visit to your repository. In the case of book collections, standard or enhanced MARC records are sufficient. Like it or not, the vast majority of manuscript collections are discovered via a Google search. There is a descriptive standard for finding aids that includes statements about the size and scope of the collection, a descriptive summary, the biographical/historical notes, date ranges, etc. Looking at this "top page" of the finding aid might persuade the patron to search through the detailed contents list. A note about related collections might send a researcher to another collection or even another repository.

Excessive restrictions on collection access might enhance the "mystique" of special collections, but it will discourage researchers. In the case where materials are too fragile for handling or photocopying, digital surrogates might solve the problem. When privacy is an issue, taking the time to isolate restricted materials from a collection that is otherwise permissible to use will help researchers a great deal. Full disclosure is another good strategy. If you know a collection has been restricted or sanitized by the subject, heirs, or dealer, make a point of telling the researcher before she or he travels across the country to dig up juicy details that have been expunged or locked away.

Connect with Genealogists

The first instinct of many reference librarians is to run and hide when a genealogist comes into the room. This is because many genealogists are considered inexperienced or "high-maintenance" by library staff. We want "real" researchers, meaning serious scholars writing a book, a dissertation, etc. The fact is that many genealogists are quite knowledgeable and can get to what they need quickly and relatively painlessly.

In her article entitled "Genealogists and Records: Preservation, Advocacy, and Politics," Aprille Cooke McKay disputes the second-class citizen status that genealogical researchers have in many archives and public records repositories. McKay maintains that on the contrary, librarians and genealogists have many goals in common. These include well-preserved and accurately described records with safe and easy access. They also appreciate adequate and stable funding for digitization projects and collection development and maintenance. She points to the work of organizations such as the Federation of Genealogical Societies (FGS) and the Church of Jesus Christ of Latter-Day Saints, who lobby on local, state, and federal government levels for open access to vital records. FGS efforts were integral in the 1984 decision of Congress to restore independent status to the National Archives by separating it from the control of the General Services Administration. The Mormon Church offers inexpensive and responsive genealogical assistance to researchers from all over the world.

Finally, the cultivation of relationships with genealogists might give rise to donations of manuscript materials important to a repository, such as ethnic or regional collections. Librarians can also tap into volunteer labor and significant funding sources by maintaining a cordial relationship with those who have adequate financial resources to be able to do "research for fun." Genealogists can turn out to be strong advocates, political allies, and even generous benefactors in the long run.[5]

Community Outreach

Academics often get wrapped up in their own areas of specialization and are therefore accused of ignoring the "real world" around them. It's true that with limited resources, our first priority should be curriculum and faculty support activities. Nevertheless, as educators, one of our responsibilities is to teach our charges how to be good citizens in a democratic society. Reaching out to the local community not only sets a good example but it also improves town-gown relations. If, as is the case here in Gainesville, Florida, a community is asked to cater to the needs of 50,000 college students, there should be some outreach done that enriches the life of that community in return.

Typical community outreach activities include open house events, lectures open to the public, and exhibits related to local history and culture. Curators often solicit materials from local business people, politicians, and civic and religious groups for special collections. All these yield long-term dividends not only in the area of community relations but also in development and collection building.

At the University of Florida, our librarians and archivists often make presentations to outside groups highlighting Special Collections materials. The curator of our Belknap Performing Arts and Popular Culture Collections, Jim Liversidge, held a film festival at a local retirement community. The curator of the P. K. Yonge Library of Florida History, James Cusick, gives a weeklong workshop in St. Augustine each summer for K–12 educators through the Landmarks of American History Program, funded by the National Endowment for the Humanities and the Florida Humanities Council. Our liaison to the African American community, Joel Buchanan, spends a lot of time talking to local civic groups and community leaders about preserving, collecting, and donating materials to our repository. As curator of literary manuscripts, I made three public presentations last year centered around Florida authors whose papers we collect. The first two were about Marjorie Kinnan Rawlings: one to a teachers' group as part of their in-service training and one to the general public at the public library headquarters as part of their One-Book One-Community program. The other presentation was at a screening of a film based on a novel by author John D. MacDonald. We also contributed display and biographical materials for a *Big Read* program centered on Zora Neale Hurston at the county public library.

Another example of a successful community partnership is one established between the Marjorie Kinnan Rawlings Manuscript Collection at the University of Florida and the Marjorie Kinnan Rawlings Historic State Park in Cross Creek, Florida, about twenty miles southeast of campus. Collaborative activities include developing promotional materials together, arranging tours for student and researchers by park personnel at Cross Creek, and referring visitors with questions to the collection curator. Interpretive tour leaders do their research in the manuscript collection on a regular basis, and the curator participates on many levels in activities and events at the Rawlings Historic State Park. This partnership serves to broaden the community of stakeholders in both locations and enriches research and interpretive programs alike.

A significant outcome of this collaboration was the conferral of National Historic Landmark Status on the Park. Support documents for the application were gathered from the Collection, from library administration, from the Marjorie Kinnan Rawlings Society as well as from major Rawlings scholars. Without the combined efforts of all these parties, the application would not have been successful. This process has helped to build a community of stakeholders interested in Marjorie Kinnan Rawlings as a writer, as a Floridian, as a twentieth-century woman, and as a major literary figure on the national scene.

Connect with K–12 Students

Another important aspect of community relations is service to the younger members of the community. Some ways that Special Collections can connect with schoolchildren are: assistance with history fair projects, school tours, and partnerships on grant projects.[6]

Many states are adopting new curriculum standards that mandate primary source research and analysis of many different types of resources for students in grades 5–8 and even earlier. Exposure to the "real thing" at a young age will often bear fruit by nurturing a lifelong library user or a budding scholar. Even a small effort in the community can yield great dividends, for instance when, during an orientation session for incoming freshman, a student declares: "Hey, I remember coming in here when I was in seventh grade!" If we can reach the younger students early, there is a good chance they will become allies in the future, by returning to do research or even becoming interested in librarianship as a profession.

Connect with Alumni and Other Important Stakeholders

Many academic libraries have full-time development staff or a liaison in the institution-wide development office to deal with donor relations by soliciting funds and in-kind donations, following up leads, helping with estate planning, etc. The assistance of Special Collections staff can be crucial to a healthy development program. For alumni, the quality and visibility of a top-notch University Archives Collection is integral to preserving the history and culture of the institution. In turn, the archives can be an important tool for building a strong foundation of alumni support. Hopefully, every student who attended your institution used the library sometime during their stay. Alumni are prime candidates for Friends groups and Library Advisory Boards. They also attend guest lectures and presentations during Homecoming and reunion events, and enjoy exhibits of memorabilia from the University Archives.

The University Archives should seek out famous alumni to solicit their materials before they deal with another repository or manuscript dealer. The ideal candidate understands the importance of organized record keeping, and that donated materials are not worth much if they are not adequately processed, arranged, and described, and that this activity is costly and time-consuming. For this reason, it is advisable to get a development officer involved when negotiating with a donor. In Special Collections, we host monthly tours for donor groups and/or for staff from the UF Foundation to show them our treasures and give them the tools they need when vying for donations. Getting Special Collections into a development proposal can be just as important as getting on the class syllabus!

Exhibitions

There's no doubt about it: Exhibitions are a tried and true outreach activity for libraries. Almost every library in the country has an exhibit space, or at least a little table-top display case. Special Collections departments often have items they would like to put on display, especially at institutions that collect more than just printed materials and books. Manuscripts and personal "papers" collections are very often much more than just paper. Documentary materials are often supplemented by those one-of-a-kind items that make a visual splash: an author's hand-printed map of his favorite drinking establishments, a charred sheaf of manuscripts rescued from a fire, or a politician's personal photo album. A well-designed exhibit is a wonderful outreach for "hidden" collections. It attracts researchers and other stakeholders and increases access, especially if it is well publicized and mounted in a heavy traffic area.

There are also a number of disadvantages. Displaying one-of-a-kind materials in a heavy traffic area can create security concerns. Mounting an exhibit is both expensive and time-consuming. Writing a grant to mount an exhibit can help with funding but definitely adds to the time involved. Exhibition catalogs are printed at great expense and may end up collecting dust in a corner. The exhibit can be mounted when staff members have more time during a lull in the academic calendar, but very few people are able to see it, or it may be in an area where people have to go out of their way to visit. The chief complaint with the University of Florida's Special Collections exhibit space is that we aren't open on weekends, the only time that off-campus people have a chance to visit and have access to on-campus parking.

There are ways to get around these obstacles: Have an exhibit opening reception after hours or on a weekend. Get students involved with doing some of the work. Last semester a group of our curators team-taught a graduate course in Exhibitions along with a professor of Museum Studies. The students formed teams and designed real exhibits using materials from one of our collections. These exhibits can be mounted anytime there is a slot available in our exhibit schedule.

Online exhibits are much less expensive, and some libraries report that online exhibitions have enhanced visibility and led to increased requests for information. Doing an online exhibit is an inexpensive way to substitute for, complement, or promote an in situ exhibit. Photos or scans of the display objects can be arranged on a Web page along with captions or short explanatory texts. Remember that most people will not read long passages online. A direct link to the exhibit on your library home page might increase the number of viewers. An online "teaser" exhibit can be mounted to entice people to come in person to your repository.

At the University of Florida, we mount three or four exhibitions a year centered on topics of interest to our researchers, faculty, and students and loan material to other institutions for exhibits. We usually pair it with a one-page online exhibit linked from our Department home page.

What about Advocacy?

Advocacy is closely related to outreach, and both involve getting our message out to our stakeholders. The key to advocacy is getting people to understand the value of special collections for future generations. By promoting and advocating for our collections, we are in a position to make a real impact on the lives of future generations. Advocacy ensures the future by preserving the past. Public education programs do much to instill this notion into the creators of possible future collections. Librarians and archivists advocate in many different ways: making presentations to individuals and groups; offering advice to people about books, materials, and media to help conserve their records; and volunteering to organize and describe the materials of a particular group. Another good idea is to design a documentation strategy in partnership with donors and potential donors that will not only promote collections but will also help to build new ones.[7]

"IS IT ONLINE?" INCORPORATING HI-TECH SOLUTIONS INTO SPECIAL COLLECTIONS OUTREACH

In a 2006 SPEC Kit published by the Association of Research Libraries entitled *Public Services in Special Collections*, a majority of the responding libraries reported on the immense impact that technology has had on public services in Special Collections. Online catalog records and finding aids are now much more prevalent than traditional card catalogs and other print tools, a trend that has significantly increased discovery and access. The availability of digital objects online makes it possible for users to gain access to holdings without visiting the library and without interacting with staff. The number of reference requests submitted via email is increasing exponentially and the nature of the requests is changing as are expectations on the part of patrons regarding how and when services should be provided electronically.[8] Technology also has affected how Special Collections conduct outreach, instruction, and other public programming. Many libraries are working with faculty and scholars to create digital content for use in lectures and exhibits.

More and more researchers are using the Internet as their primary gateway to information resources.[9] Printed finding aids will collect dust faithfully sitting on the shelf and won't do much to promote your collections. By necessity, information professionals in Special Collections have to focus on increasing the electronic discoverability of their collections. An easy-to-navigate and visually appealing interface is important, as well as a "one-stop shopping" search engine that searches all the finding aids from one page. Choose as many access points as feasible, but not so many that will cause a high percentage of false hits. Make it easy for the user to identify the collection name and box and folder numbers quickly. Finally and most importantly, be consistent with your finding aids, and use DACS (Describing Archives: A Content Standard) and, preferably, EAD (Encoded Archival Description) for metadata coding. EAD is an XML standard for encoding archival finding aids, maintained by the Library of Congress in partnership with the Society of American Archivists. The project created a standard for describing collections held by archives and special collections, similar to the MARC standards for describing regular books. Researchers benefit greatly when repositories display their finding aids with a degree of consistency. Specifically, researchers should be able to predict reliably the presence and location of certain descriptive elements within the finding aid display. They require less time learning to navigate and read each finding aid because the descriptive elements are presented in the same basic locations within the display. In addition, the retrospective conversion of legacy finding aids to the EAD standard has encouraged many archivists to revise their finding aids during the conversion process, thereby ensuring consistency between finding aids and, one hopes, improving the quality and completeness of the descriptions available.

Although EAD is a descriptive standard and not a display standard (i.e., it does not dictate how finding aids should be presented), the widespread implementation of EAD has dramatically changed the manner in which finding aids are presented. As more repositories adopt EAD and DACS and as we learn more about how researchers interact with descriptive archival information, it is likely that display styles will continue to be standardized. This in turn will increase the visibility and discoverability of special collections.

Another important outreach activity is digitization. The advantage is the ability to reach users 24/7 anywhere in the world. The difficulty is deciding what to digitize when just about everything is important to someone. Scanning and digitizing materials and representative portions of the different collections and mounting online displays help researchers to visualize potential projects and make an intellectual connection with our materials.

Grants and development opportunities abound for digitization projects. There is often a very strong conservation incentive for digitizing special collections, especially if they are requested frequently. Grant-seeking activity needs to be coordinated carefully, however, so that the institution doesn't overextend staff and/or equipment.

In the past decade there has been an abundance of new communication tools made available to librarians to get their message across. Some Special Collections librarians have set up a high-tech reader's advisory. Many keep track of contact information for frequent researchers, or they get information to their email lists about new materials as they are made available. Librarians can mobilize legions of users by taking advantage of the newsletters, email lists, and websites of genealogical groups. Another tool is to list possible research topics directly on the online finding aid website; these can be keyword links or more formal Library of Congress Subject Headings. Some Web pages advertise recent publications using materials from their collections.

Social networking software is being used increasingly to communicate and interact with our various constituencies, especially students. Librarians at my institution have put up videos about book conservation on YouTube, complete with book-eating insects in grisly close-ups. Many academic librarians have Facebook and MySpace accounts, and there are many online library "friends" and interest groups set up in these virtual spaces as well.

CONCLUSIONS AND FUTURE OUTLOOK

More research needs to be done to study the information-seeking behavior of special collections researchers from a social sciences perspective. We need to explore issues like who uses special collections and for what purpose and how they find out about them. Yet another topic might be investigating the effectiveness of metadata formats and systems through various research instruments, such as surveys. A study might explore various methodologies and designs for alert and advisory services in Special Collections, and design a tracking system to identify the research interests of Special Collections patrons.[10]

Online surveys that are easy to design and disseminate are another good research tool. Many librarians enjoy sharing information about outreach activities; learning from other peoples' mistakes and building on their successes is one of the hallmarks of the library profession. Thanks to these new technologies the avenues of communication have never been wider.

The 2006 SPEC Kit noted a significant number of the respondents, approximately 35 of 67, discussing an increase in public programming and outreach activities, including exhibitions, tours, and open house events in Special Collections repositories. Several libraries are concentrating on encouraging greater use of materials by K–12 and undergraduate students, with the expectation that if they engage the students early on it will lead to repeat visits throughout their academic careers. For example, multiple libraries participate in annual history fairs such as those associated with National History Day. Multiple libraries also emphasized outreach to first-year students. Some of these libraries have witnessed an increase in usage as a result of outreach activities. A few respondents, however, pointed out that the increase in public services and outreach has led to a decrease in other activities, such as the processing of materials. They expressed concern that staff members are becoming overworked and stretched thin as Special Collections units focus on labor-intensive public services and outreach responsibilities.

The data gathered by the survey is useful in that it provides a general overview of the current state of reference and public services in Special Collections. The comments provided by respondents are particularly useful because they reveal future directions and trends.

Outreach activities are expensive, and a coordinated plan for activities is integral to a successful program, even for the best-funded repositories. If you are in a large institution with many departments, it might be best to have a designated person, or a unit like Public Relations or Education, coordinating all outreach activities. This will prevent conflicting events being held at the same time, duplicated effort, and an unbalanced calendar. However, it is obvious that Special Collections librarians are taking advantage of a variety of known opportunities, or creating new opportunities, to reach out to their various constituencies. For their part, researchers are thinking creatively about new ways to use Special Collections resources and this certainly will have an impact on the nature and number of outreach activities.

NOTES

1. The tension between these sometime conflicting priorities is described in Julie Grob, "RBMS, Special Collections and the Challenge of Diversity." *RBM* 4, no. 2 (Fall 2003): 74–108. Grob calls for an action plan within the Rare Books and Manuscripts Section of the Association of College and Research Libraries (ACRL), a division of the American Library Association (ALA). This plan was subsequently drafted and adopted in 2005.

2. The "aura" surrounding Special Collections with regard to access is discussed in Daniel Traister, "Public Services and Outreach in Rare Book, Manuscript and Special Collections Libraries." *Library Trends* 52, no. 1 (Summer 2003): 87–108. Traister also points out that: Our readers tend to remain astonishingly less skilled than we like to imagine them at using tools that represent books rather than books themselves" (87). This also applies to finding aids, the tools of representation for manuscript collections. This situation is described in Elizabeth Yakel, "Listening to Users." *Archival Issues* 26, no. 2 (2002): 111–127.

3. A discussion about bibliographic instruction strategies for undergraduates has been broached by Pablo Alvarez, "Introducing Rare Books into the Undergraduate Curriculum," *RBM* 7, no. 2 (Fall 2006): 94–103.

4. See Leslie Hurst, "The Special Library on Campus: A Model for Library Orientations Aimed at Academic Administration, Faculty, and Support Staff." *The Journal of Academic Librarianship* 29, no. 4 (July 2003): 231–236. Hurst outlines a pragmatic, needs-based approach to designing library orientation for support staff and administrators in the university environment.

5. For specific information about the unique relationship of record keepers and genealogists, see Aprille Cooke McKay, "Genealogists and Records: Preservation, Advocacy, and Politics." *Archival Issues.* 27:1 (2002): 23–33, or Elizabeth Yakel and Deborah A. Torres, "Genealogists as a 'Community of Records'." *The American Archivist* 70, no. 1 (Spring/Summer 2007): 93–11.

6. See Michelle Visser, "Special Collections at ARL Libraries and K–12 Outreach: Current Trends." *The Journal of Academic Librarianship* 32, no. 3 (May 2006): 313–319. Visser surveyed 115 Association of Research Libraries (ARL) institutions to gauge the level of participation in K–12 outreach and the perception of such among academic librarians.

7. A detailed study on recent trends in documentation strategies can be found in Jennifer Marshall, "Documentation Strategies in the 21st Century? Rethinking Institutional Priorities and Professional Limitations." *Archival Issues* 23 (1998): 59–74.

8. Seventy-nine ARL libraries responded to this survey regarding Special Collections policies and procedures done by Florence Turcotte and John Nemmers, *SPEC Kit 296: Public Services in Special Collections* (Washington, D.C.: Association of Research Libraries, November 2006).

9. As early as 2002, 30 percent of the users of the Western History Collections at the University of Oklahoma named the Internet as their main access point to identifying collections relevant to their research. See Kristina Southwell, "How Researchers Learn of Manuscript Resources at the Western History Collections." *Archival Issues* 27, no. 2 (2002): 91–109. She predicted that this percentage would increase, as it surely has.

10. For an analysis of the nature, number, and types of reference questions asked of Special Collections staff from local and remote users, see Kenneth Lavender, Scott Nicholson, and Jeffrey Pomerantz, "Building Bridges for Collaborative Digital Reference between Libraries and Museums through and Examination of Reference in Special Collections." *The Journal of Academic Librarianship* 31, no. 2 (March 2005): 106–118. An older study that focused specifically on the Southern Historical Collection and General and Literary Manuscripts at the University of North Carolina at Chapel Hill was done in 1995 and followed up in 1999. See Kristin Martin, "Analysis of Remote Reference Correspondence at a Large Academic Manuscripts Collection." *The American Archivist* 64 (Spring/Summer 2001): 17–42.

10

UNIVERSITY LIBRARY OUTREACH IN AN URBAN SETTING: FORMING PARTNERSHIPS WITH CULTURAL INSTITUTIONS AS A COMMUNITY SERVICE

Lothar Spang and Sandra G. Yee

Outreach programs aimed at diverse populations are an invaluable service that universities located in large urban areas can provide communities. But partnering with nearby museums or other types of cultural agencies to devise specialized programs is an outreach means largely unexplored in university library systems in the United States. As of 2008, the professional literature listed fewer than ten university libraries that, in partnership with cultural entities, have created programs that combine resources to present comprehensive treatments of specific topics and, at the same time, reach previously underserved populations.

The library system of Wayne State University (WSU), Detroit, has long been a leader in the creation of programs of special interest to the varied populations of metropolitan Detroit and beyond. Today, the Libraries, by partnering with neighboring cultural institutions, universities, schools, charitable foundations, and even a newspaper, have created a series of programs that are offered free of charge to online users who otherwise, due to expense or distance, might not have access to the services and activities available through these resources.

Among the Libraries' partners are the Detroit Public Library, the Detroit Historical Museum, the Detroit Institute of Arts, the Henry Ford Museum/Greenfield Village, Meadowbrook Hall (estate of the Dodge and Firestone families), the Motown Museum, the Peace and Justice Resource Center, and even the Detroit Public Schools. Also included are the University of Michigan, Michigan State University, and the *Detroit News*. Funding for these partnerships has been provided by entities such as the Institute of Museum and Library Services (IMLS), national humanities foundations, and various public and private institutions and organizations.

Successes with the initial programs between Wayne State Libraries and its partners have set the stage for partnerships with additional cultural institutions in the immediate area. Digitization projects at Wayne State Libraries are now pending with the Detroit Symphony Orchestra and the Michigan Opera Theater. These two projects, when completed, will offer students and the public unprecedented access to music productions past and present and serve as a hands-on means of instructing students in the digitization of specialized collections.

The successes at WSU Libraries in partnering with local institutions and agencies illustrate how such cooperation is implemented and documents the benefits that accrue to university, schools, and cultural entities alike in such a partnership. Of special interest to academic librarians: the Wayne State experience documents how university libraries are poised to play a leadership role in devising innovative ways to reach new populations through digital technology.

CAPITALIZING ON PREVIOUS PARTNERSHIP EXPERIENCE

Entering partnerships with cultural entities was deemed feasible at Wayne State only after the Libraries had years of successful cooperation with libraries, local and statewide, in ventures aimed at improving research services for the local community. As early as the 1950s, WSU Libraries and the Detroit Public Library merged their health care collections, housing the new collection at Wayne State's Medical Library, with the understanding that residents of the Detroit area would have full access to it. This provided Wayne State researchers and the Detroit area with an unprecedented information resource.

By the mid-1970s, with the introduction of the Online Computer Library Center (OCLC), the online worldwide cataloging utility, as a viable bibliographic resource, Wayne State Libraries, cognizant of its strategic location in the central business/cultural center of Detroit, formed a leadership team with the University of Michigan and Michigan State University to develop a new statewide organization, the Michigan Library Consortium. This consortium, open to academic, public, and private libraries, was organized to provide a statewide cataloging utility that aided interlibrary loan among all participating libraries. Detroit area residents for the first time had ready access to the wealth of information available in libraries throughout the state. Housed at WSU Libraries during its formative years, the consortium now has its own facilities near the state capitol in Lansing and has expanded to provide member libraries with cataloging support, joint purchasing opportunities for supplies and equipment, workshops and training opportunities, and, in the new era of technology access, allows all residents of Detroit and Michigan equal opportunity to use online databases, digital books, and journals. At the Wayne State location, the partnership provides a timely access to information resources, giving students, researchers, and the general public improved research capabilities at the statewide level.

The success of these partnerships at the statewide level was a central factor in the Wayne State Libraries' assistance and leadership in the development of the Detroit Area Library Network (DALNET) in 1985, a local network of academic, public, and special libraries that includes law and medical libraries not part of the statewide system. This offering of a full range of local services to network members through the sharing of resources and innovative technology supplies Detroit area residents with a state of the art information resource.

Digital technology, especially since the mid-1990s, revolutionized all of these earlier partnerships by expanding the Libraries' ability to provide virtual access to an even broader community of local users. Archival materials previously unavailable could now support classroom instruction, research, and general information purposes alike for diverse users locally and globally. Such capability, and the successes of the earlier partnerships with libraries, meant that the Libraries could confidently invite Detroit's various cultural institutions, newspapers, universities, schools, and charitable foundations to create innovative programs that would serve diverse populations as never before.

CULTURAL OUTREACH FROM AN URBAN CENTER

Geography initially played an integral role in developing each outreach initiative at WSU. The key location of the university in the cultural center of Detroit, with additional cultural and educational institutions situated nearby, allowed the staff of the Libraries and these institutions to develop especially close working relationships that have been instrumental in helping the Libraries to develop successful digital initiatives. The resulting programs now provide professional researchers and community residents alike with specialized information sites and the training in the research skills needed to navigate ever changing information and technology resources.

WAYNE STATE LIBRARIES' COOPERATIVE DIGITAL PROGRAMS

Virtual Motor City

The Walter P. Reuther Library of Labor and Urban Affairs, based at Wayne State, houses the *Detroit News* Photo Archive Collection, a documentation of American social history, including the automobile industry, from 1868 to 1980. In 1988 *The Detroit News*, one of the premier photojournalistic resources freely available from a national level newspaper, donated some 800,000 photographic slides from its collections to the Reuther Library and transferred the copyright on them to WSU. Such copyright ownership allowed WSU Libraries to make available views of Detroit from 1900 to 1988, as seen by *News* editors, writers, and photographers, to various subject investigations and audiences in *Virtual Motor City* (http://dlxs.lib. wayne.edu/cgi/i/image/image-idx?c=vmc;page=index). The digitization of this special collection means that, as never before, Detroit area residents and the larger world can view the city's earliest transportation systems, its first automobiles, first assembly plants, the retooling for World War II, local politics and politicians, sports, local architecture, daily life, the beginnings of Motown, and the urban problems of the late twentieth to early twenty-first century.

The staff of WSU Libraries and the Reuther Archives have added considerable metadata to the photo archives, making them easily accessible. Students use the digital photos to add informational items to essays and term papers, and the public is able to view photos that otherwise would be unavailable. Funded by several grants, including one from the Library of Michigan, technical access to this site is made possible through the Michigan Electronic Library.

The assessment of *Virtual Motor City*, as given by the Dean of Wayne State's Honors Program, Jerry Herron, testifies to the program's appeal:

The *Virtual Motor City* is an invaluable resource for scholars generally, and especially for the Wayne State University Honors College. Our students undertake a curriculum that is city based and service oriented, with special emphasis in the first two years on Detroit history and culture. It is crucial that students get a hands on sense of the city, not only what is here today, but what was here yesterday. Of course, they do reading and documentary research, both individually and in groups. But there is no substitute when it comes to seeing the past, vividly and alive, as it was lived, day by day. And that is what the *Virtual Motor City* provides, a window into a world that, while it may be vanished, is no less consequential as the origin of all that we are today. (Herron 2008)

Virtual Motor City, the Libraries first digital program done in a cooperative venture, proved that by sharing resources and staff expertise, partners in such a venture are able to provide increased access to their primary clientele as well as the general community of users.

Digital Dress: 200 Years of Urban Style

This three-dimensional exhibit of the women's, men's, and children's clothing from Detroit and fashion centers across the United States through the past two centuries is a result of the collaboration among three resources in the Detroit area (http://www.lib.wayne.edu/geninfo/units/LCMS/dls/grants/ddgrant.php). Included is the Henry Ford Museum, a member of DALNET and a participant in a shared catalog system with WSU. The Henry Ford Museum digital dress collection, a part of the Museum's larger dress collection, is funded by an IMLS grant offered to each of the partners because of their cooperative effort. This digital history of costume (over a 200-year period) includes the clothing of the Ford family and others. The second partner is the Detroit Historical Museum and its dress collection, which, through this IMLS grant, catalogs the costumes of important Detroit women through history, and remains an important education source for fashion merchandising students. The third partner is Meadowbrook Hall, the home of former auto industry pioneers the Dodge and Firestone families, which houses a dress collection that includes the costumes of Mrs. Dodge and Mrs. Firestone. WSU contributed the Dorothea June Grossbart dress collection. The entire digital collection is composed of some 5,000 images of men's, women's, and children's clothing and accessories representing fashion during a period of urban transformation.

Collaborative efforts to digitize the costume collections from these three sources allowed WSU Libraries to present a 40,000-item display of occupational, formal, and recreational wear, as well as examples of clothing of everyday citizens and even union activists. These examples provide a stark documentation of costumes and accessories of the races and classes of Detroit and American culture through the past 200 years, creating an unprecedented resource on this topic.

The Web portal enhances and expands multi-institutional collections of cultural history for all age groups and educational purposes. Fashion designers, theater personnel, and social historians and students marveling at "old clothes" have found this a fascinating site. Fashion merchandising students have called the site "inspirational." In turn, for all collaborators this virtual resource unifies individual collections and provides a first of its kind means of accessing materials while preserving and protecting existing collections for future generations.

Detroit Plays: Social History through the Development of Toys

The WSU Libraries' partnership with the Detroit Historical Museum allowed the digitization of the museum's toy collection dating from the 1840s (http://www.lib.wayne.edu/resources/digital_library/toys/index.html). This tracing of the evolution of mechanical toys, dolls, cars, wagons, bicycles, and Glancy toy trains uniquely reveals the social history of Detroit and America in the past 200 years. Mechanical toys, which make up a substantial part of the collection, are represented in video segments made possible by digital technology. One of the most popular depictions on the site is the motorized mouse, which predates Disney animation by years. Making these toys available digitally helps the museum showcase its hidden collections to all citizens of the city, the state, and beyond. It is a one-of-a-kind portal that provides a unique perspective on cultural history in the United States.

Herman Miller Consortium Collection

The Libraries' collaboration with the Henry Ford Museum allows virtual access to the Herman Miller Consortium, a collection of 750 representative pieces of furniture from the Zeeland, Michigan-based manufacturer dating from the 1920s to the present (http://dlxs.lib.wayne.edu/cgi/i/image/image-idx?page=index;c=hmcc). This record of an important American manufacturer of home and office furniture documents a unique part of American cultural history, that of home furnishings.

Writing the River

This one-of-a-kind portal to poetry written by Michigan, Detroit, and Windsor, Ontario poets from the 1960s to the present is funded by collaboration with the National Endowment for the Humanities. This project includes work published by small local presses and reflects urban life as seen on both sides of Detroit River during the turbulent late twentieth to early twenty-first century era. The site is the first such effort in the United States to cross national boundaries (http://www.lib.wayne.edu/resources/special_collections/local/wtr/index.php).

Chapbooks Information Literacy Initiative

As a result of the success with the initial digital sites just described, WSU in 2006, using available Web space in a Digital Commons project done in conjunction with Detroit Public Schools, organized the instructional program, *Chapbooks Information Literacy Initiative*. Designed to provide students with an opportunity to create, design, and digitize their own written and artistic works, this site has become an important means for public school staff in Detroit and suburbs to teach students information literacy skills while nurturing the development of creative interests (http://digitalcommons.wayne.edu/chapbooks/).

Motown Historical Museum

This digitization project resulting from the Museum's partnership with WSU Libraries is underway and, when completed in late 2008, will allow users to trace the history of Motown, the record empire begun by Barry Gordy in the 1960s. The Museum (also known as Hitsville U.S.A.) documents the careers of artists such as the Miracles, the Temptations, Marvin Gaye, the Supremes, Martha and the Vandellas, and others who helped define Motown's unique sound, and explores Motown's profound influence on the music industry from the 1960s to the present day. Artifacts never before shared with the public will be available on this site.

Peace and Justice Digital Resource Center

The Library's initiation two years ago of a digitalization program, *Peace and Justice Digital Resource Center*, in cooperation with the university's Center for Peace and Conflict Resolution, produced a new type of community outreach program. This resource has 29 active community groups in the metropolitan area that can use Digital Commons Web space and technology to post their calendars, papers, and other organizational information for use by the community at large.

Unlike the other Wayne State Libraries' partnership initiatives, the Resource Center allows groups to submit current materials under their own name. The Libraries' role is to train staff from these groups, explaining the protocols for inputting their messages. To date, two groups have already been trained in these methods, and sessions for additional groups are planned.

By using the Libraries' Digital Commons, these community groups have their own Web pages and, thus, a broader audience. In turn, researchers and students, through the central resource, have ready access to the papers of these organizations, an option previously unavailable. The versatility and flexibility afforded by Digital Commons, therefore, has proven to be a key to developing special outreach programs to community groups.

PROGRAM ASSESSMENT

Evaluations of Wayne State Libraries' Partnership Initiatives

The *Virtual Motor City; Digital Dress; Detroit Plays: Social History through Toys; Herman Miller Furniture; Writing the River;* and *Chapbooks Information Literacy Initiative* sites have been in operation three years or less, beginning with *Virtual Motor City.* In 2007 the value of these partnerships was reflected in a summary of use data compiled by Joshua Neds-Fox (2007) of Wayne State Libraries' New Media and Information Technology Department, which revealed that 1.2 million pages of these combined digital initiatives were looked at by 64,300 users worldwide, 3,500 of whom were local faculty and students (see Tables 10.1, 10.2, and 10.3). WSU Libraries and its partners, therefore, have become an important part of the education system of the Detroit metropolitan area as well as a respected worldwide information resource.

Table 10.1
External Use of Wayne State Libraries' Digital Initiatives

Month	Unique visitors	Total External Visitor Statistics			
		No. of visits	Pages	Hits	Bandwidth
Jan 2007	4598	7213	79349	626811	3.46 GB
Feb 2007	4441	7272	84896	682900	3.83 GB
Mar 2007	5403	9248	172271	1575085	8.37 GB
Apr 2007	5495	8432	94394	687884	3.68 GB
May 2007	4839	7241	70391	596691	2.85 GB
Jun 2007	4142	5972	62949	494002	2.49 GB
Jul 2007	4966	8826	120298	947549	5.11 GB
Aug 2007	4999	8990	94249	723675	4.05 GB
Sep 2007	4946	9154	79360	646507	3.48 GB
Oct 2007	5153	8540	197264	803429	8.15 GB
Nov 2007	5755	8060	105848	711764	4.33 GB
Dec 2007	4942	7579	100344	792167	4.44 GB
Total	59679	96527	1261613	9288464	54.24 GB

The Means Used in the Wayne State Libraries' Initiative

Early on, the Library System selected Proquest's Digital Commons platform for its institutional repository. At first projected to house only theses and dissertations, prepublication research of faculty, student research, and digital archival projects, this repository has been expanded to provide community wide resource sharing. It has proven to be a durable and permanent location to house information that is

Table 10.2
Internal Use of Wayne State Libraries' Digital Initiatives

Month	Total Internal Visitor Statistics, 2007			
	Unique visitors	No. of visits	Pages	Hits
Jan 2007	362	515	13209	100028
Feb 2007	387	529	12000	92163
Mar 2007	295	407	10970	95593
Apr 2007	304	431	10958	86122
May 2007	245	366	8398	70799
Jun 2007	225	341	7329	52282
Jul 2007	207	316	9214	75772
Aug 2007	230	358	9315	71898
Sep 2007	322	494	8248	50648
Oct 2007	382	560	9785	79360
Nov 2007	389	547	9026	56689
Dec 2007	204	286	8962	46750
Total	3552	5150	117414	878104

Table 10.3
Total Use of Wayne State Libraries' Digital Initiatives

| Month | Unique visitors | Total Visitor Statistics, 2007 | | | |
		No. of visits	Pages	Hits	Bandwidth
Jan 2007	4960	7728	92558	726839	3.93 GB
Feb 2007	4828	7801	96896	775063	4.24 GB
Mar 2007	5698	9655	183241	1670678	8.91 GB
Apr 2007	5799	8863	105352	774006	4.23 GB
May 2007	5084	7607	78789	667490	3.13 GB
Jun 2007	4367	6313	70278	546284	2.71 GB
Jul 2007	5173	9142	129512	1023321	5.38 GB
Aug 2007	5229	9348	103564	795573	4.36 GB
Sep 2007	5268	9648	87608	697155	3.72 GB
Oct 2007	5535	9100	207049	882789	8.48 GB
Nov 2007	6144	8607	114874	768453	4.58 GB
Dec 2007	5146	7865	109306	838917	4.83 GB
Total	63231	101677	1379027	10166568	58.51 GB

searchable by local and worldwide users alike. In 2006 two librarians from Hokkaido University, Sapporo, Japan, visited Wayne State Libraries to see how they could expand their institutional repository, based on the Libraries' experiences. Hokkaido University's digital repository, begun in 2004, included only scholarly and academic papers. By deploying the latest technologies to service their 2,000 full-time researchers and 18,000 students, the professional staff hoped to provide a wide array of services to their university and the larger world, as the Wayne State Libraries were able to do through Digital Commons.

WSU Libraries have gone beyond the traditional educational and research capabilities commonly described as the benefits of an institutional repository. Digitization projects have been used creatively to support and advance the university's urban mission. Thus Digital Commons has been used to develop community partnerships that provide invaluable access to information beyond print for countless users.

Julie Klein, a teaching fellow in the Office of Teaching and Learning (OTL), Wayne State Libraries, in summarizing an OTL grant proposal reported (2008) that:

Although the Collections are accessed thousands of times per month, their use in online instruction is limited by technological barriers. On the national scene, this challenge has resulted in widespread under use of digital archives and inadequate mapping of the knowledge base for using collections (*Use and Users of Digital Resources*, 2005–2006), http://digitalresourcestudy.berkeley.edu/; *Using Digital Images in Teaching and Learning*, 2006, http://www.academiccommons.org/imagereport). Furthermore, many teachers lack technical knowledge and support for working with digital learning objects.

Through this grant proposal the OTL staff is seeking to develop a

Digital Learning and Development Sandbox that will enable students and teachers in universities, colleges, high schools, and educational departments of museums, libraries, and archives to create online learning experiences using our Digital Image Collections. (Carr 2003)

The result should be a richer interactive learning experience for students and teachers.

Program Costs

Matthew Decker (2008) of the Technology Resource Center, WSU Libraries, reports that:

The digitization projects undertaken by Wayne State Libraries in conjunction with local institutions had one-time costs that were not generally included in the per item cost. Depending on the project, and what was already available, the purchasing of computers, scanners, cameras, lighting, backdrops, and other supplies was not always necessary. The costs of digitizing varied according to medium: Photographic negatives, depending on size, generally a minimum of 300dpi, 8″ × 10″, averaged $1.50 per item. Slides, with a minimum 600dpi, 8″ × 10″, averaged $1.00 per item. And photographs, with a minimum 400dpi at actual size, averaged $1.80 per item.

Because of the original photography used for the *Digital Dress* project, and the video format used for the *Toy* digitization, these two projects had higher expenses. For *Digital Dress*, the minimum 6 MP camera resolution, results in 3,009 × 2,000 pixel images, minimum of three images per item, averaged $12.50 per item (higher for non-Wayne photographers). The video format, MPEG4, for the *Toy* collection averaged $25 per item.

Public Relations vs. Marketing in Cooperative Endeavors

The digital initiatives hosted by the WSU Libraries offer public relations benefits for the partners but can also serve as marketing venues for these same partner institutions. A statement in a 2005 brochure by the Tampa Bay Business Committee for the Arts, "Art and Culture add $521.3 million to the Tampa Bay economy," confirms what WSU and its partners have discovered: marketing the arts is a valuable community activity.

Realizing that the digital programs presented by the university are only a subset of its larger collections, researchers, students, and community users soon learn to view other resources available at the libraries and their participating partners. Collaborative partnerships, therefore, are uniquely poised to offer users access to information previously unavailable, but they are also in an unprecedented position to market their unique collections to the community and world beyond. Collaborative digitization projects are an important gateway.

Additional Benefits of Partnering with Cultural Institutions

University library cultural institution programs are creative means of meeting library system and university mission and strategic goals of serving varied communities. Access is expanded to "hidden" collections. The kinds and formats of materials available to students, faculty, the community, and beyond can be expanded. And, significantly, without university library collaboration, many partners would not be able to complete digitization projects. Through the uniqueness of their partnerships with cultural entities, universities are seen as demonstration sites for successful collaborative programs that can be replicated by other institutions and libraries.

Partnerships between university libraries and cultural institutions are, therefore, a win-win situation for all participants.

A NEW ROLE FOR UNIVERSITY LIBRARIES

The programs resulting from the partnerships between WSU Libraries and local cultural institutions illustrate how combining digital technology resources can allow each of the participating partners to reach new local and worldwide audiences. Such cooperation underscores how university libraries, in partnership with an array of cultural entities, can have ever increasing opportunities to play a vital role in the widespread dissemination of information and education to diverse populations.

An unforeseen benefit, learned from the Wayne State Libraries' experiences, is that the sharing of resources enhances the collections and services of all participants, a benefit that, in turn, encourages additional collaborations. One example: Each of the partners in Wayne State Libraries' collaborations has become a training site for fledgling librarians and information specialists, funded by an IMLS grant, an indication of the importance of collaboration in outreach endeavors. As David Carr (2003), Director of IMLS, notes, "The IMLS leadership during the last decade ... recognized the many ways that museums and libraries serve broader social educational and personal needs."

Jennifer Gustafson (2007), IMLS grant coordinator, WSU, emphasizes that "The IMLS grant is specifically designed to help offset a current shortage of librarians working in underserved communities, as well as the looming shortage of library directors and other senior librarians, many of whom are expected to retire in the next 20 years."

The collaborative programs initiated by WSU Libraries also illustrate how participants can contribute constructively to preserving cultural history while at the same time providing maximum access to holdings. For universities, as teaching institutions, such access also means that teaching information literacy skills can be achieved through the use of previously unavailable subjects of unique interest to varied types of users. Collaboration with cultural entities, therefore, defines a new role for university libraries in the Digital Age.

REFERENCES

Carr, David. Quoted in "Comment on Carr," by Marsha L. Semmel, *Curator* 46 (April 2003): 130–131.

Decker, Matthew. Email to coauthor (Spang, L.), March 6, 2008.

Gustafson, Jennifer. Email to coauthor (Spang, L.), June 13, 2007.

Herron, Jerry. Personal communication to coauthor (Yee, S.), February 19, 2008.

Klein, Julie. Email to coauthor (Spang, L.), February 21, 2008.

Neds-Fox, Joshua. Email to coauthor (Spang, L.), March 10, 2008.

Tampa Bay Business Committee for the Arts. *Cultural Institutions as Economic Engines.* 2005. http://www.pinellasarts.org/pdf/bca_brochure.pdf (accessed February 17, 2008).

11

WORKING TOGETHER: E-WE:MCIKTA: THE ARIZONA STATE MUSEUM LIBRARY AND THE TOHONO O'ODHAM NATION

Alyce Sadongei, Mary E. Graham, and Marlene (Marly) Helm

INTRODUCTION

In June 2007 the Association of College and Research Libraries (ACRL) approved standards for academic librarians that continue to define their role in very traditional terms of "developing collections, providing bibliographic access to all library materials, and interpreting these materials to members of the college and university community" (ACRL 2008). Yet academic librarians are seeing their traditional roles being expanded significantly by the introduction of new technologies, the call for diverse and nontraditional instructional methods, and the need to expand services beyond the walls of academia. Today, academic libraries are no longer just about books and walls but more importantly about space and service. These expanding roles for the academic librarian are forcing them to change and learn new skills, especially as they move to more frequent interaction with extra-library patrons, partners, and programs.

This change to enhanced outreach and collaboration is not new to the staff of the Arizona State Museum Library (ASML) at the University of Arizona. Like the academic library community, the professional museum association was similarly challenged to make their programs more relevant, inclusive, and reflective of a public-oriented mission (Hirzy 2002, 12). This call to change by the museum field issued in 1992 was easily embraced by ASML staff.

Serving as both an academic library to the university and as a specialized library to the museum, ASML staff has a history of willingness to share information and initiate communication beyond the university walls. The staff is guided by values that lend themselves to collaborative and outreach work such as cultural sensitivity, respect, and a welcoming hospitality. This attitude of openness and welcoming is especially critical to counter perceptions of privilege that often inform extra-library community members who may have limited experience in the culture of academia. These values, coupled with the critical factors of mission, staff, funding, geographic location, and changes to the museum field, have laid the groundwork for two demonstrative collaborative projects that ASML conducted with the museum cultural center and the library of a Native American tribe indigenous to the Southwest, the Tohono O'odham Nation. These projects and their success factors show how expanding the walls of academia leads to the breakdown of physical walls and, subsequently, cultural barriers.

BACKGROUND

As mentioned, ASML is both an academic and a specialized library. Its research collection, officially established in 1957, is focused in the areas of archaeology, anthropology, and the ethnology and material culture of the native peoples of Arizona and the Greater Southwest region of the United States, including the borderlands of California and Texas and northern Mexico. The collection is especially strong in ethnological and archaeological conservation/preservation, Spanish exploration and mission development, museum studies literature, and the management and preservation of cultural resources. There are also strong comparative peripheral collections on Mesoamerican cultures and Old World material culture. ASML holds collections bequeathed from renowned archaeologists like Emil W. Haury and Byron Cummings, historian The Reverend Victor Stoner, early Native American art historian Clara Lee Tanner, and Spanish colonial art historian Pál Kelemen.

ASML provides academic, research, and programmatic support to a vast constituency, including university faculty and students, museum staff, community users, outside researchers, tribal members, and contract archaeology firms. ASML is a department within the Arizona State Museum (ASM) that operates as a unit within the University of Arizona.

The State Museum was established in 1893 by territorial legislation to collect and preserve archaeological resources and specimens of mineral wealth, flora, and fauna in Arizona. Over the years the collecting scope shifted to include primarily archaeological and ethnographic material of the State and its early inhabitants. The archaeological collections are world renowned and were excavated by eminent Southwest archaeologists whose collective work helped to define and shape the study and application of Southwest archaeology, as currently studied in academia. Tribal involvement with the State Museum can be traced back to several of the university's field schools that employed tribal members as part of the field crew. The field schools operated in their prime from the 1940s to the 1960s.

TOHONO O'ODHAM NATION

The Tohono O'odham Nation is a sovereign Native American tribe whose ancestral lands covered Arizona and Mexico, including the greater Tucson basin. Today, its reservation is more than 4,000 square miles, comparable in size to the state of Connecticut, and is situated approximately 60 miles west of Tucson.

Tohono O'odham means Desert People. The Tohono O'odham regard their language and cultural traditions as central to their collective identity. Knowledge of cultural practices contributes to the well-being of the community. Their desire for a tribal museum had long been discussed, and in 2000 the tribal government officially endorsed the idea and earmarked funds for its development (Thomas 2000). After years of planning to establish community consensus regarding the location, mission, and building plan, the museum opened in June 2007. In addition to the new museum, the Tohono O'odham Nation also maintains the Venito Garcia Library and Archives (VGLA), a business park, community recreation facilities, and three casinos.

MEMORANDUM OF AGREEMENT AND MUSEUM-TO-MUSEUM COLLABORATION

In 2005 the Tohono O'odham Nation and the ASM entered into a Memorandum of Agreement (MOA) that allowed for ASM staff to work in cooperation with staff from the new museum/cultural center to identify areas of training and placement for Tohono O'odham interns. The MOA also provided for ASM staff to share expertise in areas of architectural building design, programmatic and staff needs, exhibition development, library development, and collections care. The agreement provided for transportation so staff could make site visits to each other, approximately a one-hour drive, one way.

The name of the new Tohono O'odham tribal museum is Himdag Ki: Hekïhu, Hemu Im B I-Ha'ap (Cultural House: Past, Present, Toward the Future). Its mission is to preserve and honor the Tohono O'odham way of life for current and future generations of Tohono O'odham. The cultural complex includes two buildings: one houses the museum's exhibit area and art gallery, library, archives, repository, and gift store; the other has an elders room with fireplace and kitchen, artist studios, which support a residency program, and conference/class rooms. The buildings are linked by walkways that lead to an outdoor circular storytelling/performance area, two traditional ramadas, and a covered patio. Tribal gaming revenue funded the construction and operation costs for the $15 million state-of-the-art facility.

The Tohono O'odham interns selected to work at ASM did so with specific goals in mind. Each placement reflected the interests and future work sites of the interns at the Himdag Ki. The intern assigned to work at ASML learned basic cataloging, classification and book processing, and reference work. Tohono O'odham interns assigned to other areas worked in the Museum's Public Programs Department, Information Technology Department, and the Office of Ethnohistorical Research. Beyond receiving hands-on experience, these interns were seen by Tohono O'odham community members as becoming stewards for the tribal culture, equipped to apply what they learned to the Himdag Ki.

In addition to providing training to the intern destined for the Himdag Ki Library, ASML initiated a publication exchange program with the tribal library, whose mission is to build a comprehensive collection of current and historic Tohono O'odham materials. Realizing that the new library would need books and journals and that both institutions have similar collection foci, ASML began compiling materials for a publication exchange program. The library gets many duplicate donations, and these were set aside and designated for exchange. ASML also weeded its collection for triplicate and quadruplicate copies for exchange. To date,

ASML has contributed over 800 items via the program, representing nearly 40 percent of the Himdag Ki Library's current collection of over 2,000 titles.

Informal collaboration continues between the two institutions through professional consultation in collection development, cataloging, and conservation/preservation. This informal collaboration continues to help the new institution to answer those how-do-you-do-it type of questions.

WHY IT WORKS

In practical terms, the relationship with the Tohono O'odham Nation was set in motion approximately twenty years ago. At that time, ASM was in negotiations with the Tohono O'odham Nation over the repatriation of human remains that were in the museum's collection and had been excavated many years earlier. This negotiated return occurred three years prior to the passing of the federal Native American Graves Protection and Repatriation Act (NAGPRA) in 1990.

NAGPRA requires all museums that receive federal funding to return human remains and funerary objects, sacred objects, and objects of cultural patrimony to tribes who are culturally affiliated with those objects and human remains. The law outlines a process for repatriation, which includes consultation with tribal representatives. The law also enables a tribe to identify which items are sacred or of cultural patrimony as opposed to the museum curator. NAGPRA introduced a radical reversal of concepts related to ownership and cultural authority. It also recognized that some museum objects had entered museum collections under less than sterling conditions.

Although the negotiations were punctuated by emotion and intense regard for the human remains by both ASM and the Tohono O'odham Nation, a new type of communication had been established that moved beyond anonymous cultural informant to publicly recognized partner. This relationship was later strengthened by the signing of another agreement in 1994 that created a partnership allowing ASM to curate and hold in stewardship a collection of Tohono O'odham artifacts that were given to the tribe. This agreement stipulated that the collection would be returned to the tribe after a museum was built on the reservation to adequately house and store the objects. The Norton Allen collection, named after the individual who collected the objects, has begun to be transferred to the Himdag Ki. The most recent MOA effectively brings to fruition aspects of the first signed agreement.

DIGITIZATION PROJECT

The latest project that highlights the collaborative work between ASML and the Tohono O'odham Nation was to digitize materials from the museum's photography collection. ASML received a Library Services and Technology Act (LSTA) grant from the Arizona State Library to digitize a collection of photographs from the 1970s to 1980s taken by ASM photographer Helga Teiwes. Because the images represented daily life and customs of the Tohono O'odham people, the library wanted to ensure that the photographs were not culturally sensitive and that their corresponding metadata was accurate.

The Tohono O'odham Nation's VGLA worked with ASML on this project. VGLA is a small public library that has a computer commons, circulating and reference collections, and a Special Collections containing archival materials of book and nonprint media relevant to the tribe and the Southwest, manuscripts, vertical files, sound recordings, photographs, videotapes, and Tohono O'odham language resources.

ASM's Helga Teiwes photography collection is well known and popular with the Tohono O'odham community. Many tribal members still remember the visits by the museum's photographer. Drawing on the expertise of staff from VGLA as well as from representatives of the community, ASML met periodically for several months to view the photographs, discuss their subject matter, and determine cultural sensitivity. The meetings were held at VGLA. By working directly with tribal community members, ASML received extremely valuable insight into identifying people in the photographs and providing Native language terms for many of the daily activities.

Communication was critical to this project and ASM's assistant curator for Native American Relations was integral to the project. The position was created in 1998. The curator's previous work with the VGLA's librarian and archivist made the initial contact and the subsequent follow-up for this project relatively easy. As part of the consultation project, ASML chose to offer an honorarium to tribal consultants for providing their cultural expertise. The honorarium recognized their cultural knowledge and provided a modest compensation to tribal representatives for their time and travel.

It was also important for ASM staff to conduct the meetings on the reservation, thus saving the expense and time of driving for tribal members. Funding from the grant provided for transportation costs and honoraria and for student wages to enter the cataloging metadata.

During the project, ASM staff had the opportunity to meet tribal community members and to observe the working operations of VGLA. Seeing the context of the tribal library and archive assisted ASML staff in broadening their awareness of the diversity of library and archive operations. Tribal library and archive staff were able to work directly with the assistant librarian/cataloger and to increase their professional contacts at ASM. Face-to-face contact is still of primary importance to many communities, whether they are tribal or rural. This is especially true in the case of communities who may not be constantly inundated with the use of communications technology. On the Tohono O'odham Reservation, although Internet access and email are available, cell phone coverage is still sporadic.

REASONS FOR COLLABORATION

There are several key elements that have contributed to ASML's ability to engage successfully with tribal communities. These include museum and university missions, staff, funding, geographic location, and changes to the museum field.

Mission

ASM's mission seeks to promote understanding of and respect for the peoples and cultures of Arizona and the surrounding regions. The mission of the University of Arizona is to discover, educate, serve, and inspire. The university also strongly encourages outreach and service from its faculty and professional staff. Seeking to incorporate both ASM and the University of Arizona's missions, ASML has made outreach and collaboration a part of its public services.

Staff

Staff members need to have the appropriate skills to carry out collaborations with nonuniversity communities. ASM is unique in that since 1998 a staff position has been designated to work with tribes on a consisent basis. The assistant curator for Native American Relations, who also happens to be Native American, solidifies ASM's commitment to be inclusive of tribal communities.

Prior to the hiring of the assistant curator for Native American Relations, ASML staff members have consistently demonstrated an openness and enthusiasm in providing consultations, tours, or assisting visiting researchers and extra-library patrons. Tribal members, whether or not they are enrolled university students, are made to feel welcome. Grounded in librarianship principles of access to all, ASML staff also demonstrates the ability to recognize cultural concerns that are not based on Western standards of access and democracy. ASML's director and assistant librarian were both educated at the University of Arizona's School of Information Resources and Library Science (SIRLS) at a time when ethnic minorities were being actively recruited. The concept of a diverse patron base was emerging, and students were encouraged to broaden their awareness of other cultures and worldviews. The result is that the senior library staff is able to create and direct an atmosphere of respect, cooperation, sensitivity, and openness in the library's practice at the museum. ASML staff are all actively engaged in various library and museum professional groups and they keep abreast of changes and challenges to the field. The staff members also serve as adjunct instructors in the SIRLS program and regularly mentor student interns and employees. The ability of ASML staff to assess economic and political factors (both internally at the university level and externally via local, state, and federal agencies) and to communicate effectively with these staff and their departments is another reason why ASML has been able to initiate collaborations with other groups.

Funding

The museum's staff has a creditable record in receiving grants for collaboration from state and federal sources. Both the Arizona State Library and the Institute of Museum and Library Services (IMLS) have categories designated specifically for collaboration. The State Library has a category specifically for working with tribal libraries/communities. In the case of the digitization project, working collaboratively with the Tohono O'odham Nation actually improved the grant's chances of being funded and clearly defined its scope of work.

From 1999 to 2005 ASM was awarded two consecutive National Leadership grants from the IMLS. These grants were to assess the training and development needs of tribal libraries, archives, and museums within the states of Arizona, New Mexico, Utah, Colorado, and Nevada and to create appropriate partnerships and programs with state libraries, museums, and other agencies to respond to the needs articulated by the tribal communities. The grants were awarded to ASM in partnership with the Arizona State Library and directed by the assistant curator for Native

American Relations. These projects elevated the visibility of ASM in its outreach and service to tribal communities. The grants also funded two national conferences targeting tribal libraries, archives, and museums and created a directory for these organizations. ASML staff contributed to the conferences and directory and as a result are part of the network of tribal libraries, archives, and museums along with other nontribal institutions. Grant funding has been essential to cover the costs of collaborative projects undertaken by ASM.

Geographic Location

The University of Arizona was established in 1893 as a land grant institution, thus research and resources benefit communities statewide. The University of Arizona strives to recruit and retain Native American students and offers a variety of programs and services targeting this population, including an American Indian Studies program, an International Indigenous Law and People program, the Native Nations Institute (research and policy focus), and the American Indian Language Development Institute, to name a few. The School of Information and Resource Science also manages Knowledge River, a specialized program designed to encourage Native American and Hispanic library students to enter the field. Native American faculty are employed throughout the university's colleges and departments, including the director of ASM, hired in 2004, who is a member of the Hopi Tribe. A unique aspect of ASM is that it was the first museum to be located in the region that had been and still is inhabited by the cultures being studied (Parezo 1984). Located in the southern part of Arizona, the closest Native American reservations to ASM and the university are the Pascua Yaqui Tribe and the Tohono O'odham Nation. Twenty other Native American tribes are located throughout the state.

The twenty-two sovereign tribal nations situated within Arizona have grown in population and political and economic influence over the last 15 to 20 years. Contributing to the shift has been the introduction of gaming to Arizona tribes in the early 1990s. Increased revenue has supported basic infrastructure improvements, primarily to social service, health, and education-related tribal programs. Several tribes, however, have opted to use new revenues to support the creation of tribal museums, libraries, and archives or make improvements to existing ones. Within Arizona, twelve tribes have a museum, nine operate a library and/or archive, and six have some sort of culturally related office or program. Five of the tribes have both a library and/or archive and a museum.

ASM is cognizant of its proximity to tribal communities in the Southwest. It also recognizes the relevance that ASM collections have to descendant and current communities. Outreach is a natural outgrowth that complements the university's goal of making the institution relevant to tribal communities. ASM is also viewed as an accessible resource for tribal libraries, museums, and archives within the state in terms of proximity and of staff willing to share expertise.

Changes to the Museum Field

In the years following the passage of NAGPRA, ASM and other museums across the country adjusted to the paradigm shift that the law created. Legally required consultations expanded to include dialogue regarding other aspects of museum practice. Tribal representatives were invited to consult with staff and participate in the planning of museum education programs and exhibits. Tribal consultants working with ASM staff have informed exhibit development, provided guidelines for the care and handling of sensitive material in the collection, and served as guest lecturers and educators for the student docent program.

Tribal involvement with ASM was formalized with the creation of the Southwest Native Nations Advisory Board. Each of the twenty-two federally recognized tribes in the state is invited to designate a representative, and ASM's assistant curator for Native American Relations assists the board.

CONCLUSION

The formal collaborative projects that ASML has had with the Tohono O'odham Nation have enabled ASML to further its mission and institutional goals, as well as those of the museum and the university. ASML staff also benefited by learning about another culture and its people and was able to provide increased access to its resources. The Tohono O'odham Nation's Himdag Ki's Library benefited from the technical assistance and hands-on experience that they received from ASML staff. In particular the tribal interns' knowledge and familiarity of university resources has expanded.

The collaborative projects and the experience of ASML in working together with tribal communities can benefit the academic library field by providing a model of cooperation that is grounded in the basic tenets of access, respect, sensitivity, and openness toward others.

REFERENCES

Association of College and Research Libraries. *Standards for Faculty Status for College and University Librarians.* 2007. http://www.ala.org/ala/acrl/acrlstandards/standardsfaculty.cfm (accessed March 31, 2008).

Hirzy, Ellen. "Mastering Civic Engagement: A Report from the American Association of Museums." In *Mastering Civic Engagement: A Challenge to Museums.* Washington, D.C.: American Association of Museums, 2002.

Parezo, Nancy J. and Martha A. Brace. "The Arizona State Museum." *American Indian Magazine* 10, no. 1 (Winter 1984): 26–31.

Thomas, D. Conversation with A. Sadongei, Phoenix, Arizona, June 8, 2000.

ADDITIONAL READINGS

Haury, Emil W. "Reflections on the Arizona State Museum: 1925 and Ensuring Years," n.d. manuscript.

Raspa, Dick and Dane Ward (eds.). *The Collaborative Imperative: Librarians and Faculty Working Together in the Information Universe.* Chicago, IL: ALA/ACRL, 2000.

Wilder, Carelton S. "The Arizona State Museum History." *Kiva* 7, no. 7 & 8 (1942): 26–29.

12

—◆—

REACHING OUT THROUGH DIGITAL LIBRARY PROGRAMS: THE EVERGLADES DIGITAL LIBRARY EXPERIENCE

Gail Clement

INTRODUCTION

This chapter examines the community outreach opportunities that digital library programs can offer in academic settings. The ensuing discussion pays particular attention to the ways in which academic library outreach is being redefined in the digital age. This chapter draws chiefly from a case study of the Everglades Digital Library and its associated collections at Florida International University, but it could have been written about a host of other digital library programs under development in universities and colleges today. Most every academic digital initiative can be a tool of outreach and engagement by exposing library collections, services, and expertise to the global Internet for their discovery, use, and further promotion. Digital collections serve as outreach vehicles when they push high-value library resources out to an audience who otherwise could not access them. Virtual reference desks serve a public outreach function by connecting off-campus users with needed information to solve a problem or make a decision. Digital library interfaces invite new users and new contributions into the library's sphere, engaging public involvement through blogs, wikis, annotations, tagging, and file uploading. Digital library staff members become agents of outreach by contributing their expertise and elbow grease to the creation of community information systems. In these ways and many others, academic digital library programs can help their parent institutions demonstrate their worth, showcase their most valuable assets, find new bases of support, and positively impact the communities they serve—all worthy goals of a community outreach program.

There are hundreds of digital initiatives involving college and university libraries today, many of which reach, engage, and help users beyond campus. One example among the many is Central Florida Memory, a regional digitization project that aims to improve campus and public access to local history and culture by digitally seaming together content from the University of Central Florida, neighboring historical societies, and the local public libraries. The project's positive impact on the community has advanced the University's civic mission as a public metropolitan university. As an added benefit, project partners have gained valued experience and knowledge from each other's contributions (Scharf 2003).

University digital initiatives targeted to the K–12 community have gained in popularity, providing academic librarians the opportunity to do things not usually supported in institutions of higher education. For example, participants in the Digital Heritage Cultural Community project at the University of Illinois initiated their digital project for elementary classrooms as a means of "focusing on a community outreach project; forming new partnerships with previously unserved or underserved groups; and identifying and assessing collections for digitization" (Bennett, Sandore, and Pianfetti 2002). The value of educational outreach within digital library programs has been emphasized by the Library of Congress and its American Memory Program and echoed by other agencies that fund digitization projects, such as the Institute of Museum and Library Services. Indeed, the availability of external grant funding can be a powerful incentive for academic digital library programs to pursue a K–12 outreach strategy. Yet there are other inducements to develop and sustain digital projects that support curricular needs: legislative mandates for academia to support public education; university self-interest in recruiting new students; and university research/curricular interest in digital libraries as a means of improving education.

Development of community information systems is another type of digital initiative linked to outreach. These systems can bring together, in one central online location, a diversity of information resources to meet a targeted information need on behalf of the community. Academic libraries may need to reach out to partner institutions with complementary resources to create a critical mass of content not available within the library's own walls. One notable example of the many community information systems on the Web is *Rangelands West*, a digital archive and subject portal developed by land grant colleges in the western United States to serve the information needs of ranchers, farmers, environmentalists, range managers, and the university community (Jones, Ruyle, and Hutchinson 2003).

Another successful digital library outreach model implemented in academic libraries is virtual reference desks that serve a range of user needs on and off campus. Using a host of networked communication tools (electronic mail, live chat software, and, more recently, online communities and virtual worlds), the public can connect with subject experts and with each other to share knowledge and address common concerns. An example of a virtual reference desk that serves a community outreach function is the Fire Institute Library at the University of Illinois, which assists fire departments, firefighters, and other fire/emergency-related users in the successful and effective performance of their jobs (Ruan and Sung 2003).

Integrating more interactive interfaces into digital library systems gives academic libraries additional opportunities to reach and engage users. The Digital Forsyth photograph archive, developed by Wake Forest University, Winston-Salem State University, and local partners, demonstrates the benefits of blogging software to foster "community participation in the content, description and organization of the digital library" (Mitchell and Gilbertson 2008). The Portal to Texas History project at the University of North Texas draws in hundreds of new users to its collections by adding relevant links to Wikipedia articles (Belden 2007). On a broader level, the promise of virtual worlds to revolutionize digital libraries has been recognized by members of the Digital Library Federation (DLF), a consortium of mostly academic libraries involved in digital initiatives. DLF Executive Director Peter Brantley has posited, in his blog posting "DLF moving into Second Life," that "Second Life may represent a revolutionary breakthrough for digital libraries as they seek more powerful and flexible ways for scholars and people to use information" (Brantley 2007). No doubt the emergence of participatory media and more collaborative interfaces will have an important impact on digital library development and the outreach strategies that academic libraries deploy to connect campus, community, and content.

The remainder of this chapter focuses on one particular digital library program that uses, to some extent, the range of outreach strategies described above. The Everglades Digital Library (EDL) is a collaborative and evolving online library dedicated to meeting the need for reliable and comprehensive Everglades-related information. EDL partners fulfill their vision to serve the research and educational needs of their own constituencies and to fulfill their public service missions as tax-supported institutions. Yet no one institution or library could possess, on its own, the content, technologies, resources, and expertise required to meet the extensive needs for Everglades-related information.

The large-scale investment of public funds to save the Everglades, the complexity and duration of the Everglades restoration program,[1] the international attention focused on the ecosystem and its inhabitants, and the competing interests of a large and diverse array of stakeholders create tremendous demands for information in support of research, planning, decision making, evaluating, reporting, and education. Therefore, at the heart of the EDL program is an unrelenting outreach strategy. It is through partnerships, resource sharing, and a laser-sharp focus on user needs that EDL continues to develop and be sustained.

BACKGROUND

Florida International University (FIU) is an urban, public research university located in southeastern Florida, midway between the international metropolis of Miami and the expansive wilderness of the Florida Everglades. Founded in 1972 as a unit of the State University System of Florida, FIU was chartered "to serve the greater community ... in a manner which enhances the area's capability to meet the ecological, cultural, social and urban challenges which it faces" (Florida Administrative Code 1974). Guiding the university's development are five key strategic themes: International, Environmental, Urban, Health, and Information.

The FIU Libraries support the university's mission by providing the means for the discovery and the pursuit of knowledge to a broad constituency within and beyond the campus. The FIU Libraries welcome unaffiliated visitors to use library resources without charge during all hours of operations. On-site visitor privileges include use of computers and databases for research, Internet access, reference desk assistance, and use of most library materials within the building for as long as needed. Nonaffiliated visitors also participate in the array of exhibits, lectures, and other public programs regularly hosted at the FIU Libraries.

The Libraries' Digital Collections Center reflects the university and library's broad commitment to public service through its mission to "build online collections of enduring value for university and global users by identifying, digitizing, and preserving information resources of scholarly, educational, and civic interest." Reflecting the university's strategic themes described earlier, digital initiatives have focused on the South Florida environment, local history and urban development, and the history and culture of Florida and the Caribbean. A staff of one librarian and two paraprofessionals develop and manage the operations of the FIU Digital Collections Center. Information technologies to support these digital initiatives include locally hosted systems for digital capture, conversion, processing, storage, and Web delivery, and a digital asset management system and digital preservation archive managed by the Florida Center for Library Automation in Gainesville, Florida.

The flagship program of FIU's digital initiatives is the EDL, a collaborative effort involving library, museum, agency, school, and nonprofit partners. Components of EDL include: (1) an evolving digital collection of material contributed by FIU and its partner institutions; (2) a virtual reference and referral service; (3) a Web portal to Everglades-related resources on the Internet; and (4) an outreach/publicity program offering workshops and presentations, handouts, and exhibits. With no dedicated staff of its own, the program draws from the expertise and efforts of library personnel from across the FIU Libraries, including Digital Collections, Reference, Government Documents, Geographic Information, Systems, and Special Collections. The EDL program also relies on expertise from a network of dedicated partners, champions, and users, including FIU faculty and students, agency scientists and outreach personnel, K–12 educators, and colleagues in libraries and museums across the region.

As digital libraries go, EDL is not remarkable for the size of its budget, the expanse of its collections, or the sophistication of its technological systems. Characterized in its early years as "A Nice Little Digital Library," the project was profiled in *American Libraries* because it "focused on something so mundane as useful content" (Schneider 1997). Today, what distinguishes EDL is the longevity of its operations and the worldwide extent of its impact. EDL is one of the longest running digital libraries on the Internet. Its website sees as many as 100,000 hits per month, representing visits from seventy-nine countries and most every Internet domain (government, military, educational, commercial, business, nonprofit, and more). It has been acknowledged in best-selling books, acclaimed documentaries, news articles, countless lesson plans, textbooks, and on the websites of authoritative agencies. It has attracted over $1 million in external funding, including awards from the Library of Congress, the Florida State LSTA program, the U.S. Department of the Interior, and mini-grants from local organizations and foundations. Most significantly, it continues to meet the real information needs of students and scholars, filmmakers and photographers, government decision makers, teachers, landowners, activists, tourists, and the interested citizenry, day after day, byte by byte.

The broad appeal and heavy usage of the EDL accrue, in some part, from the special significance of its underlying subject matter. The Florida Everglades is a unique ecological treasure, juxtaposed against one of the country's largest metropolitan areas. As the largest subtropical wilderness in North America, the Everglades has been designated a UNESCO World Heritage Site, an International Biosphere Reserve, and a Ramsar Wetland of International Importance. Extending across the lower third of the Florida peninsula, the greater Everglades ecosystem touches sixteen counties from the Kissimmee chain of lakes south of Orlando, across Florida Bay, and out to the reefs beyond the Florida Keys. It is the freshwater source for the region's 7.5 million human residents and numerous visitors and home to over 50 threatened/endangered species. Thanks to a century or more of dredging, diking, and draining, the highly endangered Everglades is now the site of the largest environmental restoration project in world history. Any information service purporting to serve the stakeholders of such a large-scale undertaking would likely find a receptive audience.

EVOLUTION OF THE EVERGLADES DIGITAL LIBRARY

The genesis for the EDL is a community outreach success story, with protagonists representing the largest public university library in South Florida and the research center from the neighboring national park. In the early 1990s FIU's librarians were devising a plan to develop an "Everglades Center of Excellence" for the region in response to the growing need for regional environmental information among their constituencies. Building collections and services in support of this vision was stymied by the large volume of fugitive materials unavailable to the library and its users—grey literature, historic data and images, maps, and rare government reports. Around the same time, the research director at Everglades National Park was looking for information services to supplant those lost through the closure of a longtime park library. The two parties forged a partnership to allow each organization to accomplish what neither could do alone. The concept of an "Everglades Information Network" formalized the sharing and exchange of resources, expertise, and labor between institutions. FIU Libraries offered access to collections and resources (to the extent allowable by database licenses), along with reference, instructional, and collection management support. The author joined the park's library committee in an advisory capacity, providing consultation and support on matters concerning information access, collection management, and preservation, and she facilitated greater coordination with the National Park Service's library consortium.

The park's research center provided an inventory of information resources available in the park's library, archives, museum, and in the file cabinets of individual scientists. Park staff, many of them lifelong residents of the region and career-long park employees, participated in a valuable needs assessment process to identify the types of materials that would help them perform better research or develop better exhibits and visitor programs. The "two-way street" paved between park and campus provided a critical conduit for exchanging ideas, sharing resources, building community, and ensuring that the information services produced through the partnership were as useful as possible.

The promise of the early Web compelled the new partners to ponder the possibility of creating virtually what did not exist in analog form: a Library of the

Everglades. A proposal to develop a prototype digital library was approved, with seed funding provided by each institution. Expected beneficiaries included researchers, cooperators, and interpretive staff of Everglades National Park; the faculty, staff, and students of FIU; and the greater community of researchers, resource managers, decision makers, educators, students, and concerned citizens both within South Florida and beyond. EDL opened its doors at the address everglades.fiu.edu, and the site was registered with the Internet search engines of the day. Branding for both partners was built into the website along with contact and background information for each respective organization. Conversion of park materials took place on-site, to the specifications prescribed by the FIU Libraries and under the watchful eye of the park curator.

The launch of the EDL website in 1996 coincided with congressional passage of key legislation in support of Everglades restoration, and demand for Everglades-related information exploded. A new interagency task force, responsible for coordinating the efforts of the numerous federal, state, local, and tribal agencies working in South Florida, conducted an assessment to identify science information needs in support of Everglades restoration. Among the best ideas emerging from this process was a recommendation to use and fund information specialists to benefit science, management, and public awareness.

Everyone, it seemed, aspired to develop an Everglades information portal: the number of websites, publications databases, geographic information systems, and decision support systems dedicated to the subject multiplied. Invitations to attend meetings with agency information managers provided opportunities for EDL librarians to contribute expertise on such issues as metadata, data curation, georeferencing standards, and controlled vocabularies. Cross-agency concern for common data management standards and protocols lent support for two library-initiated proposals: the *Everglades Online* thesaurus (Clement 2005) and a comprehensive bibliography of agency publications. Yet the library's vision for an integrated community-wide information portal was not favored among agency information managers, who preferred to maintain their own autonomous systems, relying on cross-links between websites to connect users to the disparate sources of relevant information.

Concerned with the barriers to information retrieval posed by the proliferation of Everglades-related websites and databases, EDL librarians sought to bring together relevant information regardless of where the resources resided. The Everglades Online database was thus established as a *webliography* of Everglades resources. It opened to the public in 1997 with 2,000 records representing the holdings of the EDL, selected Internet resources from other agencies, and key printed resources not available online. The database was developed on the statewide platform for online public access catalogs maintained by the Florida Center for Library Automation (FCLA) and was Z39.50 compliant, facilitating its interoperability with other service providers through a federated search. In time, the Everglades Online data set was migrated to a more flexible Internet portal solution—the Collection Workflow Integration System (CWIS). CWIS is an open-source application created to help build collections of the National Science Digital Library and offers features that favor the sharing of Everglades information resources across information providers: Dublin Core metadata support; ability for approved users to add new metadata records and for all users to add annotations and ratings; and export of metadata records to other search engines via the Open Archives Initiative Protocol for Metadata Harvesting (OAI-PMH). Thanks to the CWIS portal, users can now find Everglades-related resources not only from EDL but also from a host of scholarly search engines and scientific subject gateways, such as the National Science Digital Library, the marine sciences harvester Avano, and the open archives harvester OAIster.

With core infrastructure established, efforts were refocused to build a more comprehensive digital collection. The fortuitous announcement from the Library of Congress regarding a new American Memory/Ameritech competition to fund collaborative digitization projects gave impetus to reach out to neighboring repositories with significant historical content. The result of this outreach effort was the Reclaiming the Everglades project, a digital compilation of 9,291 texts, photographs, and ephemera from collections at the University of Miami, the Historical Museum of Southern Florida, and FIU. FCLA provided in-kind support to host the special digital collection and to export metadata records to the Library of Congress's American Memory website. Educators and scientists who championed the project provided helpful letters of support attesting to the research and educational value of the proposed collection. To this day, FIU continues to add historical materials to Reclaiming the Everglades as these resources become available through targeted acquisitions efforts. The collection sees heavy usage from users worldwide.

As the collections continued to grow and diversify, EDL librarians pursued educational outreach efforts to ensure that the online materials would be useful to schoolteachers and students. The first step was coordination with the interpretive staff at Everglades National Park, whose successful "Parks As Classroom" program reaches hundreds of thousands of schoolteachers and students each year. The park rangers provided expert guidance in linking Everglades-related themes to Florida's curricular standards, helping librarians select and organize digitized materials relevant to classroom use. Collaborations with FIU College of Education faculty also further strengthened the digital library's K–12 outreach program, providing opportunities to test digital resources with teachers-in-training, public school personnel, and student participants at various environmental education events.

Collaboration with educators at both the Park and the University facilitated connections to other environmental educators as well. EDL librarians were invited to join the Everglades Education Consortium, a network of individual professionals and organizations interested in promoting and disseminating educational information and public programs on the Greater Everglades Ecosystem and the Everglades restoration effort. Interaction with this diverse group has provided invaluable insights into the information needs and concerns of educational and outreach professionals statewide. One particularly beneficial outcome of this involvement was the group's decision to adopt the EDL CWIS portal as a cross-agency clearinghouse for educational resources.

In-depth interaction with user and stakeholder groups also led EDL librarians to the inevitable conclusion that user needs could not be satisfied by library collections and information technology alone. Providing seamless access to a comprehensive library of relevant information was confounded by numerous factors out of the control of the project partners: the ineligibility of valuable content to be digitized by the library (mostly due to copyright restrictions); the natural dispersion of useful information across multiple providers and systems; and the heterogeneity of information resources requiring different storage and display features. EDL librarians recognized that human intervention was required to help users jump the seams between the many resources available to meet their needs.

The Ask An Everglades Librarian virtual reference service was conceived as an online reference desk where patrons could interact with librarians in real time. The project was funded as the state's first prototype virtual reference service through the Florida Library Services and Technology Act (LSTA) program. Funds were used to purchase and install virtual reference software; train a team of librarian volunteers in virtual reference protocols; hire a dedicated science librarian to cover the desk for part of each day and provide backup support to other librarians; compile a ready reference shelf to answer the most common questions; and develop a help desk website. Additional presentation equipment and Web design services were purchased in the second year of the project to facilitate outreach to Florida classrooms (Waters and Weiss 2003).

Usage data during the grant-funded period revealed that the service achieved its objectives to serve the diverse information needs of the broad community. Approximately 40 percent of inquiries represented research questions from governmental, academic, scientific, publishing, media, and art communities, and over 30 percent came from K–12 teachers and students. The project also met the objective to prepare FIU's public service librarians for working in a virtual reference environment. As a consequence of the Ask An Everglades Librarian experience, the FIU Libraries established a library-wide virtual reference service and joined a cross-institutional reference cooperative.

The Ask An Everglades Librarian service continues to see steady use by a broad range of visitors. User comments gathered through the reference service offer a critical source of feedback to improve the overall quality of the EDL program. Requests have provided the impetus to move an item to the front of the scanning queue; hunt down an unknown fugitive document (and, when possible, add it to the digital collection); repair a broken link; add a missing page; and even form new relationships with other subject experts and information providers. Visitors who received research assistance for one inquiry have provided the expertise needed to help users working on other problems. The ability to connect users not only to valuable materials but to each other has been a particularly successful element of the Ask An Everglades Librarian service. Moreover, the active engagement of users who have their own valuable knowledge and perspectives has directly improved the EDL's collections and services.

FUTURE DIRECTIONS

The work of the EDL is far from complete. As with most digital libraries today, the program faces considerable challenges in recruiting quality source materials that are eligible for digitization; sustaining existing digital resources over time; migrating content to new and more powerful digital asset management systems; exposing data for the widest possible discovery in an increasingly content-overloaded Internet; and meeting the increasing expectations of a demanding public.

Outreach continues to be a critical content recruitment strategy and several new approaches are being tested. One innovative approach under consideration is the "roadshow" public scanning event, in which individual collectors are encouraged to contribute relevant artifacts to the digital library through a scan-while-you-wait-operation. The Mass Memories roadshow uses this approach to recruit local heritage materials for a digital database maintained by the UMass Boston Library (University of Massachusetts Boston 2006). In South Florida, a community scanning event was piloted with good success for the digital project Ephemeral Cities, a model for developing an historical digital atlas based on three Florida cities. Carried out by the Monroe County Public Libraries, in partnership with digital librarians at FIU and the University of Florida, the "My Town Event" was advertised in the Key West newspaper. Community members were invited to bring their historical artifacts to the public library to be digitally captured, documented with descriptive metadata, and added to the online collection. According to Keys librarian Anne Rice, who coordinated the scanning for her library, more than 100 participants contributed a wide range of "treasures," motivated by the opportunity to share cultural heritage materials with a broader audience without relinquishing them. Participating citizens also learned how to care for their treasures from the FIU Libraries' archivist, who remained on hand to oversee the proper handling of the aging materials. Even after the event's conclusion, citizens have continued to ask about bringing items to the library for digitization. Librarian Anne Rice has remarked on the community building and public relations benefits of the "My Town Event" (Rice 2008).

Another promising direction for the EDL is expansion of the Ask An Everglades Librarian virtual reference desk to provide even better service and resources for the broad community of users. One initiative being explored is to join forces with the Ask An Everglades Scientist service offered by the outreach unit of an ecological research group on campus. Closer collaboration between services would provide the EDL with even more advanced subject expertise, while offering the participating scientists needed protocols and methods for managing user interactions, responding to repeated questions, and effectively handling academic integrity issues. The merger of both services into a collaborative "Ask An Everglades Expert" service would be greatly facilitated with an online collaboration environment that could help manage the back-and-forth communications between librarian, scientist, and user. An online collaboration system would also offer all participants a more engaging and fun environment in which to interact. Various tools and solutions to support a shared "Ask A" service are being evaluated at the time of this writing.

One area of future work that has not yet been formally addressed within EDL is digital preservation of born-digital materials. Specifically, EDL librarians are concerned with the impermanence of important information resources delivered on the many disparate websites across agencies and repositories. The need for preservation of these born-digital reports, photographs, maps, and educational materials has been evidenced by repeated requests received through the Ask An Everglades Librarian. Users have asked for help in locating resources they used to find on a given website. In one case, the request came from the very agency that produced the original report some ten years ago. The ever-changing political, natural, and technological backdrop against which the EDL program operates increases the risk that born-digital assets will be lost from users' reach. EDL librarians hope to investigate ways in which the digital preservation system in place for digital resources they develop could be extended to those produced by other information providers on their own systems. Extending this capability beyond campus would serve the community of users very well over the long term.

CONCLUSION

The case study of the EDL illustrates the many ways in which digital library programs can advance the public outreach and civic objectives of an academic library. The "online" location of digital library collections, services, and interfaces provides a powerful means to reach and engage users and stakeholders regardless of their location. The increasingly interactive nature of the Web invites a greater level of user involvement in shaping digital collections, services, and environments. When needs-focused collections and user-friendly technology combine with librarians' collaborative spirit and service orientation, a digital library program becomes a powerful tool of outreach and engagement. Just as importantly, the contributions made by an engaged public can improve and enhance the collections, services, and systems that the academic library can provide, both to its university constituents of faculty, staff, and students and to the broader community beyond the campus perimeter.

NOTES

1. The formal name for the Everglades restoration effort is the Comprehensive Everglades Restoration Program (CERP), a federal-state initiative involving numerous federal, state, tribal, and local agencies over a multidecade time span.

REFERENCES

Belden, Deanne. "Are you using Wikipedia to draw users to your online materials?," Library 2.0 Blog, comment posted May 29, 2007. http://library20.ning.com/group/governmentdocuments/forum/topic/show?id=515108%3ATopic%3A29392 (accessed April 21, 2008).

Bennett, Nuala A., Beth Sandore, and Evangeline S. Pianfetti. "Illinois Digital Cultural Heritage Community—Collaborative Interactions among Libraries, Museums and Elementary Schools." *D-Lib Magazine* 8, no. 1 (January 2002). http://dlib.org/dlib/january02/bennett/01bennett.html (accessed March 31, 2008).

Brantley, Peter. "DLF Moving Into Second Life." Peter Brantley's thoughts and speculations Blog, posted May 29, 2007. http://blogs.lib.berkeley.edu/shimenawa.php?cat=127 (accessed May 13, 2008).

Clement, Gail P. *Everglades Online Thesaurus: A Standard Vocabulary for the South Florida Ecosystem.* http://digitalcommons.fiu.edu/glworks/1/ (accessed May 13, 2008).

Florida Administrative Code, 1974. Florida International University, *Florida Statutes,* Chapter 6C8-1.

Jones, Douglas, George Ruyle, and Barbara Hutchinson. "Building a Collaborative AgNIC Site as an Outreach Model: Rangelands of the Western U.S." *Reference Librarian* 82 (2003): 125–140.

Mitchell, Erik and Kevin Gilbertson. "Using Open Source Social Software as Digital Library Interface." *D-Lib Magazine* 14, no. 3/4 (March/April 2008). http://www.dlib.org/ dlib/march08/mitchell/03mitchell.html (accessed March 31, 2008).

Rice, Anne. Personal communication, March 19, 2008.

Ruan, Lian and Jan S. Sung. "Meeting Changing Information Needs of Illinois Firefighters: Analysis of Queries Received from Outreach Reference Service." *Reference Librarian* 82 (2003): 69–105.

Scharf, Meg. "The Central Florida Memory Project: Collaboration and Digitization." Presentation at the EDUCAUSE Annual Conference, 2003, Anaheim, CA. http:// connect.educause.edu/Library/Abstract/TheCentralFloridaMemoryPr/38086?time= 1208520168 (accessed March 31, 2008).

Schneider, Karen. "A Nice Little Digital Library." *American Libraries* 18 (1997): 76.

University of Massachusetts-Boston. *The Mass. Memories Road Show Handbook: Procedures and Protocols for a Public Scanning Project.* August 2006. http://www.msp.umb. edu/MassMemories/handbook/MMRSHandbook.pdf (accessed April 20, 2008).

Waters, Megan and Susan Weiss. "Integrating Virtual Reference Services into Dispersed Digital Resources: The Everglades Information Network/Ask An Everglades Librarian Experience." In: *Navigating the Shoals: Evolving User Services in Aquatic and Marine Science Libraries: Proceedings of the 29th Annual Conference of the International Association of Aquatic and Marine Science Libraries and Information Centers (IAMSLIC),* eds. Markham, James W. and Andrea Duda, 105–110. 29th Annual Conference of IAMSLIC 5–9 October, 2003 at Mystic, Connecticut, USA. http://hdl.handle.net/ 1912/2014 (accessed April 19, 2008).

ADDITIONAL RESOURCES

American Memory Program, Library of Congress, http://memory.loc.gov/ammem/index. html

Central Florida Memory, http://www.cfmemory.org/

Collection Workflow Integration System (CWIS), http://scout.wisc.edu/Projects/CWIS/

Comprehensive Everglades Restoration Program, http://www.evergladesplan.org/index.aspx

Digital Forsyth, http://www.digitalforsyth.org/

Digital Heritage Cultural Community, http://images.library.uiuc.edu/projects/DCHC/

Digital Library Federation, http://www.diglib.org/

Ephemeral Cities, http://web.uflib.ufl.edu/epc/

Everglades Digital Library, http://everglades.fiu.edu/

Everglades Education Consortium, http://www.floridaearth.org/index.cfm?fuseaction= pages.eec

Everglades National Park, http://www.nps.gov/ever/

Everglades Online thesaurus, http://digitalcommons.fiu.edu/glworks/1/

Illinois Fire Institute Library, http://www.fsi.uiuc.edu/content/library/

Mass. Memories Road Show, http://www.massmemories.org/

Rangelands West, http://rangelandswest.org/

13

OREGON RURAL COMMUNITIES EXPLORER

Lena E. Etuk and Laurie M. Bridges

In 2001 a partnership was established between Oregon State University (OSU) Libraries and the Oregon University System Institute for Natural Resources with the goal of creating a natural resources digital library that would provide Oregonians with access to reliable and up-to-date information. An assessment of the needs of citizens, policy makers, and educators revealed that users wanted access to information in a multitude of ways, such as using GIS (Geographic Information Systems) mapping tools, creating charts and tables, as well as accessing digital data, photos, reports, and publications (Salwasser and Murray-Rust 2002). After several years of collaboration, assessment, and discussion a digital library prototype was unveiled in 2004 with the first geographic (or basin) portal, the Willamette Basin Explorer (www.willametteexplorer.info). The Oregon Explorer was launched in 2007 as the natural resources digital library that provides the statewide framework for users to learn about other places and topics (www.oregonexplorer.info). Many basin and topic portals are now accessible from the Oregon Explorer including the North Coast Explorer, Umpqua Explorer, Land Use Explorer, Wildlife Explorer, and most recently the Rural Communities Explorer (RCE). The RCE (http://oregonexplorer.info/rural/) is a digital collection of community-based information designed to help Oregonians engaged in work in rural communities make informed decisions about issues including vitality and change.

The RCE allows individuals to access county- and community-specific social, demographic, economic, and environmental information about rural Oregon in a framework of rural community vitality. The information is presented through quantitative data, qualitative stories about rural areas, and archived research on rural Oregon and rural issues. The portal serves as a forum for rural residents and community leaders of all types to learn about, explore, and engage with their own and other rural communities across the state.

This chapter describes the details of the Oregon RCE project to inform the work of others seeking to do academic library outreach. To do so, we discuss the project's history, the information available through the portal, the dynamics of collaboration on the project, and the nature of the project's outreach mission. Ideally, the lessons learned from the Oregon RCE project can help establish a set of best practices for doing academic library outreach beyond the campus walls.

HISTORY OF THE PROJECT

The success of the RCE is the result of a collaboration among various stakeholders, including faculty from the OSU Rural Studies Program with joint appointments in OSU Extension Service; librarians and Oregon Explorer staff from the OSU Libraries; staff from the Institute for Natural Resources; financial support from the Ford Family Foundation; and input from residents of rural Oregon communities.

The project began in 2005 when University Librarian Karyle Butcher became aware of the OSU Sustainable Rural Communities Initiative. An excerpt from the initiative reads:

The Rural Studies Program at Oregon State University has developed a statewide, multi-disciplinary program from five colleges and the Extension Service to develop a new and unique model of University engagement with rural communities. This model involves partners from other universities, governments, and the nonprofit sector in creating new educational opportunities, applied and fundamental research, and outreach that address the needs of rural communities. (Oregon State University 2008)

Upon reading the initiative, Butcher began to envision a possible partnership with the Rural Studies Program that would align with part of the libraries' strategic plan, "In recognition of the growing need to provide information to support colleges and programs involved in economic development activities, OSU Libraries will expand its role as an information broker in the state" (OSU Libraries 2004). Butcher immediately contacted Bruce Weber, the director of the Rural Studies Program, with the idea of creating an Explorer portal that would house important rural Oregon information that could be accessed by the general public. Butcher and Weber conversed about the idea with staff over the next several months, and in July 2006 a meeting was set up among Weber, Lena Etuk, a social demographer from the OSU Extension Service–Family & Community Development (FCD) program who is also a member of the Rural Studies Program, and Janine Salwasser, the OSU Libraries' natural resource digital library program director, who heads up the Oregon Explorer team. In this initial meeting participants discussed possible strategies for the creation of an Oregon RCE portal and the needed functionality for a phase one product.

After several planning meetings, additional library members were added to the RCE team, including Ruth Vondracek, head of reference consulting and innovative services, Laurie Bridges, the business librarian, Tim Fiez, a systems architect/

lead programmer, and Marc Rempel, a programmer/GIS analyst. Kuuipo Walsh from the Institute for Natural Resources later joined the team as project manager.

A creative brief for the project was developed to document the project objectives, target audience, key messages, data and documents, tone and perception, as well as deliverables and milestones. A mock-up of the RCE portal home page based on the Oregon Explorer template for basin and topic portals created by a local design firm was created. When the mock-up was presented, it created an initial wave of excitement among the team members, which helped further motivate them as they began to see their vision becoming a reality. The mock-up was also used to explain the project to potential users and to gather support from funding sources.

Finding funding for the RCE was a top priority from the onset of the project. After a timeline and budget was created, the Ford Family Foundation (http://www.tfff.org/) was identified as a possible contributor. The director of the Rural Studies Program set up a series of briefing meetings in early 2007 between the RCE team and representatives from the Foundation to inform the Foundation of the project and to solicit ideas and input. Ultimately, these meetings, along with ongoing conversations, led to a $25,000 grant in August 2007 from the Ford Family Foundation for the first-year development of the RCE.

As the team collaborated on the creation of the RCE infrastructure and architecture, Weber and Etuk worked to develop the content of the site, identifying the necessary content through informal needs assessments conducted in 2006 and 2007. In the summer and fall of 2006, Etuk conducted informal needs assessments among three user-audience groups, the first from among OSU Extension FCD county and campus faculty and the second among OSU Extension Administration. The faculty and administrators were asked to identify their various information needs related to social demography that would help them better serve or understand the communities in which they work. The feedback from both groups were assessed to yield the following areas of need for information: poverty, health challenges, older adults, social context surrounding health, food, populations of color and ethnic minorities, migration, family, education, and general social and demographic trends by county or community.

The areas of need generated from these two initial needs assessments were narrowed on the basis of data availability. Subsequently, specific indicator variables were identified for their ability to illuminate the topics. This list of variables was presented to a third group of faculty on the OSU campus for their input; these faculty members specialize in rural research and represent a broad array of expertise and research focuses. Based on this meeting, the list of variables changed only slightly. Finally, the complete list was sent out to five Extension FCD county faculty members for their written feedback. Based on their feedback some minor changes were made.

Following Etuk's needs assessments among potential users of the RCE affiliated with OSU, Weber worked to determine indicators of rural community vitality. He settled on a list of measures and indicators based on a review of the literature and several meetings with residents of rural Oregon communities. Many times throughout the research process it was recognized that many stakeholders desired information that no federal or state agencies actively collect. It also became apparent that the specific definition of community vitality must represent the unique context, needs, and vision of the local community. Clearly, there was a need for new data to serve rural Oregonians and a need for the community to be involved in the determination of what should be collected. These insights have informed the strategy of the research team throughout the duration of the RCE project. The two researchers, Etuk and Weber, decided to build a Web-based database system tool that could be built on in the future and that could accommodate change. The first step was to create a database of secondary data for indicators available for all communities across the state, and the second step would be to work with the communities to add to the RCE database by uploading community-generated data that measure community-defined vitality.

Once the first version of the portal was created and made live on the Web, Weber and Etuk presented it to a group of rural community members from across the state for their input. The group was asked to comment on the data and information available on the site, the geographic specificity and flexibility of the site, the functionality with respect to data manipulation and the extent to which the user can interact with the site, and other general topics. The feedback from this initial usability assessment was incorporated into later versions of the RCE.

The OSU Libraries' natural resource digital library program director then worked with Weber and Etuk to identify a group of users in the target audience for the RCE. The target audience falls into three broad categories: engaged and civically active rural community members, rural elected officials, and rural program managers (of nonprofit organizations, community service or outreach organizations, or other organizations serving rural Oregon). Representatives from these groups were invited to participate in a series of one-on-one usability tests of more mature versions of the site. In addition, an OSU Rural Sociology class tested the usability of the site in a classroom setting. Focus groups are planned to evaluate the site post-launch and recommend features for future phases of development. The results of each of these usability assessments have and will continue to inform the functionality, structure, and attributes of the RCE.

FEATURES OF THE OREGON RURAL COMMUNITIES EXPLORER

The Oregon RCE provides a forum for rural leaders to learn and explore the dynamics and composition of rural communities through data tools and archived research findings; access others involved in rural communities; and to use the RCE as a tool for community change. To provide this forum, the RCE features a unique variety of information, tools, resources, and functionality.

A Social Science Framework

To present a broad array of information about rural Oregon communities in a useful and informative manner, the RCE is designed around a framework of community vitality. A vital community broadly defined is a community that has the capacity to identify and solve collective problems and to realize a balance of positive outcomes in the social, environmental, and economic realms. To convey this notion of community vitality and to reveal the ways in which it can be affected, the portal features a visual model informed by social science research.

The model portrays the relationships among a community's conditioning influences, its resources and assets, its capacity, the actions undertaken within it, and its (economic, environmental, and social) outcomes to inform users about the resources, processes, and actions necessary to affect community change. By using this visual map an RCE user can see the overarching system of relationships among these aspects of community functioning. The user can click on any of the model's components to find out which variables serve as indicators for each and what the corresponding data are for communities, counties, and the state of Oregon.

One-Stop Shop for Local, State, and Federal Data

There are three types of quantitative data available through the RCE that allow users to learn about the vitality of a community. The first is data gathered by agencies external to Oregon, namely the U.S. Census Bureau, the U.S. Department of Agriculture, and the U.S. Federal Deposit Insurance Corporation. The second type of data is gathered by Oregon Departments of Forestry, Human Services, Education, and other state agencies. The data from state and federal sources were selected on the basis of their ability to serve as indicators in the model of community vitality.

Prior to the creation of the RCE, data from state and federal agencies were dispersed across the Web, making it difficult for the average person to locate and use information about rural areas. The RCE makes it possible for an individual to avoid navigating through numerous separate websites to access information pertaining to each issue in which they are interested. Providing so much information in one place also makes it possible for people quickly to explore relationships among issues whose data were previously housed in disparate locations. For instance, by housing high school dropout data in the same place as teen pregnancy data, a user is conveniently able to see how and if the trends may relate to each other.

The third type of data available through the RCE is gathered by rural Oregonians themselves to measure community vitality specifically. These data speak to the four elements of community vitality (community capacity, social outcomes, environmental outcomes, and economic outcomes) that are not collected by external agencies. Community-generated data are only available for the rural communities that have collaborated and engaged with OSU's Rural Studies Program faculty to do community-based monitoring of vitality. The data are collected using a participatory approach to research and outreach that seeks to build the capacity for community change by engaging communities in a process of defining community vitality and its indicators, collecting data, and using the data to plan for community action. These indicators are designed to reflect each community's unique context and vision for the future.

Geographic Specificity and Flexibility

The data available in the RCE that have been collected by external agencies and are used as secondary data were manipulated by the working team to grant users of the RCE the ability to examine 723 specific communities in Oregon and some flexibility to manipulate the boundaries of the community under examination.

Users may explore the social attributes of up to 723 named places and 36 counties in Oregon by relying on the geographic crosswalk constructed by members of the RCE team. The crosswalk links each community to four units of geography. The first unit approximates or directly corresponds to the boundaries of the community itself, the second geographic unit corresponds to the school district in which the community lies, the third geography corresponds to the county in which the community is located and, finally, some communities have been subdivided into neighborhoods for which data are also available. Prior to the creation of this geographic crosswalk, the average individual had difficulty accessing information at each of these geographic scales, but particularly at the scale of the community itself if the community was not an incorporated town or city.

Community

To understand better the aspect of the crosswalk that links communities to geographic units that approximate or directly correspond to the boundaries of the community itself, it is important to have a basic knowledge of the U.S. Census Bureau and their data. The U.S. Census Bureau conducts the decennial census of the U.S. population. It gathers data from all households for the purpose of enumerating the total population. This agency compiles the most comprehensive database of information about characteristics of the United States population, complete with addresses, in the nation. Though the addresses of census respondents are hidden to all researchers using census data, the bureau uses the address information to assign aggregate population values to various geographic areas that cover the country. The largest of these geographic units is the nation, and the smallest is called the census block, with twenty units in between. One of the geographic units in between is called place, and the U.S. Census Bureau recognizes 309 villages, towns, and cities in Oregon as places. There are, however, 414 unincorporated towns and villages in Oregon that are not recognized by the U.S. Census Bureau. Before the creation of the RCE, the average Oregon user of census data would find it incredibly difficult if not impossible to access information about an "unrecognized" town or village with the Census Bureau's data tool. The lack of information about these 414 towns and villages placed rural communities at a distinct disadvantage.

To make the RCE a revolutionary tool for rural residents, a geographic crosswalk was created to link these 414 unrecognized towns and villages to the census' sub-county geographic unit of census tracts. Census tracts may contain more than one small community, but they do provide greater geographic specificity than county boundaries and better sociogeographic boundaries than zip codes. The RCE was designed to alert the user if the community being examined corresponds to the boundaries of a census tract, in which case the data presented may also correspond to other communities close to the community of interest.

The data topics available for the 309 places recognized by the U.S. Census Bureau are the same topics available for all census tracts. With the RCE geographic crosswalk, individuals interested in the information about unrecognized communities can access the data about the census tract that contains the community just as easily as individuals who are interested in information about a recognized community.

School Districts

Some of the information housed in the RCE database relates to the schooling outcomes of communities. These data are organized according to schools within school districts. Schools tend to serve the youth of many communities, not only the community in which the school itself is located. For this reason, information about schooling outcomes is provided to each community served by the respective school district. The geographic crosswalk assigns each of the 723 named communities in Oregon to a school district for easy access to these educational data.

Counties

The U.S. Census Bureau is the only agency that collects information to such a degree of geographic specificity. Most federal and state agencies provide data at the county level only. For the variables whose data have been gathered by an agency other than the Census Bureau, if a user indicates his or her interest in community-level data, the county data are shown and prominently noted as such. The team decided early on that if a user requests information about their community, information available at the county level only is an appropriate substitute for community-level data.

Neighborhoods

The geographic crosswalk available in the RCE also allows users to access data about neighborhoods in communities that contain more than one census tract. In communities with large populations, the Census Bureau divided the city into census tracts that correspond roughly to neighborhoods. For users interested in the distribution of population characteristics across neighborhoods within this limited number of communities, the RCE provides data through the mapping tool of the site.

Geographic Flexibility

A great deal of effort has been put into the geographic capabilities of the RCE. One feature grants access to information for 723 specific communities in Oregon. An additional geographic feature of the site was designed to serve the needs of specific users as well as to recognize the porosity of community borders in rural areas. The feature grants the user some flexibility with respect to the geographic boundaries of the community under examination by allowing communities to be combined to get aggregate indicator statistics. So long as users do not wish to aggregate unlike geographic units, such as counties with places or places with communities whose data correspond to census tract boundaries, they may combine raw data for any number of communities to get statistics for the total area.

Digital Archives

The interactive statistical database of the Oregon RCE is an important component of the portal as it grants users the ability to do their own quantitative research about rural communities. There are also other types of information, such as texts, data sets, photos, and maps that are housed in an academic library system, which can improve the public's understanding of rural issues and communities. At OSU this information is stored in OSU Libraries' digital online archive, ScholarsArchive@OSU (http://ir.library.oregonstate.edu/dspace/). ScholarsArchive@OSU was developed as an institutional repository for collecting, preserving, and making publicly available the intellectual output of the university. The archive also makes publicly available documents written and submitted by rural community members. To provide users of the Oregon RCE access to the digital resources of the OSU Libraries, the portal provides entry into ScholarsArchive@OSU.

In 2006, as the RCE project was just getting off the ground, ScholarsArchive@OSU already housed a considerable number of publications about rural Oregon. Materials in ScholarsArchive@OSU are maintained in perpetuity, and a system is set up to accept future research publications. The archive was a natural choice for the retrieval of currently available materials about rural issues and Oregon's rural communities and for the archival of future materials. From the RCE portal a user can pull information from ScholarsArchive@OSU by searching for a topic plus the term "rural" or the name of a community (e.g., Lakeview). Results of the search will be sorted into bins based on the material format (e.g., reports/pubs, data sets, photos/videos, maps, etc.).

ScholarsArchive@OSU includes faculty, graduate, and undergraduate students' research, as well as information from individuals outside of OSU. The ability of community residents to submit local information to ScholarsArchive@OSU was first implemented with the Umpqua Basin Explorer (www.umpquaexplorer.info). The option of submitting materials by individuals outside of OSU is now available from the home page of any Oregon Explorer portal, including the RCE.

The process for submitting locally authored material through the RCE is first to register with ScholarsArchive@OSU; once approved by a librarian, a community member can follow step-by-step instructions (available from the home page) to upload reports, publications, data sets, or stories and create a metadata record that describes and categorizes what is being uploaded. After these steps are completed and the materials are submitted, a library staff member or member of the RCE team will review it and add the content to the repository. Stories that are submitted to ScholarsArchive@OSU and written in an informative and journalistic style about rural communities in Oregon are featured on the main pages of the RCE.

Additional Resources

The RCE also grants users access to additional resources that are intended to encourage and facilitate individuals' engagement in their communities or information gathering about their communities. There are guides that instruct people how to interpret statistics, manipulate data in database management software programs such as ArcGIS and MS Excel, and access additional data from federal and state agencies. Via the RCE users can also find out about human and organizational resources in their communities they may contact for information pertaining to development or community change. Finally, the RCE provides a link to an online discussion forum about rural communities and issues facilitated by Rural Development Initiatives, Inc.

Rural Studies Program staff and Oregon Explorer team staff are committed to keeping RCE a useful, living portal by agreeing to maintain it. The Oregon Explorer team has designed a Remote Administration Tool for sites such as the RCE. This tool allows password-protected access to software that enables select administrators to edit and add to the portal content. The remote administration capability enables the site to be kept fresh by the people directly connected to the content and adds long-term value to collaborative, short-duration development projects such as phase one of the RCE.

THE DYNAMICS OF COLLABORATION AND OUTREACH

Collaboration

The RCE was made possible through the collaboration of a diverse group of people and resources. The project would not have gotten off the ground without the efforts of the group convener, Karyle Butcher, the university librarian. After she initiated a set of conversations, the RCE team collaborated continually, with monthly meetings augmented by small groups and individuals working on various components of the RCE. Each component, including obtaining funding, creating the site content, establishing the quantitative GIS database, creating the site design and architecture, obtaining copyright releases, and assembling and managing the digital collections in ScholarsArchive@OSU, was assigned to an individual or small group to complete. There was a high level of trust and autonomy among the collaborators to complete each component of the project largely because everyone agreed on the final product and the shape, structure, and mission of outreach. Without the diversity of expertise and shared mission of each of the nine collaborators, the dynamics of the collaboration would have been much more difficult to manage.

Other aspects of the collaboration itself and the partners ensured a productive dynamic within the RCE team. The large team size, along with the broad and sometimes overlapping expertise of the many members, mitigated the potentially detrimental effects of staff turnover over the life of the project. Collaboration was also made easier because of the focus of the OSU Libraries, Extension Service, and the Rural Studies Program as information centers readily available to disseminate useful and relevant information to audiences inside and outside the campus walls. Given this shared focus, the team simply had to work together to devise creative ways to make the RCE a useful tool for communicating research-based information to the public. The presence of Extension Service and Rural Studies Program faculty, whose mission it is to reach out to and engage with audiences outside of the university setting, guaranteed that this shift was a smooth one for the library team members. Finally, a productive collaboration dynamic was ensured because of the current emphasis at OSU on using new technologies to provide audiences outside the campus walls access to information. Thus, partners were fully supported by their home departments in creating the RCE as a Web-based tool. These observations underscore the importance of having a large group of collaborators who share a common mission, are supported by their institutions, and who can also capitalize on their unique perspectives to complete an outreach and engagement project.

The dynamics and product of the collaboration were also influenced by the financial support available for the collaborators. This project exemplifies the financial collaboration inherent in a public-private partnership. The Ford Family Foundation's $25,000 grant for phase one of the project was key to the initiation of the RCE. OSU faculty and staff in the Rural Studies Program, the Libraries, and Extension Service also contributed many hours of FTE (Full Time Equivalent) staff to complete the first phase. For this team to have spent so many hours in initiating the RCE indicates not only that the team members were personally devoted to the mission of the project but that their department heads and program leaders were as well. Indeed, to work on a project beyond the amount financed by grants at a public university means that the hours were financed through state money and library gift funds. The RCE collaborators were able to leverage the resources of both private and public funding to complete the project and were clearly motivated to create the portal no matter the finances. This funding structure guarantees the Oregon RCE itself will be accountable to the public as well as the private donor foundation and that each team member has a personal stake in the final product.

Outreach

The direct collaboration of the OSU Libraries, Rural Studies Program, Extension Service, and the Institute for Natural Resources to leverage diverse resources led to the creation of a Web-based information tool for use by people outside the walls of the OSU campus. The tool serves the outreach aims of the Library, Institute, and Program faculty while also serving the engagement mission of the Extension faculty to work with rural Oregonians to jointly define and research the components and dynamics of community vitality. Ensuring the ability of the RCE to serve the outreach and engagement needs of the team members involved a number of processes and actions.

First, crafting the RCE into a premier tool for the dissemination of information about rural communities across Oregon involved assessing the needs of the end users. Needs assessments and meetings with rural community leaders and others engaged in serving rural Oregon informed the foundation of the RCE. The Rural Studies Program faculty also served a vital function in providing insight into the site content and design. Their past research had put them into contact with rural community members (the end user) as well as with research particularly informative to the exploration of rural issues. The RCE system was therefore built to serve the needs of users as well as be consistent with the academic community involved in rural issues and communities. Second, the RCE team members had to devise a strategy for the effective marketing of the final product. Because the team engaged in needs assessments, meetings, and usability tests with end users of the RCE, it was not difficult to spread the word about the portal. The launch of the RCE during a rural Oregon event was the main method used to ensure the RCE would reach the audience for which it was designed. The team also used press releases, conferences, email announcements, and postings on the OSU Libraries' and Rural Studies Program websites for publicity.

Third, the Rural Studies Program and Extension faculty pushed the RCE to move beyond outreach and toward engagement. This is a new trend in the realm of

Land Grant Universities, which seeks to engage actively in two-way dialogue with communities outside of the university to promote the relevant production of knowledge and mutually beneficial involvement of the university in the community (Kellogg Commission on the Future of State and Land-Grant Universities 1999). For the RCE, a move toward engagement meant creating a tool with a structure flexible and dynamic enough to be used in a number of different ways. On one hand, the site has to serve the traditional outreach function of informing rural community members about what is known about rural issues, communities, and vitality, so they may make informed decisions. But the portal also must function as a tool to inspire community members to ask more questions about their community and seek answers to those questions in collaborative partnership with faculty members, particularly those with joint appointments in the Rural Studies Program and OSU Extension Service.

Finally, the RCE must be a long-term, dynamic site with the ability to serve as a repository for new information gathered by researchers and community members into the future. Therefore, the collaboration between OSU Libraries, the Rural Studies Program, and the Institute for Natural Resources must continue beyond the initial phase of the project. The long-term collaboration for the RCE portal will result in a site that is constantly enhanced with new data, tools, and a fresh understanding of user needs. This dynamic structure and mission of the RCE, which provides access to the resources and knowledge of the university and the community outside the university, allows the RCE to be truly relevant as a tool for rural residents working toward a vital future.

CONCLUSION

Academic libraries typically have experience with and are experts at doing informed outreach and information dissemination for audiences inside the halls of academia. The Oregon Explorer program legacy has given OSU Libraries and the Oregon University System Institute for Natural Resources the unique experience of applying the same principles and methods of outreach to communities throughout Oregon. Indeed, each Oregon Explorer portal project has given OSU Libraries the opportunity to learn more about new audiences and their information needs. The Oregon RCE portal is no exception. The RCE has been a new type of partnership for the OSU Libraries as they paired with faculty with joint appointments in OSU Extension Service and OSU Rural Studies Program. These faculty members were interested in moving beyond one-way outreach and toward creating two-way lines of communication between the university and rural communities about community vitality and change.

The emphasis on engagement pushed the framework of the RCE to become a forum for community members to learn about rural issues and communities, as well as share information from their own perspectives. Such a two-way street benefits research on the university campus as well as rural Oregonians eager to learn from their compatriots.

Each element of the collaborative outreach process, the skills of the team members themselves, the funding structure, the working relationships, the shared missions of the partners, and the unique perspectives of each member, shaped the structure, functionality, and information housed within the RCE. This type of partnership and a concept of outreach that emphasizes engagement have ensured that the RCE can deliver on its mission to be a public and unbiased information system that can reveal

- the dynamics of rural community systems and change;
- how and if a community is moving toward its vision of a vital future;
- targets for policy or program influence and actions; and
- strategies for rural community change

through the regular collection, maintenance, and analysis of community-level data, rural research, stories, and other information by rural community residents and OSU.

REFERENCES

Kellogg Commission on the Future of State and Land Grant Universities. *Returning to Our Roots: The Engaged Institution. Third Report.* 1999. http://www.eric.ed.gov/ERICDocs/data/ericdocs2sql/content_storage_01/0000019b/80/17/3c/18.pdf (accessed October 9, 2008).

Oregon State University. "Rural Studies Program Homepage." http://ruralstudies.oregonstate.edu/program.htm (accessed March 12, 2008).

OSU Libraries. *Oregon State University Libraries Strategic Plan 2004.* 2004. http://hdl.handle.net/1957/7991 (accessed March 20, 2008).

Salwasser, J. and C. Murray-Rust. "Assessing the Need for a Natural Resources Digital Library." *Issues in Science and Technology Librarianship* no. 33 (Winter 2002). http://www.istl.org/02-winter/article2.html (accessed March 24, 2008).

14

ENGAGING THE COMMUNITY THROUGH AN ONLINE DIGITAL ARCHIVE: GULF COAST COMMUNITY COLLEGE'S MEMORY COLLECTION

Matthew Burrell

Academic institutions have an important historical connection with the community in which they exist. A college is not an entity that exists alone. Institutions are created through a need for education in the region, and they are sustained by the continuation of that need. An educational institution has a local presence that could be strengthened by the library to increase awareness of the institution and the connection to the local community. This awareness could be produced through a historical archive collection, available online, that members of the community could be a part of and connect with the college. In this chapter I make the case that academic libraries can create and make available online digital archives of materials from the college and from members of the community. The first section deals with finding unique connections between the college and community. The second explains the equipment, training, and materials needed to begin an archive in an academic setting. The third part of the chapter explores ways an institution could engage the community through the library's archival project. In the final section I explore approaches to continuing the project and suggest criteria for a formative evaluation.

CONNECTING THE COLLEGE WITH THE COMMUNITY

The college is a part of the community. The relations between the community and the college are entrenched in the lives of people who attend, teach at, work at, or may have family members and friends who play a role in the institution. It employs the population of the region, is an economic force, and impacts local and regional industries, politics, and education (Steinacker 2005). Lifelong education and the prospect of educational possibilities for the community are also significant. The history of the institution does not have to be long to have an impact. Schools just ten years old will show signs of local impact. Finding a historical connection with the community includes linking local leaders, the high schools in the region (who supply students to the college), important events in history tied to the college, and the public face of the college. The public face is what the community sees, reads about, and watches on the local news. It comes from the school's contribution to the area's culture, its sports teams, and the impact of the institutional knowledge shared with other learning organizations. The college supplies an educational and cultural anchor in a community. When looking for historical significance, consider the events that have taken place at the school. Place the school in the context of world and local events. What was printed in the student newspaper during significant times in history? How has the school changed since it was established? What came before? These are suggestions for beginning to create the school's link with the community.

SETTING UP YOUR DIGITAL ARCHIVES

The first step in setting up your archives is to put a team together that has interests in archival preservation and the history of the institution. Look over the materials the library owns or has collected for the archives. Decide what materials you will work on first. There are several instructional websites online that can help you.[1] In the beginning you should digitize items that your users will find interesting. Priority should, of course, be given to important materials in poor condition, but spending time on this part of the archival collection may defeat your purpose. Put items that demand individualized attention aside for conservation at a later time.

Collect materials that involve students (the largest part of the collection). One of the strong points of your archival collection is the "find me" aspect. Early in our project we found that the tendency of anyone looking at it is first to do a search on their own name. From board members to cheerleaders and magazine editors, the first search that is done is on their own name. If they are successful in finding themselves they are completely sold on the entire project. Other items to collect are pictures of the faculty, grounds, sports (including basketball, football, and intramural games), events such as a Christmas ball, elections of students, and student organizations. Gather school annuals, student newspapers, faculty dissertations, sport pennants, and blueprints for early buildings. You will find ample materials from the president's office, including awards, proclamations, presidential memos, faculty handbooks, and narrative early histories of the school. Be careful not to gather so much that your team gets lost in the materials. Begin slowly and as you progress and become proficient, gather more materials.

These materials will form the basis for your archival collection. Divide your collection into categories important to your institution and the region. Gulf Coast Community College has categories for administration, students, faculty, publications, facilities, and newspaper articles. You may want to give groupings or item subcategories to further divide the collection, such as school annuals within publications and athletics within students. We found that broad category terms were best in that there is little indication about what might be collected or found to be important for future digitization. For example, a faculty dissertation about local history is also the history of the first location of the college. This publication by

Dr. Peggy Dorton Pelt, *Wainwright Shipyard: The Impact of a World War II War Industry on Panama City, Florida,* consists of interviews with shipyard workers and Bay County residents during the World War II years. It fits into publications but also local history and facilities and is important to local historians and student research. We found that creating a subcategory for faculty publications allowed us to collect the dissertations of any employees who wanted their materials accessible. This unlocks an area for further archival collection of faculty writings. Avoid conflict with local history organizations by collection and digitizing only your own institutional objects. This chapter addresses possible collaboration with your local history organization later.

The first items added to the collection should be photographs or negatives that are identifiable and that illustrate the history of the school and its relationship to the local community. At the beginning of your archive project, the photographs that you are placing online should have at least two verifiable aspects. Look for a date, subject, name, location, or other characteristic of the photograph that you can verify with a school annual, personal knowledge, catalog, or within the photograph itself. When identifying photographs, record as much information about that item as possible. Users may look for unusual items within the photographs, such as telephone, furniture, food, or other objects. It is crucial that the information you attach to an item and place in your archives be correct. If there are errors, users will find the entire collection suspect. Make sure the dates are correct. If you are concerned that a detail may not be correct, do not digitize that item. Save it for a later time. After your collection has been established, you can start to add photographs for which you have only one identified part, but at the beginning you want to be able to attach a large amount of information.

At Gulf Coast we found that little more than 5 percent of the photographs were identifiable, and even fewer were worthy of adding to the collection. Each identifiable photograph is treated as a separate object. Using a plastic clip, attach a data sheet to the photograph. On the data sheet list the date, subject, title, photograph size, and a short description. As you write the description, you should identify the picture as if it were lost in a pile of photographs and you needed someone else to find that exact picture. For example, "It is a black and white photograph with a horizontal crease near the bottom. The photo is of a young woman with dark hair wearing a light colored blouse typing on an Underwood typewriter in a small office. The nameplate on her desk reads Wendy Dover. There is a picture on the wall of three young children on a beach." This descriptive information will be helpful later when you identify the photograph in the collection. The process of making the picture ready for digitization is the most difficult part of the process. Scanning and placing the object online takes just a small amount of time compared to the important work of identification.

The information provided about each object is called metadata. As librarians, we are used to MARC records. Similarly, there are standard ways to identify objects that are digital in nature. There are metadata standards to use that help you to understand the information you need to record about the objects you are placing in the collection. Dublin Core and Open Archival Information System (OAIS) are metadata tools. They are used as a standard for data collection, identification, and retrieval. Dublin Core has fifteen main element sets that may be applied to each item. These elements include the title, subject, description, source, publisher, format, and identification of the item.[2] When you collect information about the photographs or other objects, list the elements on the data sheet and leave additional areas for notes. On the lower part of the sheet and working down, leave room for the initials of the person completing each of four steps: identification, verification, scanning, and preservation. Each of these is a major point in the process. If there is a problem with how something is completed, the individual who completed that part of the process can be identified to clear up any misunderstandings.

TRAINING

Funding may be available for student assistant employment in the archives. Work in the archives attracts students in the visual and performing arts, technology, digital production, and photography programs on campus. Working with Photoshop, scanning, and digitization may fit well into a student's area of study. When hiring students look for those with a computer background or interest. Students who do not have strong technology skills are useful in the preservation and filing procedures of the digitization process. Training students may take a whole semester, so a commitment from the student to work for three or more semesters is a good idea. Hire and train students for particular parts of the digitization process so that they become expert in those areas. For example, a student trained to use Photoshop to scan, repair, and upload photographs will become proficient in that area. Performing digitization on school annuals or newspaper articles requires a different process. Text documents require proofreading, scanning at a different resolution from photographs, and uploading. Likewise, students who are involved in the nontechnical side of the project, preservation and filing, will come to understand the reasoning behind carefully handling items and correct storage processes.

EQUIPMENT AND STORAGE NEEDS

Setting up the institution's archives requires basic equipment. To start you will need two relatively high-end computers, a server to store the digitized objects, one or two scanners, and software. I am purposefully being vague about the equipment because technology changes so rapidly and prices continually drop. At least one scanner should be $11'' \times 14''$ and at least one should be able to handle transparencies. A secure area to hold the equipment, ample work space, and storage cabinets are necessary. Storing materials before and after digitization involves deciding how best to preserve the items and avoid damage. Store large photographs, blueprints, and newspapers flat. Microform cabinets with the dividers removed are excellent containers. Buffered paper is used between pages of newspapers and documents to keep acid from transferring through the pages. Place photographs within leaves of buffered paper and then enclose them in acid-free folders within filing cabinets.

The work area is set up in a linear manner, making the process flow in a logical way. Imagine an object moving left to right with individual stations for each part of the process. Begin with sorting and identification on the left and working toward the right. Follow the course with the photograph till it reaches the end, preservation and filing. A second work area will help keep the text processes separate. Use this area specifically for newspaper articles, monographs, and other text-based objects. Again, start with identification, scanning, OCR application, proofreading, and uploading. Follow this with preservation of the object. Procedures written for each step are necessary. Every process should be backed by an exact written procedure that is kept in a manual for students to refer to if questions arise. Setting up well-written standards early in the project and adhering to them will help avoid problems later. As questions arise, make note of them in the procedures manual. It is difficult and time-consuming to change a part of the procedure after having scanned in a couple of hundred items.

The software that your team decides to use will minimally include Photoshop licenses for each computer, an optical character recognition, or OCRs, program for the text documents, database software, and software to organize and display your digitized objects. Gulf Coast Community College uses CONTENTdm, an OCLC product. With CONTENTdm, we are able to scan items and upload them to the server as a tiff file, include the metadata, and then display the items for the user in JPEG2000 format in the browser window.[3]

When purchasing the materials you need, remember that outsourcing is also a viable alternative to the expensive costs incurred with hardware. For example, we have fifty student newspaper issues that are be printed on regular newspaper-size sheets. For three years the student newspaper was in this large format. Our scanner was not large enough to digitize this format. We used a local blueprint shop to make the digitized copies for us. They were able to save them in tiff format. This is not a way to scan older, brittle newspapers. In this case we had excellent copies and more than one of each issue. Another example of outsourcing is when you have a small amount of microfilm to scan. You may have the equipment and resources to scan your own microfilm, but it may be best to outsource this part of your project.

PROCEDURES

The archive team should prepare the procedure manuals before starting your project. The procedures are then refined and detailed early in the project. As you move into the application of the procedures, evaluate the manuals and make the necessary revisions to ensure standards are kept. Start with the identification procedures and how you will verify the elements of an object. Your first photographs identified are those that come from a personal collection of a faculty member, the photography club, or the library itself. The photographs may be marked or in an album dated and persons and events identified. Be careful not to fall into the false impression of believing that what is written on the photograph is necessarily correct. Verify the identifications through another source. If it is a faculty member that has been identified, check the school's catalog and make sure the name is spelled correctly, the date fits the information, the class being taught, or any other relevant information is correct.

In your procedure manual, create a standard nomenclature for your items that indicates some basic parts of the object. A nomenclature schema that is useful at Gulf Coast Community College is a file-naming convention that begins with the two-digit year of the creation of the object followed by a letter that indicates the category. For example, in our collection, an "a" is a plain text document, "b" signifies a photograph, "c" is a college annual, "d" is a newspaper article, and so on.

Next in the file name is a four-digit consecutive number for that category followed by a single check digit. A photograph taken in 1957 may have the file name 57b42581. This number stays with the object throughout the procedure including preservation. On the back of the photograph (or document) is the file name written in light pencil.

Once the photograph is identified and given a unique file name, the photograph moves into the scanning process. There are standards that you need to follow about how items are handled during scanning. Some basic rules include scan an item only once. Save the original scan before any repairs are applied in Photoshop. Keep the original scan because it is unknown if in the future there will be a process for digitally repairing parts of your picture. When you scan photographs, scan them with a black border around the entire photograph. Place dull solid black paper behind the photograph when scanning. This is done so your end user can see the very edge of the photograph. The photograph is more appealing, and it also gives you the opportunity to add a watermark below the picture.

Digitizing negatives follows the same conventions as photographs, but frames are not necessary other than to hold a watermark and make the photograph visually appealing. Some of your best photographs will only be available as negatives or slides. The original photograph of a past president or major event may have long disappeared, but you may find negatives of the missing picture in better condition than the photographs. One of your scanners should have the capability of scanning 35mm negatives, transparent positives (35mm slides), and large-format picture negatives popular in the late 1940s and 1950s.

Use Adobe Photoshop to correct the damaged photograph that came from bad storage procedures, rips and tears in the document, or scratches on the negative. This is the step that will take the most skill and the longest time. It is paramount that no additional data are added or taken away from the photograph. It is not ethical to take something out of a photograph when you are digitally archiving. Students who are working on this stage of the process may feel a compulsion to fix someone's hair, modify colors, or erase something in the background. Students may feel the need to scan in grayscale, removing any color that is part of the photograph. We cannot be sure that the original photograph did not include any color, so scan everything in color.

Once the photograph is scanned, copied, corrected, and uploaded, preserve the item so that the photograph is available in the future. When preserving photographs, use the available standards developed by the Library of Congress, large universities, or archival organizations and societies.[4] Proper storage and location information is an essential part of your project. Once correctly preserved and stored, the photograph will remain in the best possible condition for future generations.

Procedures for working with text documents are slightly different from photographs. Text documents decay faster and are difficult to work with. They may have been glued into an album, become yellowed due to acid damage, or be extremely brittle with age. Scanning newspaper articles may not be possible because of the deterioration of the paper. In some cases, the color of the paper is very similar to the color of the text on the paper. OCR may be useless. Proofreading the document is tedious work for a student.

All of your original scans and the repaired scans must be backed up. This is a very important part of the process. Back up your data on a separate hard drive, DVD, or another location other than the server you are using to keep your items for end-user display. Use database software such as Microsoft Access to record the location of the original scan. The person who is preserving the object could also have the responsibility of maintaining the database. The database could also hold all of the information on the data sheet and be accessible should you need to revisit the original item. There will be times when there is a request for a tiff file for publication, or a community member may want to make quality reproductions of a photograph.

ENGAGING THE COMMUNITY

There are several ways the institution's digital archives can be used to engage the community. When you are in the early stages of the identification process, you will have the opportunity to ask for help from the community. There will be people who have worked at the institution or graduated years ago who will be able to assist with identification of those photographs for which there are no obvious ways to tell what they are, but seem to be important. For example, a photograph of a speaker in an auditorium filled with students is an event, and there may be someone who could identify who it is, or why the event took place. Set aside photographs that you have little or no information about, keeping them in folders of similarly aged pictures for groups to browse through. There are members of local churches, women's clubs, alumni associations, and historical organizations that you can draw from to ask for help. Involve the media in getting the word out about the collection. Record the names and affiliations with the college of those who come in to help. Thank them publically, present them with a letter of thanks from the president of the institution, and then bring others in. Set aside an area apart from the archives for people to work. The archive team should decide a predetermined amount of time, how the information will be used, and the number of people you have at one time. If you have more than two or three at a time, consider the large amount of time people will be reminiscing about the school rather than actually working to identify photographs. The object of these identification sessions is to engage the community, not necessarily to get free work completed.

Ask community members for their own items to be added to the collection. They also have been collecting items about the school. Return the item to the donator and recognize in the published collection that the item was a loan and the lender's name. For example, Gulf Coast Community College is located in Panama City, Florida. One of the first graduates of the school, Ann (Dorothy Johnson) Robbins, loaned several photographs to the collection. Some of the photographs were of a snowball fight that took place in the first year the school existed. She was able to identify most of the people in the photographs. People will search the collection and may come across the loaned photographs, which may entice them to add their own materials.

The collection becomes a part of the local community through its use as a supplement to existing local history. Consider working with the historical society. Notify the genealogy society that there are items they may find of interest online. Ask if a librarian can address the club. The local newspaper may have a weekly history editorial that could make use of several parts of your collection. Your images of the institution's sports, major events, or dignitaries may be an opportunity to add where the collection can be found through the library's Web page, and how the reader can assist the library.

As your collection grows, you will find people are accessing your collection through other websites or from a search engine. When your collection is live, you are engaging the local community as well as the larger community of the Internet. The collection will be important to people and create a connection when they see photographs of friends, relatives, or themselves in the archive. Local elementary and high schools may perhaps use the collection for an instructional aide when teaching about history. Notify public and school librarians about the collection.

CONTINUE AND EVALUATE

The collection will grow slowly. As items are added, consider branching out to other objects to collect and archive. You will be scanning photographs, text documents, monographs, and student newspapers and also preserving those documents. The collection will be noticed by the administration because of the free advertising the school is receiving in the media. For the future of the collection, continue to ask for help from the community. Consider placing videos or audio tapes in the online collection. Many colleges have radio stations. These stations may have kept reel-to-reel tapes of major community events. The tapes will need to be digitized and preserved before they deteriorate.

To evaluate the impact of the digital archive on engagement in the community, look at the amount of newspaper and media attention the collection gets. Place a Web report script on the Web page to measure the use after announcing to the community the news about the collection or changes to the collection. Google has a free tool that will measure where the end user is going, how much time is spent on the site, and even what keywords were used when a search was performed that led them to the collection.[5]

Creating an online archival collection is important to the community as well as the institution. The preservation of institutional memory and the important documents and photographs for future generations should naturally take place. As a benefit of the archival project, the institution engages the community through the library. As collectors and disseminators of information, librarians have the ability and knowledge to best provide access to historical information today and into the future.

NOTES

1. Moving Theory into Practice: Digital Imaging Tutorial. http://www.library.cornell. edu/preservation/tutorial/ is one tutorial website I would recommend. Other sites include OCLC for help with outsourcing parts of your collection and CONTENTdm.

2. The Dublin Core Metadata Initiative. http://dublincore.org/

3. CONTENTdm information can be found at the website http://www.contentdm.com/. OCLC has different plans available, so you can house the software and items in-house on your own server or at OCLC.

4. There are several organizations where you can find how best to preserve your archival objects. For example, The Society of American Archivists is found online at http://www. archivists.org/.

5. Google Analytics is a free tool that tracks the use of your Web page. http://www.google.com/analytics/features.html.

BIBLIOGRAPHY

Steinacker, A. "The Economic Effect of Urban Colleges on their Surrounding Communities." *Urban Studies* 42, no. 7 (June 2005): 1161–1175.

Part 4

EVENTS AND EXHIBITS

15

THE NEA BIG READ COMES TO VALDOSTA!

Yolanda Hood and Emily Rogers

We began in Fall 2006 as a small group of academic librarians sharing an interest in "one book, one community" reading programs and a university mission to "promote the economic, cultural, and educational progress of our community and of our region, through excellence in service outreach" (Strategic Research 2007). A year later, by mid-November 2007, we had completed programs featuring more than a dozen book discussion groups in bookstores, libraries, churches, private homes, the local military base, and an arts center. A kickoff festival celebrated our community's diversity, and a children's festival hosted a visiting storyteller and author along with local talent. Student volunteers performed dramatic interpretations of the novel and assisted with book groups and special events. Our keynote address celebrated the closing of the program with a reception, prize giveaway, and performances. How did librarians and other faculty at Valdosta State University (VSU) help bring about this transformation of Valdosta, Georgia, into a city joined together in reading *Their Eyes Were Watching God?* In large part, the change came about through successfully applying for and implementing funding from the National Endowment for the Arts (NEA) Big Read.[1]

Collaboration is at the heart of The Big Read, which is "an initiative of the NEA designed to restore reading to the center of American culture. The NEA presents The Big Read in partnership with the Institute of Museum and Library Services and in cooperation with Arts Midwest" (National Endowment for the Arts 2008). Valdosta's application process started when Dr. Wallace Koehler, director of VSU's Master of Library and Information Science program, suggested that Dr. Yolanda Hood, then reference librarian for marketing at VSU's Odum Library, apply for a grant from the NEA Big Read. A core group of academic and public librarians and VSU English department faculty considered reading options that seemed best suited to Valdosta, a south central Georgia city of almost 45,000 residents within a metropolitan statistical area located sixteen miles north of the Florida state line. Because of Valdosta's regional proximity to author Zora Neale Hurston's home in Eatonville, Florida, our committee selected her novel *Their Eyes Were Watching God*.

As one form of community outreach, VSU librarians had already met regularly with librarians from the South Georgia Regional Library system, local school systems, and Valdosta Technical College to consider opportunities to collaborate and combine resources. Other outreach projects include participating in the American Library Association's *Let's Talk About It: Jewish Literature* program and, for National Library Week, hosting annual Read Fests that invite more than 150 prekindergarten students and teachers to campus to share reading and other fun activities with VSU's librarians and College of Education faculty and students.

This history of collaboration proved valuable when in March 2007 VSU's Office of Grants and Contracts reviewed two VSU applications for The Big Read: not only Odum Library but also faculty from the Middle, Secondary, Reading, and Deaf Education Department in the Dewar College of Education (COE) planned to apply for grants. Both groups recognized the wisdom of combining proposals to align resources and avoid duplication. The library's initial plans for community book discussions, movie viewings, lectures, festivals, and workshops for middle and high school teachers expanded to include the COE faculty's "Readers into Leaders" program for developing public school students into discussion group leaders and encouraging reluctant readers. This joint application emphasized how The Big Read would enable the applicants to fulfill three broad goals: (1) to create a platform for the interchange among literature, literacy, and community; (2) to provide members of the Valdosta community an opportunity to utilize the resources of Odum Library and VSU; and (3) to provide an enjoyable, shared intellectual experience that would also foster a sense of community. In June 2007 the NEA awarded Valdosta The Big Read grant for programming to run October 14 through November 10, 2007.

WHY COMMUNITY READING PROGRAMS?

Despite popular belief, reading is not an isolated practice. Records of the existence of reading salons, groups, and clubs stretch as far back as the eighteenth century (Ross, McKechnie, and Rothbauer 2006). The act of reading—along with the desire to talk about the reading experience—invites a sense of community. However, in light of heightened media attention, especially from celebrities like Oprah Winfrey, and the Web 2.0 technologies of the late twentieth and twenty-first centuries, readers are more aware of the communities that center around reading and have far more options for participating in them. Now, a reader in Oregon can join a book club in Mississippi simply by logging on to a message board or a chat room. If readers want to feel more socially and physically connected, they can participate in community reading programs.

Community reading programs owe much of their current success to Nancy Pearl, author of *Book Lust* (2003) and former executive director of the Washington Center for the Book at the Seattle Public Library. Pearl is also renowned as the real-life model for the Librarian Action Figure toy. Her mission, according to her Action Figure Trading Card, is "to promote and celebrate the written word," partly by developing one of the nation's most successful community reading programs, the Seattle Public Library's "If All Seattle Read One Book" program, now "Seattle Reads" (Washington Center for the Book 2008).

Community-wide book programs, in which an entire community is invited to share experiences reading the same book, seem a natural development from the early 1990s' increase in adult book clubs or reading groups, often held at bookstores, public libraries, or private homes. Community reading programs' widespread popularity is evident in the Library of Congress's Center for the Book Web list of "One Book, One Community" participants (2008) and in the NEA's Big Read initiative offering grants up to $20,000 to support community-wide reading of classics such as *Fahrenheit 451, The Great Gatsby, Their Eyes Were Watching God, To Kill a Mockingbird*, or *The Joy Luck Club*. These reading programs aim to create common ground for community members who have the chance to read, discuss, and attend programs about the same book. Pearl explains in the American Library Association's guidebook, *One Book One Community: Planning Your Community-Wide Read*, the motivation for citywide reading programs:

People can go for days at a time not talking to anyone outside their immediate family. There are precious few opportunities for people of different ethnic background, economic levels or ages to sit down together and discuss ideas that are important to them. This project provides that opportunity. (2003, 4)

Some community book programs have partnered public and academic libraries, such as the summer reading program through Appalachian State University and Watauga County Libraries in North Carolina, and the Bowling Green Public and Western Kentucky University Libraries' One Book programs. A recent twist on the community reading program is the "One Book, One Campus" program, with members of a campus community sharing a common title and reading experience. Barbara Fister, academic librarian at Gustavus Aldolphus College in Saint Peter, Minnesota, describes the development of these programs, also known as "common reading" programs: "Some assign a book to be read by incoming first-year students for a discussion during orientation; others use the book in first-year seminars or hold a campus-wide event for the entire community" (Fister 2007, 1; see also Twiton 2007; Laufgraben 2006).

Despite these goals, however, Pearl claims that a community reading program is "not an exercise in civics; it's not intended to have literature cure the racial divide" (Rogers 2002, 16). But other programs do admit to loftier goals: as Mary Dempsey says of the Chicago Public Library's program, "If you can get a city excited about a book or even disagreeing about a book, then you've made a significant contribution to the cultural life of that city" (Rogers 2002, 16). The NEA's Big Read draws its motivation from its 2004 report *Reading at Risk: A Survey of Literary Reading in America*, which identified more than a 10 percent drop in literary reading by adults between 1982 and 2002; for young adults (aged 18 to 24), the decline was even more dramatic: 28 percent (National Endowment for the Arts 2004). The NEA claims its goal for its Big Read program is to "revitalize the role of literature in American popular culture and bring the transformative power of literature into the lives of its citizens" (National Endowment for the Arts 2008).

VALDOSTA READS

The committee that worked together to bring the NEA Big Read to Valdosta believed that a community experience of sharing one book had the potential to build bridges across generations, with immigrants new to the region, and among literate and nonliterate populations.[2] With an estimated illiteracy rate of between 20 and 30 percent, the South Georgia area needed a positive experience with reading and books (Welch et al. 2003). Our committee believed this reading program was an opportunity for the community to share something in common, so we decided to plan and promote a series of events that would cross racial and class lines. These included a kickoff event in a newly remodeled park in the middle of a mostly working-class and minority neighborhood; reading discussions located in places that were often overlooked, like a low-income senior citizens' apartment complex; a children's festival to encourage the participation of the youngest members of the community; and audio books and a movie adaptation for those who needed reading help. The activities encompassed more than just reading discussions to show how literature can be a vibrant and integral part of everyday life.

To receive the grant funds and complete the discussions and activities, Valdosta had to send a team to the NEA Big Read training, held in Minneapolis, Minnesota, home of Arts Midwest, a nonprofit regional arts organization that partners with the NEA and the Institute of Museum and Library Services to support this program. The training consisted of a day and a half of discussions about the NEA Big Read, past programs, and ways to make the current grant recipient programs successful. Workshop topics included publicity/marketing, community and military collaborations, and further funding sources. The training also provided an opportunity for grant recipients to share their NEA Big Read activity ideas and trade tips for success. Our Valdosta team returned well-equipped to implement a month of exciting literacy programming for a community of nearly 100,000 people.

Stage One: Establishing Partnerships

As a first step, we needed to develop several more partnerships, create publicity and marketing strategies, and identify hosts for discussion groups. Our program director wanted to be creative in establishing community relationships. We also knew that requests are most likely to succeed when they are *specific* rather than general, which meant that we needed to anticipate what potential partners might be able to offer. Finally, our biggest concern was how to reach the population outside of the academic community, who might not typically participate in a community-wide reading program.

In South Georgia, football is *huge*, and 2007 would see the county high school team win the state championship while the VSU team won the NCAA Division II national championship. If we could enlist the help of the football community, we would reach a significant number of prospective participants in the program.

Developing this relationship was relatively easy. We contacted the administrator in charge of public relations for the VSU football team, Shawn Reed, by email, explaining the NEA Big Read, who should participate, and how influential the football community could be in making it a success. As the time and energies of all partners have to be considered, *specific* requests proved the most effective: Would the stadium announcer announce Valdosta's participation in the NEA Big Read during home games? Would volunteers be allowed to distribute promotional materials for the program at stadium entrances? Would an announcement of the NEA Big Read in Valdosta be posted on the athletic program's two large electronic billboards located in heavy traffic areas in the city? VSU athletics administrators recognized that the football team would be helping to promote a program to help the whole community and encourage young and old to pursue reading as a pastime. They appreciated the chance to be affiliated with a community-wide literacy effort and considered our requests relatively simple to grant.

Another interesting partnership was established with VSU's College of the Arts. During a new faculty orientation gathering, we approached the dean of the College of the Arts, Dr. John Gaston, explained the grant, and made *specific* requests while emphasizing the benefits to the college. For instance, a program of dramatic readings from *Their Eyes Were Watching God* would add another interpretation of the book, entertain the community, and give theater students the opportunity to hone their acting skills. The dean found a faculty member, Deborah Morgan, to be the point-person; she enthusiastically used the program as a teaching opportunity. As a part of this partnership, the theater group performed several dramatic readings, including a premier at Odum Library and shows at the youth festival and keynote. Committee members and Odum Library agreed to feed the actors at each performance. Again, this partnership was relatively simple to establish. Frequent emails and phone calls helped to keep the lines of communication open and to schedule the performances.

Moody Air Force Base, ten miles northeast of Valdosta, gave us an opportunity for a community partnership. The NEA Big Read encourages outreach to the military, and the grant proposal included plans for outreach to the base and military families in the area. Early on, the base's participation seemed threatened by a requirement to include a credit line for the Boeing Corporation's support of military participation at that time. Careful negotiation among our librarian liaison to the base, Shilo Smith, officials at Moody, and Arts Midwest administrators led us to add to the credit line "The Big Read for military communities is made possible by Boeing" and some follow-up wording for local materials: "No federal endorsement implied." We were grateful this partnership worked out: Our committee expanded to include the librarian and other representatives from the base, all of whom participated actively in planning and events. We were able to distribute promotional materials at the base library and the annual air show in October, and the base hosted a book discussion group and movie viewing.

One of the most fascinating buy-in/partnership efforts, however, occurred at a unique local event: a new traffic light celebration. Mayor John Fretti of Valdosta encouraged the efforts of the committee and wrote a letter of support for the grant proposal. Because of the mayor's very busy schedule, however, it was difficult to meet face to face to discuss further support from his office (two meetings had been scheduled but canceled due to emergency business). We decided that the only way to make our requests known would be to "ambush" the mayor, and we found our opportunity in an announcement that VSU and local officials, including the mayor, would inaugurate the new traffic light at the busy main entrance to VSU. Afterward, we followed the mayor, reminded him of his letter of support for the NEA Big Read, and made our *specific* requests: We wanted him to appear at the kickoff festival and participate in a local book discussion. An hour of footwork earned the full support of the mayor and the city's public information officer, Sementha Mathews. She opened the doors for press opportunities and community contacts (e.g., a local women's shelter) that we might not have found on our own. She also participated in committee meetings, initiated contact with the nearest NBC television affiliate in Albany, which aired the public service announcement provided for us by the NEA Big Read, and arranged to have the mayor officially open the kickoff festival and visit a discussion group.

Not all partnerships went exactly as planned, however; creating a partnership with the public schools proved to be more difficult than we had imagined. The original proposal included the Readers into Leaders program, which would select a range of students (diverse in abilities, ages, races, gender, etc.) to be trained to lead book discussions and volunteer at events. Any book discussion host site could select its own facilitator or request a facilitator from the Readers into Leaders group. Our committee envisioned this part of the programming as a way for the students to feel a sense of ownership of the community-wide read. We also hoped that the students would help inspire their parents and other adults who had not read for pleasure in quite some time. COE faculty took charge of this aspect of the proposal because they already had partnerships with many schools and school initiatives.

Unfortunately, by the time of the official announcement of the grant, in late June 2007, most of the public schools had chosen the literature that they would use in their curriculum for the next year, and schools were out for summer break. It proved very difficult to recruit students who were highly motivated to read the book on their own and attend a weekend workshop to learn how to facilitate book discussions. Teachers, concerned with testing schedules and time restrictions, were not able to change their curriculum plans. The best results came from a few literature classes at the county and city schools, where *Their Eyes Were Watching God* was already on the fall schedule. Those teachers who were using the book in their classrooms received teacher guides, reader guides, copies of the books, and posters. Some students did actively participate in several discussion groups, volunteer at the Children and Youth festival, and attend the keynote address.

Stage Two: Planning and Promoting

Once partnerships were in place, we moved on to planning and promoting the literacy program further. Along with training, the NEA Big Read provides grant recipients with banners, reading guides, posters, bookmarks, public service announcements, templates for press releases, and CDs of readings, music, and commentary on the novels. Grant funds supported purchase and distribution of 600 paperback copies of the novel along with multiple film DVDs and audiobooks. We created a list of frequently asked questions to explain the purpose of the NEA Big

Read, the book selection, and ways community members could participate. In addition to the promotions at VSU football games and Moody Air Force Base, volunteers distributed materials and gathered data about local reading habits at the annual Harvest Fest at Valdosta Technical College and the nearby Hahira Honeybee Festival, events that attract thousands for fall festivities. Volunteers staffed banner-draped promotional tables at a local literacy fair at Sam's Club and among Saturday morning shoppers outside a busy Wal-Mart. We took advantage of campus events such as new faculty orientation and the VSU Centennial Celebration. Several of us enjoyed using our project director's icebreaker: "All of Valdosta is reading this book; are *you*?" Committee members spoke at a civic round table luncheon and area club meetings. Reading guides and event calendars found distribution points not just at area bookstores and libraries but also at Valdosta beauty salons, stores, restaurants, a senior citizen center, an arts center, area churches, and school systems in several nearby counties.

Resources from the NEA Big Read also allowed us to fund visits from two authors, Joyce Carol Thomas for the Children and Youth Festival and Valerie Boyd for the keynote address. Contacting and creating contracts with guest speakers, in our experience, showed both sides of a coin. Our keynote speaker was Boyd, author of *Wrapped in Rainbows: The Life of Zora Neale Hurston* (2003). At the time, Boyd was a visiting professor at the University of Georgia. Our project director simply emailed Boyd, told her about our grant, and requested that she speak. Throughout the whole encounter with Boyd, we were impressed with how approachable and warm she was. She was very easy to work with, and VSU's legal office readily accepted her terms for a contract.

For the Children and Youth Festival, sponsored by the Valdosta-Lowndes County Library, Joyce Carol Thomas was the visiting author. Thomas was the obvious choice for us, as she had adapted into children's picture books several of the stories that Hurston had collected on her fieldwork trips. Her participation was harder to obtain, however, because the contract was negotiated through her publisher, and the university's legal office had many questions and revisions. Special requirements in the contract, such as providing vegetarian food and ice water in a glass, made us nervous about satisfying her expectations, but Thomas proved to be as warm and pleasant as Boyd.

Opportunities for electronic marketing allowed us to reach diverse audiences as well as to draw upon the skills of Odum Library colleagues Cliff Landis and Sherrida Crawford. Everyone who visited the Odum Library home page during the program saw the NEA Big Read banner ad and could visit links to promotional material for events and sponsors through the library's Web page and RSS feed. Electronic publicity continued through the Big Read blog, which featured photos from events and links to more information about Hurston's life and work and our calendar of events. Through the blog, participants had the chance to review and offer feedback on events.[3] We also distributed announcements through VSU email lists and the university's news bureau.

Stage Three: The Major Events

A kickoff event is a key to success for any NEA Big Read, and we started well by securing the mayor and a great location in a city park with ample parking and a small amphitheatre. Our kickoff included activities for children and adults as well as readers and performers with diverse appeal. The emcee was Nadine Whitfield, a COE faculty member who dressed and spoke as author Zora Neale Hurston throughout the event to help bring the novel to life. Locating performers was more difficult, for our kickoff fell on the weekend before short fall breaks at VSU and public schools. Unable to book school performers, we relied on contacts in the mayor's office, area churches, and VSU employees who were longtime area residents to suggest possibilities. Our performers, an eclectic but entertaining mix, included a recorder trio, step teams and cheerleaders from area churches, and the Valdosta Asian Cultural Association's youth lion dancers. Miss Teen Valdosta, Greta Smidt, sang and spoke about the freedom Americans have to read, and VSU English major and poet Ricky Davis credited Hurston with inspiring his own creative writing. Between performances, volunteer readers, including COE Dean Philip Gunter, VSU attorney Laverne Lewis Gaskins (also a local author), the director of VSU's African American Studies program, Dr. Shirley Hardin, and literacy and library workers, teachers, and elementary and middle school students read short excerpts from Hurston's novel and stories.

The kickoff also provided an opportunity to distribute more promotional materials and copies of the books. Committee members Maureen Puffer-Rothenberg and Shilo Smith created attractive gift bags containing a copy of the book, a map to discussion group and film locations, a calendar of events, and a reader's guide. We asked book recipients to sign up for book discussion groups and fill out event questionnaires provided by the NEA; they were then entered into a prize drawing for a beautiful basket of books and gift items about Zora Neale Hurston and the Harlem Renaissance. This drawing would occur at the keynote, a way to encourage continued interest in our programs and attendance at our final event. Throughout the kickoff we also drew from these names for free copies of *Their Eyes Were Watching God*, promotional T-shirts, and other small prizes. Overall, the kickoff was one of our best attended events and gained the most thorough media attention of the entire program: front-page coverage with color photographs of the kickoff appeared in the next day's *Valdosta Daily Times*, followed by an editorial in support of literacy efforts in Valdosta and the NEA Big Read programs in particular.

For the Children and Youth Festival, we moved to the Valdosta-Lowndes County Library for readings and book signings with Joyce Carol Thomas. On the previous day, Thomas had visited Sallas Mahone Elementary School, where students made cards welcoming her to Valdosta and Mayor Fretti made his second NEA Big Read appearance. For the festival, our public library decorated the author's reading area with ficus trees bearing paper pears in honor of Hurston, paper suns, and yellow, green, and white balloons. The library also hosted storyteller Donna Washington, our Readers' Theatre for the group's second performance, spoken-word poetry group Poetic Magic, and games and music.

Our book discussion groups, as with most community reading programs, were the core of the NEA Big Read in Valdosta. Volunteers and committee members scheduled book groups and/or film viewings for foster grandparents, a women's shelter, Moody Air Force Base, churches, a community coffeehouse, an arts center, bookstores, senior citizens, new faculty and graduate students, and public and college libraries. Some established book groups made Hurston's novel their choice during our programming period, whereas other groups used their readers' guides and DVDs borrowed from our libraries to host book and movie discussions. The variety of hosts and locations for the groups gave opportunities for both avid and lapsed readers to participate.

Along with the kickoff, our most successful event was the closing keynote address, "An Evening Wrapped in Rainbows," at the VSU University Center. Our speaker, Valerie Boyd, spoke about the research and writing of Hurston's biography and the inspiration she drew from Hurston's life for her own creative work. Boyd even grew sentimental about her own VSU connection: She had summered here as part of the Governor's Honors Program, a competitive program for gifted Georgia students while in high school. Closing the NEA Big Read in Valdosta deserved a great speaker, another fine performance by the Readers' Theatre, and a reception to celebrate. The prize basket went to an audience member who had also attended the kickoff, and Boyd generously talked with fans while signing copy after copy of her biography of Hurston.

Stage Four: Challenges, Assessment, and the Future

Valdosta had never before attempted a one book, one community program. Overall, it was a great experience, but we also learned a lot and had a few disappointments along the way. One of our greatest challenges occurred just before the NEA Big Read program started, when our initial project director moved to a new position at a midwestern university library. Fortunately, one of our COE faculty, Dr. Brenda Dixey, was willing to assume oversight of the remaining programming and the final grant reports, so she became the new project director to lead us through our weekly planning meetings and vigorously support the NEA Big Read in Valdosta.

One event from our original grant application proved to be too costly, both in time and in funds, to complete. We had planned to have at least one community field trip by bus to Eatonville, Florida, to visit the Zora Neale Hurston museum there and see firsthand the community that was the setting for much of Hurston's novel. This trip would help reward the Readers into Leaders for their work with our programs, as well as provide another learning opportunity for members of the Valdosta community. Unfortunately, the increased cost of transportation and the difficulty in scheduling a full-day trip led us to cancel these plans, although some program participants planned individual visits to Hurston's hometown.

Such unexpected expenses always come up in programming, but we received permission from Arts Midwest, the day-to-day administrative contact for the NEA Big Read, to divert the transportation funds to other needs, such as buying additional copies of the novel for free distribution. Grant funds also covered the cost of typing the Readers' Theatre script that Deborah Morgan adapted from the novel. The grant would not cover any expenses for food, however, so Odum Library, committee members, and funding from the Office of the Vice-President for Academic Affairs and the College of Education provided the food and receptions.

Though our committee was pleased at how Valdosta responded to the NEA Big Read, the canceled field trip was not the only scheduling problem we faced. For our next community-wide read, we will look for a time of year with fewer potential conflicts, perhaps January. Competition came not only from scheduling, however, but also from some unanticipated attitudes. Overall, the Valdosta community reacted positively to the NEA Big Read; even residents who did not participate seemed pleased to see reading and books receive so much attention. Not all, though: Some administrators with area organizations turned down opportunities to pursue book groups or movie viewings, declaring that their constituents would not be interested or simply failing to respond to repeated invitations. Although disappointing, such reactions indeed reflect attitudes of some residents toward reading or community events more generally. On the other hand, we were pleased that we encountered no resistance based on the content of the novel. Several years earlier, Lowndes County Schools had suffered a censorship battle over Barbara Kingsolver's *The Bean Trees* (McCormick 2006). Although we were warned to expect battles, we heard no reports of concerns over *Their Eyes Were Watching God*.

CONCLUSION: CONTINUING OUTREACH

Through the NEA Big Read, VSU librarians had the chance to develop and deepen relationships with faculty in the Dewar COE and the College of the Arts, local media, city government, religious and other nonprofit organizations, Moody Air Force Base, and area public schools. These relationships are extremely important because they emphasize the interconnectedness of community organizations and the importance of collaboration for effectiveness and survival. Furthermore, community partnerships like the ones formed during Valdosta's NEA Big Read are a unique example of group advocacy in action. The goal, now, is to sustain these relationships. We intend to follow up on programming, communication, and grant-writing opportunities that were suggested during our NEA Big Read collaborations. For example, Odum Library hosted a poetry café in Spring 2008 featuring Poetic Magic, an area nonprofit poetry performance group that performed at several of Valdosta's Big Read events.

Ultimately, we found that success depends on being open to unexpected partnerships and advantages, being willing to negotiate, and keeping open the lines of communication. No single campus entity could have accomplished this much community outreach in little more than a month, and our committee was fortunate to have input from many talented community members. Organizers must ask for help, and the more specific the requests, the more likely they are to be successful. Likewise, it is vital to respect and respond to residents' ideas. Above all, a shared commitment to the community, combined with expertise and funding from the NEA, empowered our library and campus to find new ways to fulfill our mission to promote education and progress in the Valdosta area.

NOTES

1. The NEA Big Read program in Valdosta, Georgia, was a joint effort of VSU's Odum Library, Dewar COE, and Master of Library and Information Science Program; the South Georgia Regional Library system; Valdosta City Schools; Lowndes County Schools; Moody Air Force Base; Valdosta Technical College; and the City of Valdosta. Additional partners included the VSU College of the Arts, the VSU Athletic Department, the Alliance for

Literacy and Literature, Hildegard's Café, and the Annette Howell Turner Center for the Arts.

2. Members of the original NEA Big Read grant committee were VSU faculty: project directors Dr. Yolanda Hood and Dr. Brenda Dixey, Shilo Smith, Emily Rogers, Dr. Robbie Strickland, Dr. Barbara Stanley, and Dr. Erin Huskey. Additional committee members and volunteers included Nadine Whitfield, Sementha Mathews, Dr. Wallace Koehler, Tamiko Lawrence, Dr. Anne Marie Smith, Maureen Puffer-Rothenberg, Sherrida Crawford, Jack Fisher, Cliff Landis, Dr. Anita Ondrusek, Ken Smith, Julie Reffel, Dr. Elaine Yontz, Christie Paulk, David Peeples, Halley Little, Holly May, April Oliver, Staff Sergeant Maria Rodriguez, Kathy Tomlinson, Charlie Oliver, and Deborah Morgan. The authors acknowledge with gratitude the contributions of all volunteers as well as the following supporters of the NEA Big Read program in Valdosta: Dr. Louis Levy, Mayor John Fretti, Dr. George Gaumond, Dr. Betty Paulk, Chuck Gibson, Dr. Philip L. Gunter, Dr. John Gaston, Dr. Barbara Gray, Carolyn Williams, Shanika Hezekiah, Dr. Shirley Hardin, Captain Dustin Hart, and Laverne Lewis Gaskins.

3. VSU's NEA Big Read information page is available at http://www.valdosta.edu/library/about/bigread.shtml, and the original program blog is available at http://bigread valdosta.blogspot.com/.

REFERENCES

American Library Association. *One Book, One Community: Planning Your Community-Wide Read.* Chicago: American Library Association, 2003. http://www.ala.org/ala/ppo/files/onebookguide.pdf (accessed February 21, 2008).

Boyd, Valerie. *Wrapped in Rainbows: The Life of Zora Neale Hurston.* New York: Scribner, 2003.

Fister, Barbara. "One Book, One Campus: Exploring Common Reading Programs." *E-Source for College Transitions* 5, no.1 (2007): 1 ff. http://nrc.fye.sc.edu/esource/4%281%29.pdf (accessed April 26, 2008).

Laufgraben, Jodi Levine. *Common Reading Programs: Going Beyond the Book.* The First-Year Experience Monograph Series No. 44. Columbia, SC: National Research Center for the First-Year Experience & Students in Transition, 2006.

The Library of Congress Center for the Book. *"One Book" Reading Promotion Projects.* The Library of Congress, 2008. http://www.loc.gov/loc/cfbook/one-book.html (accessed March 24, 2008).

McCormick, Angie. "Banned in Lowndes County: Why Two Teachers Said No." *KNOW Magazine* 5, no. 1 (2006): 23–29. http://neageorgia.org/pdf/KNOW/5.1/feature2.pdf (accessed September 12, 2007).

National Endowment for the Arts. "Executive Summary." *Reading at Risk: A Survey of Literary Reading in America.* National Endowment for the Arts, 2004. http://www.arts.gov/pub/ReadingAtRisk.pdf (accessed March 26, 2007).

———. *The Big Read.* National Endowment for the Arts, 2008. http://www.neabigread.org/ (accessed March 25, 2008).

Pearl, Nancy. *Book Lust: Recommended Reading for Every Mood, Moment, and Reason.* Seattle: Sasquatch, 2003.

Rogers, Michael. "Libraries Offer Chapter and Verse on Citywide Book Clubs." *Library Journal* 127, no. 6 (April 1, 2002): 16–18.

Ross, Catherine Sheldrick, Lynn (E. F.) McKechnie, and Paulette M. Rothbauer. *Reading Matters: What the Research Reveals about Reading, Libraries, and Community.* Westport, CT: Libraries Unlimited, 2006.

Strategic Research and Analysis Office. *Concise Mission Statement.* Valdosta, GA: Valdosta State University, 2007. http://www.valdosta.edu/sra/documents/VSU_Concise_Mission.pdf (accessed April 26, 2008).

Twiton, Andi. *Common Reading Programs in Higher Education.* Saint Peter, MN: Folke Bernadotte Memorial Library, Gustavus Adolphus College, 2007. http://gustavus.edu/academic/library/Pubs/Lindell2007.html (accessed March 24, 2008).

Washington Center for the Book. *The Seattle Public Library: Seattle Reads.* Seattle: Seattle Public Library, 2008. http://www.spl.org/default.asp?pageID=about_leaders_washingtoncenter_seattlereads (accessed April 16, 2008).

Welch, V., et al. *The Facts about Georgia: Our Health Depends on It.* Atlanta, GA: Emory Center on Health Outcomes and Quality, Emory University, 2003. http://www.sph.emory.edu/CHOQ/HGFREPORT/FactsComplete21004.pdf (accessed April 26, 2008).

16

CHILDREN'S READING CELEBRATION & YOUNG AUTHOR'S FAIR

Debra Hoffmann

Before I discuss the annual Children's Reading Celebration & Young Author's Fair at California State University Channel Islands (CSUCI), I would like to tell a little about the unique aspects of the university and library that make both places so special. Located in Camarillo, California, CSUCI is the newest university in the California State system. It opened in 2002 and graduated its first freshman class in 2007. Placing students at the center of the educational experience, CSUCI provides undergraduate and graduate education through integrative approaches and experiential and service learning and graduates students with multicultural and international perspectives. The newly opened John Spoor Broome Library enhances CSUCI's mission through active collaboration with students, faculty, and staff in developing collections, services, and information literacy skills. The Broome Library is one of the most important entities on campus, and Broome librarians are known for their visible presence both on campus and in the community and for the unique programs and services we create. In addition to providing service to the campus as librarians, we constantly reach out in partnership to other academic and cocurricular programs, serve on campus committees, and create unique events for students and faculty. There is literally nothing that the library does not want to be involved with on campus.

HOW WE STARTED

This event started in 2004 when the dean of the library and a professor from the English program decided to create an event that would be a service-learning opportunity for students in the professor's children's literature class. For the library, the goal was to reach out to the English program and highlight the library as a unique partner for such an event. More importantly, the library saw the event's potential as a community outreach opportunity; the campus had officially opened the previous year and was highly interested in ways to draw the community at large to campus.

The premise of this first event was simple. Students from the children's literature class chose storybooks to read to children who attended and created reading "spaces" with pillows and other props inside the library. The idea was to have the children who attended listen to stories read by the students at half-hour intervals and have the students who would be reading their stories do so in an effective and creative manner. The library provided the space for the event and kept it running smoothly. Approximately 30 children and parents from the community attended. Although the turnout was small, both the English class and library felt it had been successful, affording students the opportunity to interact with children from the community and bringing members of the community into the library.

I was hired as a reference and instruction librarian in 2004 and took over running the event the following year. After reviewing the previous year's event, I decided to add additional activities that would enhance the program for attendees who may want something more to do besides listen to children's books. I added a simple hands-on art project (children painted faces onto squares of paper that then became a "quilt"); a reader's theater presentation by students from a theater arts class on campus; allowed attendees to draw with chalk on the sidewalk in front of the library; and we served lemonade and cookies as refreshments. Approximately 60 parents and children attended that year—double the previous year's attendance. Advertising each year had been via press releases from the campus marketing department and word of mouth. It was gratifying to see that even with such little advertising, people wanted to attend the event and tell their friends about it too. Both the English program and the library knew we were on to something.

Because the event had doubled in size and our library at the time was extremely small, I knew that this event would have to be held in another campus venue in the future. While scouting for new campus locations in 2006, I learned that the Ventura County Reading Association (VCRA), a local area nonprofit group devoted to children's literacy, had booked their annual Young Author's Fair on our campus, to be held two weeks prior to the Children's Reading Celebration I was hoping to schedule. Intrigued, I contacted VCRA and learned that the Young Author's Fair is an annual event where books created by students from local area grade schools are showcased for community members to see. Published children's book authors speak at the fair each year, which is usually attended by over 100 parents and their children. I told VCRA about the library's Children's Reading Celebration and asked if they would consider combining their event with ours. They agreed, and the first annual Children's Reading Celebration & Young Author's Fair was born.

This initial partnership exceeded both our expectations. The Young Author's Fair had a built-in audience of community attendees (VCRA had sponsored the event for 27 years), and the Children's Reading Celebration added entirely new dimensions to their event via storytellers and arts and crafts activities. This first event was attended by about 120 children and their parents and was very positively received by attendees.

Because the Children's Reading Celebration & Young Author's Fair is made up of two different events with similar goals and missions, it complements and builds off of its components, not diminishes them. Activities for the Children's Reading Celebration each year include a variety of student storytellers, a Make-Your-Own-Book station, and a hands-on "Paint-By-Numbers" activity that knocks the participants' socks off. Each year, an artist is hired to create a large canvas filled with paint-by-numbers areas that children fill in with paint throughout the day. By the end of the event, a fully formed mural appears, usually the face of a famous literary character (past images have included Pippi Longstocking and Harry Potter). Children and their parents are blown away by the mural that is created. The Young Author's Fair showcases books created by K–6 grade students from all over Ventura County and invites two popular children's authors to speak at the event. Attendees have an opportunity to visit with the authors and purchase their books at a book fair hosted by VCRA.

In 2007 the second annual Children's Reading Celebration & Young Author's Fair was attended by about 300 people and saw the addition of a "Make-Your-Own Concertina Book" station, led by a former student who graduated from the English program. The 2008 event, with over 350 attendees, was the first at the campus' new John Spoor Broome Library. Reading therapy dogs were added to the mix, allowing children to read books to therapy dogs. The dogs were a huge hit and will be a permanent addition to the event.

The outcome of this collaboration has been threefold. In just a few short years, the library has created a highly respected and successful community outreach event that allows us to foster and sustain relationships with campus and community groups. Additional campus partnerships have developed, and the event has turned into a showcase for the library as well as the VCRA—their Young Author's Fair event now has a home as well as a larger base of participants and attendees.

INTERDISCIPLINARY AND COCURRICULAR ASPECTS OF THE EVENT

Some of the best aspects of this event for the library are its interdisciplinary and cocurricular components. As previously mentioned, the mission of the Broome Library is to enhance the mission of the university through active collaboration with students, faculty, and staff. Our unofficial mission, however, is to reach out to the campus in fresh and innovative ways to create sustainable relationships that benefit not only the library but our partners as well.

Our initial collaboration with the English program showed promise. The library was able to interact with students and faculty outside of the classroom setting and beyond the scope of traditional library interactions such as orientations and bibliographic instruction. We had always had a positive working relationship with the English program, but reaching out to students and faculty in this nontraditional way made the relationship fresher and more creative, and showed both parties that there was room for further exploration of innovative and nontraditional ways to collaborate on campus.

After the first Children's Reading Celebration & Young Author's Fair, other campus entities contacted me about partnering with the event. Part of the mission of the university is to provide students with service-learning opportunities; CSUCI's Center for Community Engagement is dedicated to providing students with experiential and service learning experiences. For students in the children's literature class each year, the Children's Reading Celebration & Young Author's Fair proves to be a service-learning opportunity unlike any they've experienced before. For their part of the event to be successful, these students must create a storytelling presentation and space for an audience of community children and their parents that is unknown to them until the time of their presentation. This forces them to think not only about which stories they will choose and why but also about the community outside of the university. Who are the children who live in this community? Where do they go to school? What are their needs? The university is bordered by several communities, each with its own range of cultural and socioeconomic issues. Forcing students to take these many factors into account as they create their presentations helps them forge a connection with the communities outside of campus that they would not have had without participating in this event.

Opportunities to collaborate with other campus programs grew along with the event. After the first Children's Reading Celebration & Young Author's Fair, I was contacted by the Educational Opportunity Program (EOP) on campus. EOP is a university program that provides college access to students whose educational and economic circumstances have limited their college educational opportunities. EOP's goal is to provide incoming students from disadvantaged backgrounds with the tools they will need to help them succeed in college and ultimately graduate from CSUCI. EOP does a lot of outreach to the community and, when they heard about our program, asked if they could be involved with it. For the last two years, volunteers from EOP have hosted a "University for a Day" table where children can get their pictures taken in a cap and gown as well as receive a "diploma" with their name on it. EOP volunteers have also given campus tours to families with older children who may be interested in attending the university in the future. The "University for a Day" table has been a huge hit with attendees. In turn, EOP benefits from being able to target their outreach efforts to many more children in one day than they may reach otherwise throughout the year.

Lastly, Alpha Nu Eta, a campus honor society, asked if they could be involved with the event. Alpha Nu Eta's goal is to promote interest in literature, literacy, language, and writing while promoting exemplary character, good fellowship, and high standards of academic excellence. The current president of Alpha Nu Eta was a graduating English major at the time of the first Children's Reading Celebration & Young Author's Fair and was doing her senior capstone project on community literacy programs. She volunteered time and donated supplies to the first event and then used the data she collected through interviews with teachers who participated in the event to complete her capstone project. Alpha Nu Eta continues to provide volunteers each year for the events. It is this interdisciplinary nature of the Children's Reading Celebration & Young Author's Fair that has been one of the keys to its success.

PARTNERSHIPS CREATED

One of the surprising outcomes of this event over the last few years has been the unexpected partnerships that have been created and sustained as the event has grown. The library is fortunate to have been able to partner with an organization that has been around for so long (27 years at the time we first partnered) and that has a good reputation in the community as well as a long history of working with schools and teachers to promote literacy. The VCRA is a professional organization for teachers, student teachers, administrators, librarians, instructional assistants, and parents to promote literacy through school and community programs. VCRA maintains a good relationship with teachers and school districts in the communities surrounding our university. Inviting VCRA to join our event brought our university to the attention of these teachers and schools, many of whom had never visited the campus before. There was a built-in level of trust among the teachers and schools because of VCRA that allowed our initial partnership to prosper from the beginning, which in turn led to further partnerships.

One partnership developed quite by accident. A woman attending our Children's Reading Celebration with her son in 2005 told me that she was affiliated with the local chapter of an organization called Altrusa International, a community-based, grassroots organization that seeks to solve the problems of local communities. The mission of the Ventura chapter of Altrusa is to address community literacy issues. She invited me to speak about our Reading Celebration at the group's next meeting. Afterward, the group pledged to participate in the 2006 event, which they did by handing out free books to all children who attended. This contact also put me in touch with a local network of families who home-school their children. We were able to invite them to participate in future Young Author's Fairs.

Since this event began, we've sent out press releases to local media, including the local newspaper, the *Ventura County Star*. Through VCRA, we discovered that the newspaper has its own community foundation, the Star in Education Foundation, a nonprofit organization dedicated to providing free copies of the newspaper to schools in the area. In 2007 a member of the foundation agreed to run free quarter-page ads about our event in the newspaper in exchange for listing the foundation as a cosponsor of the event. These ads helped increase attendance at our event dramatically and allowed us to reach out to the community in a way that we hadn't been able to before.

Some of the best partnerships are unanticipated. When a colleague at the library led an unrelated outreach event for local area high schools, she met the librarian who runs the Learning Resource Display Center for the Ventura County Office of Education. After hearing about our event, the librarian offered to advertise it to the school districts, about 150 schools, in exchange for including the Ventura County Office of Education as a cosponsor of our event. Her assistance has been invaluable to us.

BENEFITS TO THE LIBRARY, THE CAMPUS, AND THE COMMUNITY

As previously noted, the unofficial mission of the Broome Library is to create sustainable relationships and partnerships that benefit not just the library but our partners as well. For the library, the Children's Reading Celebration & Young Author's Fair helped to put us "on the map" in terms of our place on campus and in the community. When we began in 2004, the university had enrolled its first freshman class only the previous year. The library needed to define its role with regard to serving students and its place on campus, and creating and hosting the Reading Celebration helped us do just that.

Up to this point, most students on campus had used the library for research, as a place to study, or perhaps not at all. Students often view university libraries as large buildings filled with books, with librarians telling them to be quiet. Having these students in the building for this event (even if at first it was only two dozen of them) opened their eyes to the resources and services available to them and how different we are from the typical university library. "I can check out video and digital cameras?" Yes. "I can eat and drink in the library?" Yes. "Your library collection has new release DVDs and new release bestsellers?" Yes. "Can you help me create a poster online for a class presentation?" Yes. At each turn, students were surprised by the array of nontraditional resources and services available to them, and a connection was born. It opened students' eyes to the fact that our library was a cool place to hang out, that there was more to us than meets the eye. By including students in this outreach event, the library set the tone early on as a fun, innovative, and welcoming place that has something for students regardless of what those needs may be. These students also got a new perspective on what the university library is and what our role is on campus.

The event proved to be beneficial to the campus as well. One of the four "pillars" of the university is the integrative and interdisciplinary approach to the creation, discovery, transmission, and application of knowledge on campus. Because the university was so new at the time we first began, interdisciplinary opportunities were few and the creation of these partnerships was highly encouraged. Creating this event not only benefited the library but allowed the English program to partner across disciplines as well.

As it happened, the library was also able to "piggyback" with an annual student event called "Dolphin Days," a weeklong cocurricular event put on by students to foster fun and a sense of community on campus. Each year, Dolphin Days ends with a barbecue for students and their families, and I was able to schedule our event to end right as the family barbecue was beginning. Organizers of Dolphin Days were thrilled to have a built-in base of attendees for the barbecue and even offered to lead campus tours during the Children's Reading Celebration & Young Author's Fair for interested families.

A final benefit to the campus is that this event brings members of the community to the campus who might not visit otherwise. Though centrally located, the university is tucked away behind hills and is not readily visible from the street. Many people knew there was a new university in the area but were unsure where it was located. Bringing the community to campus, especially school-age children who may eventually attend the university, helps engender a sense of pride and ownership of the campus with the community. Indeed, as this event has grown, families who have attended each year feel very comfortable being on campus and have attended other events on campus throughout the year.

The benefit to the community outside of campus cannot be overstated. For a start-up university and library, building a connection with the community is critical to the success and sustainability of both. An event like the Children's Reading Celebration & Young Author's Fair bridges the gap between the university mission and the need of the community to feel that they have a stake in the university. As the event draws more and more people to campus each year, I hear comments like, "I never would have visited the campus if it wasn't for this event" or "I had no idea the university was even here." Because people are so comfortable at our event, they feel comfortable interacting with the university on multiple levels, whether it is visiting the campus for other events or supporting the campus financially. This event draws to campus a section of the community traditionally overlooked by many universities.

ASSESSMENT, SCALABILITY, AND SUSTAINABILITY

This event started small, with only about 30 children and parents attending the first year, and increased to about 350 attendees in 2008. It's an approximate increase because in all these years I have yet to conduct a formal assessment. Why not?

Initially, because the event was so small, it was easy to gauge its success and see what to do to make it better. As it grew, it was still easy to assess because it took place in one large performance hall. We knew how many people attended, which stations or activities were popular, who needed more or less space for their activity, etc. When the 2008 event moved to our new 137,000 sq. ft. library, it became clear that we need to conduct more formal assessment in the future. We have always relied on attendance numbers and verbal responses from attendees to let us know how we're doing. In 2009 I anticipate the addition of informal questioning of attendees during the event (in the form of "graffiti stations" around the library where people can leave comments about the event as it's happening) as well as a more formal questionnaire sent to participating teachers/schools as to how we're doing and what we can do to make it better in the future.

What I hope is clear is just how scalable this is. Depending on your space, staff, and budget limitations, an event like this can be as large or intimate as you would like, and the amount of what you offer can vary from year to year—it's really quite flexible! As for sustainability, because the purpose of this event is to create and foster partnerships with campus groups as well as reach out to the community, it has the inherent ability to build foundational relationships between groups that traditionally may not partner together and can be built on and sustained over time.

CONSIDERATIONS, MISTAKES, AND WHAT I WOULD DO DIFFERENTLY

So, how do we do what we do? Before creating and undertaking an event of this type, you'll want to keep in mind the following considerations.

Budget

The John Spoor Broome Library at CSUCI has a library foundation account that we use to pay for our portion of the event. CSUCI also has grant opportunities on campus to which we can apply if necessary. That being said, the most I have ever budgeted for this event is $2,500, and I have always come in under budget; $1,500 each year has gone to pay the artist who creates the amazing paint-by-numbers mural for the event (a lot of money given my budget!), but an important expenditure because this activity is so hugely popular that I would be hard-pressed to do the event without him. In 2008 we purchased a permanent display banner, a one-time expenditure of $300. Posters, postcards, and other advertising are created in-house by an amazing media specialist, so I pay only for printing. To offer free on-campus parking to attendees, I pay a flat-rate fee to campus parking services. VCRA pays for two authors to visit during the event, refreshments, a portion of the printing expenses, and table decorations. The English program pays for craft and book-making supplies, and EOP pays for their "University for a Day" supplies. Press release advertising is free through CSUCI's marketing department; newspaper ads are donated by the Star in Education Foundation.

Mistakes include missing obvious partnership opportunities that would have saved money and added greater depth to the event (e.g., partnering with the Art program on campus). I am paying a professional artist to come to campus each year when I could have art students create hands-on activities for the event as a service-learning opportunity. (I did finally approach the Art program last year, but to date no students have wanted to participate.) Even though I am a librarian, the first year I ran the event it never occurred to me to reach out to public librarians in the community as potential partners. I also forgot to include the elementary school that is affiliated with the university on my list of schools to contact in the area.

What I would do differently is partner early and often with campus and community members and make better use of networking connections from colleagues and friends. Because the library foundation fund fluctuates, I never know from year to year if money will be available for this event. I would explore a wider variety of funding options, including grants and donations from community businesses.

Time

This event, though not daunting, takes a good deal of planning to make it run smoothly. Even though I do some of the planning via email, a lot of time goes into the preparation, setup, and takedown of the event. This is in addition to the classes I teach, the meetings I attend, and the hours that I staff the reference desk each week.

Mistakes include underestimating the time involved in doing this well. Not everyone involved can meet at the same time. Some leave town for extended periods of time, some are only available to meet mornings, etc. Setup and takedown are much more time-consuming than originally anticipated. Unexpected delays in printing and deliveries always occur.

What I would do differently is double my original time estimates and be more flexible. Meet once or twice as a whole group and then conduct the bulk of interactions via email. Oversee the event but delegate more responsibility to other event partners.

Volunteers

An event like this is only as good as its volunteers, and I have been fortunate to have great student, staff, and community members volunteer each year. Students usually need volunteer opportunities and this event is perfect for that, even if the students do not end up directly participating in the event itself. Most of my volunteers are students from the children's literature class, who help set up the day before or assist at the activity areas during the event.

Mistakes include underestimating how many volunteers I need and when I need them and not keeping track of who shows up and how long they stay.

What I would do differently is request more volunteers, especially for setup and takedown. Because of our large venue, in the future I will place volunteers strategically throughout the event to ensure a smooth flow from activity to activity.

NOTHING SUCCEEDS LIKE SUCCESS

So, can you duplicate an event like this at your library? Absolutely. Regardless of the size of your library or a possible lack of funds or partnership opportunities, an event like this is tailor-made for anyone looking to try something new. Start by looking on campus to see if there is a department or student group that is already doing outreach or in need of outreach opportunities themselves. Remember, if your library is thinking about outreach, it is likely that other people on campus are as well. Share your strengths...and your budgets. It doesn't take much to maximize efforts while working with little money. Start small. Test the waters without too much impact on your time and finances by piggybacking onto existing events or working with established groups or local agencies to enhance both your event and theirs. Nothing succeeds like success. Others who may be reluctant to partner with you initially are usually eager to partner after they see an event in action, so keep at it. Small successes reap big rewards. You'll never know until you try, so get out there!

FOR FURTHER INFORMATION

California State University Channel Islands, http://www.csuci.edu
Ventura County Reading Association, http://www.vcrareading.org

17

PARTNERSHIPS BEYOND THE UNIVERSITY CAMPUS: COMMUNITY CONNECTIONS THAT WORK

Toni Tucker

Academic libraries have been interested in community outreach for more than fifty years (Schneider 2004). How academic libraries define community outreach is changing. In the early 2000s articles written about academic library outreach were limited to marketing services to the campus community (Cruickshank and Nowak 2001) or marketing traditional library services to the community surrounding the university campus (Schneider 2004), such as borrowing privileges, Internet access, and the use of materials. Academic libraries teaching literacy skills was another type of community outreach written about in the late 1990s and early 2000s (Malanchuk and Ochoa 2005). This chapter will focus on how to create partnerships with the community beyond the campus. Examples of community outreach that worked for one academic library are given.

Partnership, collaboration, teamwork, and alliances are all words used to define how one works with another whether in the same office, facility, organization, or an outside party. These words can mean different things to different people, yet they are all intertwined. For the sake of simplicity, partnership will be used throughout this chapter.

This chapter will answer the question, How can partnering with community groups or organizations make the university more relevant to the community in which it is located?

CHARACTERISTICS OF PARTNERSHIP

When we think of partnership, many ideas come to mind. In its simplest form partnership is a relationship between two people or groups. There are business partnerships in which two organizations or two or more people agree to do business together. Partnerships also exist in education. For example, there is a partnership between the teacher and the student, a librarian and a patron. To be a partner means there is an agreement to share responsibilities in a relationship. Not all partnerships are formal, requiring the signing of contracts. Many partnerships are informal; each party agrees to carry out certain responsibilities. They are generally not equal. One partner, usually the initiating partner, agrees to carry out the main responsibilities whereas several other partners may have only one task related to the partnership agreement. Most partnerships are voluntary and usually mutually beneficial to all parties or groups. Partnerships can be between two people or entities, or a large number of people or entities that agree from the beginning the responsibility of each party. The key to partnerships is that a relationship exists and all parties have some level of responsibility in that relationship.

GETTING STARTED

Creating community partnerships should be part of the university library's mission and goals. A mission statement is very broad, sending a clear message about the library's purpose and its reason for existing. Goals are how the library plans to achieve its mission. Goals should be relevant to the mission, precise and measurable. Once goals are set, objectives are then written about how to achieve the stated goals. If the university library is serious about community partnerships, the library must include them in their mission and goals document. Writing it down establishes a commitment from the library to act on the goals and hold library staff accountable for achieving them. Following are examples of a mission statement, goal, and objectives that include community partnerships:

Mission Statement: Our mission is to encourage, enrich, and enlighten the campus and surrounding communities.

Goal: Increase outreach to surrounding communities.

Objectives:

- Develop and carry out an assessment plan.
- Evaluate current library events and activities and tie them to community groups.
- Develop relationships with key personnel in community organizations.
- Host a minimum of two events in the university library that involve community groups.
- Participate in a minimum of two community events set in the community.

One person should have oversight of library partnerships to facilitate uniform communication between the library and the community. Start small the first year by learning who the valid partners are within the community and then begin to build relationships with them. Plan at least one event or activity that involves community partners.

Assess existing organizations in your university's community; don't limit the assessment to other academic, school, public, and special libraries. Look beyond the typical partners to groups such as museums, businesses, social groups, service organizations, local government, media, and health care organizations. These are only a few. Each community has a variety of organizations that would be delighted if they were aware of the university library's interest in partnering. An assessment does not have to be formal. Sit down with a group of library staff members and brainstorm community partners. Ask on the library's email list or blog for ideas of community partners. The more input you receive, the broader the list of potential partners. Imagine big. Don't limit the possibilities by thinking only about organizations that the library has worked with in the past or that have an educational component.

Initially, look at the library's current events and activities and match up community partners with areas that may interest them. Make contacts to find out who performs outreach for each organization suggested by the library team. It is important to build relationships with key people in the organizations identified in the assessment. At the outset, get in touch with those who have outreach responsibilities and request to meet with them to discuss ideas for partnering. Have one or two ideas ready to share to start the conversation. Partnering does not necessarily mean a financial commitment from either side. It may be using a community space for programming or sharing a speaker. To build partnerships, a community center may be willing to post or distribute flyers about a library event. The local history museum may be willing to host an exhibit related to a program happening in the library. Perhaps the university is having a speaker related to health care that a local hospital or clinic would be willing to support. The library can be the conduit between university events and the community.

CREATING STRATEGIC PARTNERSHIPS

Academic libraries are not particularly known for reaching out beyond the campus community to form partnerships. In has only been in the last two decades that academic libraries have felt the need to market services to their own users (Wood, Miller, and Knapp 2007). Most academic libraries now recognize the need to have public relations and marketing responsibilities as part of a library staff member's job. The American Library Association (ALA) and the Association of College and Research Libraries (ACRL) have strong marketing components. Both organizations have committees related to public relations and marketing as well as offer workshops and preconferences at annual conferences and throughout the year about how to market library services. Building on these skills, ACRL is now looking for ways to assist university librarians to reach beyond the campus community. One of the proposal selection criteria for the 2009 annual conference is to "contribute ideas for positioning academic and research librarians to be leaders both on and off campus" (ACRL).

One example of a way to begin building community partnerships is to apply for a traveling exhibit that requires partnerships with organizations beyond the academic library. The ALA's Public Program Office provides grant funding through the National Endowment for the Humanities (NEH) to host traveling exhibits for libraries and museums. Applying for one of these exhibits is an excellent way to look for community support. A main requirement of the grant is to have support from community partners that will provide programming or will promote or create an event related to the traveling exhibit. Traveling exhibits have included subjects such as Abraham Lincoln, Frankenstein, Lewis & Clark, Alexander Hamilton, Jazz, and many others. Current, past, and future traveling exhibit grants can be found at http://www.ala.org/ala/ppo/publicprograms.cfm. For the grant to be funded, community support is required. This type of partnership is a good way to show the university library as a leader in the community for collaborative projects. Programming for traveling exhibits can appeal to all levels of audience from young children to senior citizens. Imagine having around the table preschool, business, museum, public and private school, and library leaders discussing how to join together as partners all under the leadership of the university library. Even if the initial grant is not funded, partnerships have already been cultivated with community groups, allowing other ideas for partnering to evolve.

Sharing authors is another way to build community relationships. Perhaps during Women's History Month the university library hosts a female historian. Share the author with the local history museum or a local history group. If the author is not willing to speak twice, provide information far enough in advance to allow time for community groups to send information to their members about the event. Once you start attracting community members to campus, the chance they will come back increases.

Author visits to local schools is also a way to create goodwill and partnerships with the school district. Many universities have Colleges of Education (COE) that offer children's literature courses. The university library hosting children and young adult authors can be seen as supporting the programs of the COE. When negotiating with authors, include an event at a local public school. Work with the school librarian to have the appropriate age group prepared for the visit. This is a good way to build rapport with the school librarians in your community.

The partnerships discussed so far have shown the university library taking a leadership role. This does not always need to be the case. Watch for events happening in the community. By offering to distribute literature about a program or post information on the library website, the library can begin to build relationships with community organizations. The university library may offer to create a bibliography on a topic a speaker is talking about at a local service club or bring materials related to the topic to an event. Starting to build partnerships takes time and energy, but the benefits can be rewarding.

BUILDING ON PARTNERSHIPS

Once partnerships are established, it becomes easier to think of ways the university library can partner within the community and for community organizations to partner with the university library. As community organizations become aware that the university library is willing to be affiliated with community activities, they will have the library on their radar when seeking partners. The following are ways the university library can partner with community groups:

- Use exhibits as a way to share community resources.
- Help promote community events related to library activities (i.e., author events, literary activities, and book clubs).
- Prepare bibliographies for community exhibits or events.

- Cosponsor author visits.
- Collaborate on grants.
- Facilitate between campus and community events.
- Assist organizations in finding authors.
- Have library staff present in areas of expertise (e.g., on genealogical searching for local service organizations).
- Cosponsor fundraisers.
- Organize events/activities around annual weeks/months (i.e., Banned Book Week, National Library Week, or National Women's History Month).

ILLINOIS STATE UNIVERSITY'S EXPERIENCE DEVELOPING COMMUNITY PARTNERS

All of the above are well and good, but does it work? The library at Illinois State University (ISU) has been building partnerships with the community over the last seven years. ISU is in the twin cities of Bloomington-Normal (pop. 150,000) located 137 miles southwest of Chicago and 164 miles northeast of St. Louis. The university was founded in 1857 as the first public institution of higher education in the state. Today, ISU is a student-centered, multipurpose institution committed to providing undergraduate and graduate programs of the highest quality in the state of Illinois. The university enrolls over 20,000 students from 49 states and 71 countries. ISU's academic programs are supported by the services and collections of Milner Library, which contains more than 1.6 million volumes.

The central mission of ISU is to expand the horizons of knowledge and culture among students, colleagues, and the general citizenry through teaching and research. The university library's mission is for the library to serve its community of users as a dynamic force in the intellectual life of the campus and the community. Goals of the university library include "to promote the library as a cultural center for the campus and community" and "increase collaborative relationships and outreach with other libraries, museums, and agencies locally and statewide."

In light of the library's mission, a position was established in 2001 that included the responsibilities of public relations, development, outreach, and grant support for library faculty and staff. These roles blend together well; they all revolve around building relationships between library staff and grant funders, campus offices, and the community. Having one person overseeing outreach for both the campus and the community offers a unique opportunity to see a bigger picture of what is happening in both places. This allows the university library not only to be a bridge between university library and community activities but to connect other campus activities to community events.

To apply for an NEH traveling exhibit, the library was required to look beyond the campus for partners. Because the Bloomington/Normal community has a strong connection to Lincoln, the library applied for the exhibit Forever Free: Abraham Lincoln's Journey to Emancipation. Through this process the library partnered with organizations with which it had previously not been associated or with which it had loose connections, including a children's museum, county history museum, state historical site, and two large public libraries. Once the grant had been awarded, monthly planning meetings were held beginning eight months prior to the exhibit's opening. Many of the partners in the room had never worked together up to this point. It was interesting to watch the meetings go from strictly business about the exhibit to conversations about what was happening in each institution. Meetings became brainstorming sessions about partnerships. The most unique partnership coming out of these sessions was a fundraiser sponsored by the children's museum and the university library. Through sharing what was happening in the two organizations, each found out the other was planning to hold a fundraiser by hosting a murder mystery dinner. Both organizations, located within walking distance of each other, were planning to hold the fundraisers during the same month and draw largely from the same community audience. Although they seemed unlikely partners for a fundraising event, joining together created a partnership that has successfully hosted three fundraisers. After costs are deducted, proceeds are shared equally. The first two years the fundraiser was a murder mystery dinner held in the museum; the third year a trivia night was held at the university library to try to draw in more of the college-age crowd. The event was so successful, raising the proceeds by 75 percent over the murder mystery dinners, that the two organizations agreed to host a second trivia night together.

Through the traveling exhibit grant process, informal partnerships were strengthened and formal partnerships were developed. The history museum and the library had worked together in the past but in a very casual way. After working together on the grant, more formal partnerships, such as sharing authors and collections, began to take place. The library and the history museum wrote additional grants together to digitize collections. They also began marketing each other's programs. The partnership created more awareness of what is happening in the community.

The NEH and ALA traveling exhibit program brought together a group of organizations; the people representing the organizations developed long-lasting relationships that went far beyond the grant cycle. New partnerships were formed for the university library but were also created between other partners. The children's museum and the local history museum have planned events that coincide. Cultural programming that brings together diverse organizations strengthens the community by reaching beyond populations they traditionally serve. A strong community advances the university's ability to draw in faculty members and students. Everyone wins.

The university library has applied for two more traveling exhibits, and community organizations have requested to be a part of the programming. The library demonstrated that together the library and community can provide cultural events that impact the entire community. When good programming is happening, organizations want to be a part of it. The university library at ISU has become part of the cultural fabric of the local community. That the community feels welcome at the university library is proven over and over again as attendance at library events by community members increases.

ISU also has used author visits as a way to build partnerships. Public schools generally do not have the funding to bring in visiting authors but are eager for their students to have exposure to them. This type of relationship building will not bring additional funding to the university, but sharing authors is a way to build positive relationships with schools and provide a way for children to meet positive role models. Annually since 2001, the university library has been sharing an author with local schools. Seven years later, local schools have begun asking if the university library would like to host authors that are visiting the K–12 schools. Having schools share authors with the university is an unexpected consequence of being a good community member. The university library has reached out to schools as a community service; when schools have the opportunity to share back, they think of the library at ISU. It takes time to build partnerships, but the rewards benefit the entire university community.

Attending community events and engaging in conversations with community leaders led to an unusual partnership for the ISU library. An ISU librarian attended an open house at the local Community Cancer Center. The center's director was inquiring informally if anyone knew of a speaker that could engage an audience for their annual cancer survivor day banquet. Previous speakers had spoken mostly about the medical aspects, from nutrition to caregiver assistance; the director was looking for a speaker with a lighter message. The librarian suggested an author she had met at an ALA Conference and whose books she had subsequently read. The fictional character was a cancer survivor and amateur detective. From that conversation a relationship developed between the university library and the Cancer Center. The university library agreed to contact the author because it had more experience working with author visits and also wrote a proposal for a grant that required a partnership between a library and community organization to cover some of the expenses. The grant was funded and a partnership was born. The author agreed to be the keynote for the Cancer Center's Survivor Day and give a presentation at the university library on writing in the mystery genre. Both organizations benefited from the partnership and are looking at other ways to share author events. This is one example of many where a library staff member made a connection between the library and a community organization. Library staff members at ISU consistently hear about and ask to volunteer for community activities such as the library fundraisers. When they hear of opportunities or have an idea, they bring it to the outreach coordinator. It has taken time to get library staff members to "get it," but it is well worth the effort.

Banned Book Week (BBW), held in late September, is a great way to build partnerships. This time, instead of other libraries, ISU formed a partnership with a local bookstore. Over the last three years the ISU library and the bookstore have cosponsored banned book readings during BBW. The readings take place in the bookstore during weekday lunch hours. The library and bookstore staff meet throughout the summer to select fifteen readers, matching banned books that suit the selected readers. Readers are a mix of university and community members. The bookstore manager and a library staff member send letters requesting the readers respond if they are interested in participating. What makes this partnership unique is that the bookstore approached the library. The store manager, who had worked at book signings for the library, had always wanted to hold an event during BBW, and the opportunity to partner with the ISU library presented itself. In its third year, the program is considered a success. Both community and university members attend the readings. Partnering with a business that may seem like a competitor has turned out to be rewarding for the university library. The bookstore now helps financially by cosponsoring author visits. Future plans are in the works to have an author per year sponsored by the bookstore for the community on the ISU campus. It all started by sharing a program between the library and a business. Everyone wins—the university, the bookstore, and the community!

SUSTAINABILITY

The ISU library has demonstrated that partnerships can develop and grow by cultivating relationships with a variety of community groups and businesses. Starting with small steps in 2001, we have been reaching out into the local community on a consistent basis. Relationships are kept alive by continuing to look for ways to partner even in small ways. Making connections with the community needs to be coordinated by one person, yet it is everyone's responsibility at the library to keep their ears open for partnership opportunities when attending community events or visiting the local museum with their family. It is also the community's responsibility to bring forward ideas for ways their business or organization can partner with the university library. Once the ISU library put itself out into the community, the library staff and community now "get it." Partnership activities with the community are considered the norm. It did not happen by partnering occasionally. The university library consistently needs to keep itself on the community's radar.

CONCLUSION

To answer the question posed at the beginning of this chapter: How can partnering with community groups or organizations make the university more relevant to the community in which it is located? For the university library to be relevant to the surrounding community it has to be part of the community, not only participating in community events but taking a leadership role in creating events as well. Heather Young, of the Children's Discovery Museum in Normal, Illinois, states: "I feel that ISU's university library partnership brings the campus to the community. It acquaints or reacquaints community members with the University and its mission, and reminds them that the University is not an island unto itself, but rather an enormous partner of the entire community. I have always believed and cherish the fact that it brings two or more audiences together for a common purpose. We have grown our base of donors and event attendees because of the partnerships we have created. It is a win-win for both entities."

This chapter has touched on only a few ways university libraries can reach out to their surrounding communities. Each community is unique; relationships between universities and the communities they live in are unique. The university library has opportunities to engage the community that other university units may not have. Community members are already accustomed to using the resources of the university library; other campus units may not have the opportunity to welcome the community into their spaces as freely as the library. Sharing exhibits, authors, and librarian expertise are only a few ways to begin to build upon relationships already in place. Relationship building with the local community can create positive feelings not only for the university library but the entire university. The library can take a leadership role in demonstrating how to build community relationships. For over twenty years libraries have been honing their marketing skills to reach the campus. It is now time to take those skills beyond the campus and into the local community.

"You can't stay in your corner of the Forest waiting for others to come to you. You have to go to them sometimes" (Power, Milne, and Shepard 1995).

REFERENCES

ACRL 14th Annual Conference. http://acrl.org/ala/acrl/acrlevents/seattle/program/selectioncriteria.cfm (accessed April 20, 2008).

Cruickshank, John and David G. Nowak. "Marketing Reference Resources and Services Through a University Outreach Program." *The Reference Librarian* 35 (2001): 265–280.

Malanchuk, Iona R. and Marilyn N. Ochoa. "Academic Librarians and Outreach Beyond the College Campus." *Southeast Librarian* 53 (2005): 23–29.

Powers, Joan, A. A. Milne, and Ernest H. Shepard. *Pooh's Little Instruction Book*. New York: Dutton, 1995.

Schneider, Tina. "Outreach: Why, How and Who? Academic Libraries and Their Involvement in the Community." *The Reference Librarian* 39 (2004): 199–213.

Wood, Elizabeth J., Rush Miller, and Amy Knapp. *Beyond Survival: Managing Academic Libraries in Transition*. Westport, CT: Libraries Unlimited, 2007.

Part 5

DISCIPLINE-SPECIFIC OUTREACH

18

GOVERNMENT INFORMATION IN THE 21st CENTURY: A NEW MODEL FOR ACADEMIC OUTREACH

Kirsten J. Clark and Jennifer Gerke

In June 2006 the University of Colorado at Boulder, in partnership with Arizona State Library, Archives and Public Records; New Mexico State Library; Wyoming State Library; and University of Utah, received a Laura Bush 21st Century Librarian Program grant through the Institute of Museum and Library Services (IMLS). Entitled "Government Information in the 21st Century," the grant is a five-state continuing education program to train reference and public service librarians and library workers in the use of electronic government information. Many would call this a worthy endeavor in and of itself, especially with so much government information freely available online. The University of Colorado IMLS grant does more, however, and that is the topic of this chapter.

The Government Printing Office's Federal Depository Library Program has been in place for over 110 years, its backbone being the distribution of documents in print and microfilm to over 1,300 depository libraries across the United States.[1] These depositories can be found in academic, public, and special libraries, with each having designated depository librarians available to help patrons find and use government information. This system has worked for the majority of its history. However, with over 90 percent of current government information now available online, the job of the government information specialist is no longer tied to a bricks-and-mortar building. In the twenty-first century, some could argue that any library staff member could be a government information specialist with access to government resources.

A recent OMB Watch and Center for Democracy & Technology article, however, shows some disagreement with the above statement. According to their research, many government sites cannot be found through commercial search engines. Much of the information is hidden deep within agency websites and thus inaccessible to the average user. As the report states, "With as many as 80 percent of Internet users accessing government information through third party search engines, these uncrawlable sites pose a significant problem. Many Americans are failing to find authoritative government sources, or worse, concluding that the information or service doesn't exist" (OMB Watch 2007, 3). Although the report centered on the searching habits of the general public, the same could be said for any library staff that does not have a deep knowledge of how government information is arranged.

OVERVIEW OF GRANT

The "Government Information in the 21st Century" grant is an effort to meet this new need for government information expertise outside the traditional depository library setting. It centers on three development phases: (1) developing government information content modules that highlight the main resources for broad subject topics, (2) providing train-the-trainer information to government information specialists so they feel comfortable training their peers, and (3) training library staff throughout the five-state region covered by the grant, including Arizona, Colorado, New Mexico, Utah, and Wyoming. At the center of this grant is the University of Colorado. Though one could argue that any depository library could be the instigator of a grant like this one, the University of Colorado, as a large academic institution, has many of the resources needed to make the grant a success. The University of Colorado Government Publications Library also has an ongoing relationship with the depository libraries and librarians in the five-state area and is respected throughout the depository library community.

The Federal Depository Library Program contains two types of depositories: selective and regional. Though both contain documents collections and offer reference and instruction services, regional libraries provide additional support for the administration of selective libraries in their state. The University of Colorado is one such regional that has a history of outreach to other libraries in the program. In addition, the University has a Carnegie class of RU/VH (research university with very high research activity). This ranking illustrates a strong research focus on campus, including extensive grant experience. Together, these attributes provide Colorado with a strong grounding on which to build this endeavor.

Colorado houses grant administration, including the grant writer, principal investigators, and project manager, and each of the other four states involved has a state coordinator. The coordinator ensures that the state is following the grant requirements and reports back to grant administration at regular intervals. In addition, there is an overarching planning committee comprised of the principal investigators, project manager, state coordinators, and a group of librarians representing different library types. This group provides a sounding board for ideas and participates in planning the various aspects of the grant. By collaborating at the grant-planning level with representatives of all types of libraries, the grant ensures that the needs of all are being met through each of the three phases.

CONTENT DEVELOPMENT

Demographics, Environment, Small Business, History...the list of topics that can include government resources is unending. Think of the variety of reference questions asked at any library, academic or public, and there is a good chance a government information source will help answer it. With so much content, the first decision of the grant administration was to decide on the most common topics to cover in training modules for both the train-the-trainer conference and later outreach to nondepository libraries. After an initial list of topics was created by the planning committee, the group developed a survey that was sent to depository libraries within the grant region. In sending the survey to depository librarians rather than those who might be trained in the third phase, the grant drew on the expertise of those with government information backgrounds. On the basis of the survey results, the highest ranked topics were selected for the first phase of development to meet the perceived needs of nongovernment information library staff. A later survey was sent out to all library staff in each state asking for input into their ranking of the module topics. This information was later used in developing state plans for training.

The importance of the knowledge base available at the University of Colorado cannot be understated at this early stage. The University of Colorado Government Publications Library website is well known throughout the depository library field and is used by researchers around the world. To provide a template for additional module development, the government publications staff created the first module on demographics. The materials included needed to be easily adaptable to different training venues because some trainers would have access to state-of-the-art computer labs whereas others would be training in rooms with limited Internet or hands-on access.

The materials also needed to be stored on an easily accessed website where the information can be updated as new government sites are created or revised. In addition, as the next stages of the grant began, the training modules needed to be expandable to include information adapted and/or created based on real-life experiences using the modules. The planning committee chose OCLC's WebJunction as the content site. WebJunction is built on the premise of supplying training for librarians and that fit well with the mission of this grant.

Once the demographics module was in place, module development teams were created for the other nine topics in the first round of development. A full list of the modules is available at the WebJunction "Government Information in the 21st Century" site.[2] Team members were pulled from across all five states and a few from outside the grant region, with the main criterion being that they dealt with government information on a regular basis. Many teams contained members from both public and academic libraries, thereby helping to create balanced module content that focused on the government information needs of both a public library worker who is working with the general populace and the academic librarian who meets with faculty and provides bibliographic instruction for students. To facilitate work across the large geographic region, teams used conference calls, email, and, most importantly, wikis to collaborate.

Guides to government resources are an important piece of each module's content. For instance, many library staff are overwhelmed by the amount of information found on the Census Bureau website, so the demographics module contains handouts and Web pages that walk trainees through the site's main database, *American Factfinder*, as well as how to use another key resource, *American Community Survey*. Other resources include "real-life" exercises, overviews of agencies, and resource lists. The focus of the information is federal government sites, although some, such as the Legal Resources module, focus on state-level information. In addition, one module, International Relations and Foreign Information, includes sources outside the United States.

The University of Colorado's role in the module development was that of content management, especially making sure that there was continuity between the modules in both arrangement and resources. In addition, grant administrative staff made sure the topics were adequately covered. By the end of round one, ten modules had been developed for the Train-the-Trainer Conference: demographics; legal information; immigration & citizenship; environment; health & medicine; consumer information; small business; history & genealogy; crime & justice; and energy & natural resources. An additional thirteen modules were created after the conference.

TRAIN-THE-TRAINER CONFERENCE

The development of the first-round training modules occurred from Fall 2006 to Spring 2007 so they would be ready for the Train-the-Trainer Conference hosted at the University of Colorado on June 7–8, 2007. During the first day of the conference, depository librarians from the five-state region came to Boulder, Colorado, to learn about the grant, to learn methods for teaching adult learners, and to be trained in the modules by the content development teams. On the second day, trainers met with their state coordinators and used the state survey results to map out a training plan.

Attendees of the Train-the-Trainer Conference committed to teaching at least two training sessions before September 2008, the end of the grant period. These sessions could be within their library or within the same town or city. For instance, an academic library could do a session about demographics for their colleagues and a session about legal issues for the local public library. Another could provide training at the state library association's annual conference where they would reach librarians and library workers from all types of libraries and then do a session at a smaller library in a remote part of the state.

The conference provided trainers with grounding in the grant requirements, a basic understanding of the modules, and an understanding that, although each state had its own training plan, everybody was working toward the same goal. An added benefit and one highlighted again and again in the conference evaluations was the camaraderie that developed between trainers within the same state, across state lines, and from different types of libraries. Some comments from the conference evaluations include:

- "I liked to see everyone's ideas—I'm charged up to incorporate new material and engaging ways to present."
- "Seeing modules...it began to feel natural to know how to use them and how to proceed in preparing presentations."
- "Networking with others to ensure that I will not be the only one fulfilling these goals."

However, the transition from theory to practice is a big step, as many trainers found out when the third phase of the grant began.

REACHING OUT TO THE COMMUNITY OF LIBRARIANS

After the conference the depository librarians went back to their states to begin outreach to their communities. Between July 2007 and March 2008, 310 librarians were trained. Each attendee completed a short survey that asked some basic demographic questions along with questions on comfort and knowledge of government information.[3] Of the 189 individuals who identified their library type, 74 came from academic institutions, 97 from public libraries, 3 from government/state libraries, 11 from school libraries, and 4 from special libraries. In addition to attracting a diverse pool of attendees, these trainings took place in public libraries, schools, state libraries, academic institutions, and many other locations across the five states involved in the grant.

This multistate, multi-institutional outreach resulted in a variety of approaches to reaching the nondepository librarians. Some trainers focused first on reaching their home institutions (public, academic, and state). Others focused on reaching users at preestablished conferences or statewide events that in many cases had few, if any, training sessions on government information. Because these were typical outreach methods, this section looks more in-depth at the training done in nonstandard locations for academic librarians, such as public libraries.

Although there may be projects that can be successful with basic outreach, such as emails and mailings, this was not one of them. Public libraries know that there are government resources that might be useful to their users, but they may be reluctant to use valuable training time learning about e-government resources. One way the grant attempted to address this problem was through careful selection of topics, using the survey discussed earlier. The survey also served as initial promotion, piquing interest in the free training to be offered.

Even with this initial outreach, more work needed to be done to convince potential attendees that the training would be useful. Providing training in local libraries was a successful method of attracting participants. This was especially true in states the size and distribution of the five-state grant region, some of which have comparably small and geographically dispersed populations. Although cities like Albuquerque, New Mexico, or Denver, Colorado, can host centralized training, geography, such as mountain ranges, poses significant challenges. The different states have approached this problem in a variety of ways.

Librarians in New Mexico and Arizona teamed up to reach a number of the small tribal colleges on the New Mexico/Arizona border. For example, picture three trainers in a car driving across the Navajo Reservation, training at one college in the morning and crossing the mountains to train at the next one that afternoon. In Colorado, one trainer scheduled a training session in a local high school on the eastern plains and invited librarians from the surrounding counties. Librarians from these areas would need a full day of travel to go to and from a major population center. Many small libraries can ill afford to let even one employee be gone a whole day, but one or two people can make time to attend a half-day or one-hour session presented locally. The "Government Information in the 21st Century" grant also provides student stipends. The fifty dollar stipend provides financial support to cover the costs of travel and meals to and from the training session.

Another barrier to broad-based participation is the perception that finding government information is hard. Becoming an expert in government information takes

Table 18.1
Trainings Requested and Rankings

Topic	Trainings Requested	Survey Ranking
Legal Information	13	2
Demographics	10	1
Overview of Government Info	10	Not surveyed
Consumer Information	5	7
Elections & the Political Process	5	16
History and Genealogy	5	9
Small Business & Entrepreneurship	4	4
Health and Medicine	4	3
Energy and Natural Resources	3	6
Citizenship and Immigration	3	5

work and dedication, but it is important to remind participants that the goal is not to become experts in everything, but rather to become aware of resources that can be used to better answer their patron questions. The WebJunction site, with its collection of resources, links, and guides, remains freely accessible to users after the training sessions. They can return again and again to practice and enhance their knowledge. The training also provides trainees with the name of a local contact who can help with future questions.

Each training session focuses on particular areas of government information. This concentration allows the user to apply the knowledge gained to needs within their libraries. The host institution takes the lead in the selection of topics covered, which builds further interest in the process. Table 18.1 lists the various topics requested for training up through March 2008. It probably comes as no surprise that legal information and demographics are the most popular topics. The other topics chosen, except one, are the same topics identified by the surveys as being among the top ten needs. How does the "Government Information in the 21st Century" grant get people to request training? Requests come from a variety of outreach methods, including personal contacts, articles in state newsletters, and direct mailings. The most successful efforts often come through partnerships with organizations with a well-established training role in their respective states. For example, each year the Colorado Library Consortium (CLIC) provides numerous workshops that are well attended by public and academic librarians from throughout the state. This partnership allows trainers in Colorado to reach a group of people who may ignore a call from a depository librarian in Boulder.

After overcoming these hurdles, how do librarians teach librarians and, just as importantly, how do we ensure we are providing useful information? One of the consistent themes that emerged from the session evaluations is the desire for "more." When asked "Was there anything we could have done differently to make the workshop either more useful or more productive for you?" the responses included a series of what could be called the "more" comments: more hands-on practice, more printouts of websites, more exercises—with answers, more examples and sample searches, more visuals, more samples of forms, more time, more than just one or two subjects covered.

At the Train-the-Trainer Conference presenter Deb Greely (2007), from the University of Denver Education Department, spoke directly to the issues associated with training adult learners. Although adults do not learn in the same ways as children, they share many of the same needs and desires. Greely cites the need for a system that allows for "interactive, competency-based, individual and in groups, applied, and reflective" learning (Greely 2007). Many of the earlier "more" comments can be tied to these needs, especially in the areas of interactive and applied learning.

One lens for examining the needs of the adult learner is to consider the theory of "point of need" as applied to student learners. Many academic librarians conducting bibliographic instruction encounter students asking, directly after a class, how to do something demonstrated during the session. Some of this could be ascribed to distraction or teaching styles, but another factor is the lack of immediate need. In this context the theory may be that public service librarians never know what they might use and, therefore, everything could be considered "point of need." To make training relevant, trainers need to include numerous examples that illustrate potential uses for the materials.

Does this training work? According to survey data, the average comfort level with using government information before the training is 2.78 on a scale of 1 to 5, with an increase to 3.13 after the training. This increase is not as high as one might expect, but this is probably due to the fact that some trainees actually had a decrease in comfort level with government information after the training. This correlates back to the comments trainees made expressing a desire for "more" of everything. Though the training increased the knowledge of the participants, it also illustrated that some librarians may not know as much as they originally thought. This also reflects the OMB Watch report cited earlier that reveals the inability of many commercial search engines to find government information. One participant stated, "I often use Google in creative ways, hoping it will lead me to what I need." It may become clearer to participants after training that a search engine approach is not the best strategy for finding government information.

This discussion reflects the results of the first nine months of training, with six months remaining. As the grant continues, the methods used by the various states and trainers continue to be shared to achieve the desired outcome of the grant: a base of trained library staff who continue to use government information to meet the needs of their users.

SCENARIOS

Because of the complexities of administrating a grant of this size, a large research institution with the resources and collection expertise served as the lead, but the concept can be scaled down to meet the more modest needs of academic library outreach. The following section describes two possible scenarios for application of this model by smaller academic libraries.

Scenario I—Digital Projects Outreach

How can you take an outreach project focused on government information and apply it to another area? One aspect of this training is outreach on materials in the digital realm. Though this grant focuses on government information, outreach could focus on other free resources (e.g., digital projects). Many academic institutions have dedicated significant time and resources to digitize materials, many with the objective of sharing these resources with others.

These digital projects can use some of the techniques for outreach used in the "Government Information in the 21st Century" grant. First, examine the use of the online presence for the projects. This grant has focused more on face-to-face training of librarians, but there has been a lot of work in developing online training materials. The grant's navigation pages in WebJunction received 251,805 hits between March 2007 and January 2008. This is obviously a much larger group of users than the 310 attendees of the training sessions. On a basic level, digital projects could include not only help files for assistance in using the resource but also training materials on how to make the best use of a particular digital project.

These training materials can be as simple as step-by-step instructions on database navigation to an in-depth discussion of how to integrate the resource into library instruction or school lesson plans. The most popular resource on the WebJunction grant site is a set of quick links to the United States Citizenship and Immigration Service followed closely by a guide to the Census Bureau's *American Factfinder* database.[4] These materials obviously demonstrate an area of need for government resources. It is of interest that, although ten of forty-eight training sessions have contained information on demographics, only three sessions have been on citizenship and immigration resources. This finding suggests there may be a disconnect between the online users and in-person users or that those requesting training do not have a clear understanding of their training needs.

Another way to use ideas developed in this grant is to focus on face-to-face training in a local setting. Traditional library outreach to other librarians has focused primarily on library conferences or events. Although there have been some training sessions conducted at conferences, the majority of the training for the "Government Information in the 21st Century" grant have been conducted at local libraries. As mentioned earlier, smaller libraries lack sufficient personnel to support trainings in distant locations, even if it is free. Because many libraries do sponsor in-house training workshops, speaking to individual institutions about their needs provides opportunities to present resources in a way that is useful to the library. Depending on the type of resource being presented, it might be appropriate to contact school libraries. Online resources can sometimes be used to help meet state curriculum standards. This example of mixed outreach, using both online tutorials about how to integrate digital resources into lesson plans and direct outreach to school systems, is one possible model.

Scenario 2—Community Partners Outreach

The University of Colorado identified a need for training on the use of online government information. Because many libraries do not identify government information as a high priority for training, another scenario with the same limitation, working with recent immigrants, provides a useful example for comparison. In many parts of the United States, there is a strong need for training of library staff and community groups about the cultures and backgrounds of recent immigrants.

Using the "Government Information in the 21st Century" project as a model, a library could develop training modules around various aspects of immigrant life. Some of these modules could contain basic guides to resources available in the local area or state, much like those about government information created for each of the modules for this project. However, there would also need to be resources available for specific immigrant groups, such as Somali or Hispanic populations. As immigration patterns change over time, the module framework could be adapted for a new population.

Although the grant used the Federal Depository Library Program as its backbone, there are other "backbones" available for libraries to use when setting up similar programs. For the "Government Information in the 21st Century" grant, the training funds came from an Institute of Museum and Library Services grant. State library associations and regional networks are strong entities that share some of the same goals as this project. With their support, training could be included in annual conferences or incorporated into regional network training. The "Government Information in the 21st Century" model could be applied to a shared commitment between libraries and regional or state associations.

CONCLUSION

We have described our project and provided examples for outreach implementation, but the focus should be on the sharing of knowledge. Librarians all have special talents and skills that can be shared in a broader context. These skills, no matter the size of your library, combined with outreach enable all to provide the best information and services to their respective patrons.

NOTES

1. More information about the Federal Depository Library Program can be found at http://www.fdlp.gov.

2. More information about WebJunction and the "Government Information in the 21st Century" site can be found at http://www.webjunction.org/gi21. This site provides background information about the grant, the training modules, the Train-the-Trainer Conference, and the training sessions done since the conference.

3. For information on what forms are filled out, including copies of the surveys, check out the Trainer Resources on the WebJunction site, http://webjunction.org/do/Navigation;?category=17739.

4. These guides and many others can be found on the WebJunction Demographics and Citizenship and Immigration websites, http://webjunction.org/gi21.

REFERENCES

Greely, Deb. *Teaching and Training the Adult Learner.* Presentation, IMLS Grant Train-the-Trainer Conference, Boulder, CO, June 7, 2007. http://www.webjunction.org/do/DisplayContent?id=17890 (accessed March 26, 2008).

OMB Watch and Center for Democracy & Technology. *Hiding in Plain Sight: Why Important Government Information Cannot Be Found through Commercial Search Engines.* December 11, 2007. http://www.ombwatch.org/info/searchability.pdf (accessed March 22, 2008).

19

<hr/>

HEALTH INFORMATION OUTREACH TO UNDERSERVED POPULATIONS IN BALTIMORE, MARYLAND

Paula G. Raimondo, Anna Tatro, and Alexa Mayo

BACKGROUND

The Health Sciences and Human Services Library (HS/HSL) at the University of Maryland, Baltimore, supports 5,300 students and 6,600 faculty and staff members on a 61-acre research and technology complex of 62 buildings, including the University of Maryland Medical Center. The seven professional and graduate schools on campus include schools of law, dentistry, medicine, nursing, pharmacy, and social work. The HS/HSL serves all but the Law School.

The Library has had a long-standing commitment to providing excellent quality services and resources to the faculty, staff, and students at the University. In 2004 a new executive director came on board with a mandate for change. During the following year the library underwent a process of self-evaluation in which library staff reviewed the organizational structure, institutional values, and relevance to the campus and community. The outcome was a change to the organizational structure complemented by a revised strategic plan.

A new vision, mission, and strategic initiatives were announced. In a key change, the library broadened its vision of service to include providing quality health information beyond the boundaries of the campus to the city of Baltimore and throughout the state. In addition, library faculty identified "collaboration" as a core institutional value. For the first time, the HS/HSL—the only publicly funded health sciences library in the state—had a strategic initiative related to health information outreach: "Collaborate and build partnerships to create healthier communities throughout Maryland and beyond."

With this goal clearly articulated, library staff set out to create projects to lay the groundwork for outreach through partnerships. As a first step, we gathered data about the health information needs of Maryland citizens. In 2004 we applied for and received an award from the National Network of Libraries of Medicine, Southeastern/Atlantic Region (NN/LM/SEA) to assess health information needs and identify underserved populations in Maryland. To gather the data, we invited a diverse group of participants and convened a series of health information summits across the state. Our goal was to identify health information needs, review current outreach programs, develop potential outreach partners, and make recommendations to improve Maryland residents' access to health information.

Four health information outreach planning meetings were held in regions across Maryland: the Eastern Shore, Western Maryland, Baltimore City, and Southern Maryland. Eighteen people participated in the health information outreach summit in Baltimore. The group included public, academic, and school librarians, staff from community-based organizations, and health department employees. The half-day summit began with introductions; participants shared information about how they used health information in their work in the community. The executive director of the HS/HSL and the director of the NN/LM/SEA gave short presentations on the goals and opportunities offered by their organizations. In a live Web demonstration, a member of the services staff discussed the National Library of Medicine's (NLM) *Go Local*, a Web resource with links to health programs and services throughout Maryland.

To gather additional data, summit attendees participated in focus group sessions. Through these interviews, we learned about the many health information needs of Baltimore City residents. We identified underserved populations (homeless, immigrants with language barriers, teenagers aged out of foster care, employed single women with no health care, and families suffering from substance abuse); common barriers to health care access; strategies for promoting health; and strategies for delivering the health information message. Participants at the summit provided powerful examples of the lack of health information resources in Baltimore City.

A participant at the outreach summit was the associate director at the University of Maryland's Social Work Community Outreach Service (SWCOS). This organization is committed to creating innovative models of service to strengthen underserved individuals, families, and communities. Outreach through SWCOS is often accomplished in partnerships with the university, nonprofit organizations, public institutions, and private agencies throughout Baltimore and the metropolitan area. In providing outreach to the community, the SWCOS staff frequently works with people in need of health and referral information, including Baltimore residents. As a result of her participation in Baltimore's health information summit, the SWCOS associate director approached a member of the HS/HSL *Go Local* development team with an idea for a collaborative outreach project—work together to introduce *Maryland Health → Go Local*, *MedlinePlus* and other NLM products to underserved populations in Baltimore.

Baltimore is a city in need. In 2000 Baltimore had a poverty rate of 18.8 percent for families and 22.9 percent for individuals. The median income in 2004 was $30,078, which ranks 87th among the 100 largest cities (City of Baltimore n.d.). The Brookings Institution Center on Urban and Metropolitan Policy (2003) profile, *Living Cities: the National Community Development Initiative: Baltimore in Focus* reports that two out of every five Baltimore families with children live below or near the poverty line. SWCOS staff and library faculty understood the need to provide improved access to health information in Baltimore. With this in mind, HS/HSL faculty and SWCOS staff prepared and submitted a proposal, *"Health Information Outreach to Underserved Populations in Baltimore, Maryland,"* to the NN/LM/SEA. We received notice of an award in 2006; work began in January 2007.

PROJECT OBJECTIVES

Objective 1: Improve access to health information in underserved Baltimore neighborhoods by improving skills to locate the health information, resources, and services that affect their physical, social, and emotional well-being.

Objective 2: Create and support an independent network of service providers and community leaders to teach others about *MedlinePlus* and *Maryland Health → Go Local*.

Objective 3: Identify ways to improve the effectiveness of *MedlinePlus* and *Maryland Health → Go Local* to reduce health disparities.

Objective 4: Design and widely distribute support materials for *Maryland Health → Go Local*.

Objective 5: Publish or present findings of the subcontract to a wide audience.

MEDLINEPLUS

MedlinePlus (www.medlineplus.gov) is NLM's consumer health information website. The site contains free, authoritative information intended to educate consumers and help them make informed medical decisions. The information comes from NLM, the National Institutes of Health, and other government agencies and health-related organizations. The site is reviewed at least every six months, and new links are added every day.

MedlinePlus offers drug information, a medical encyclopedia and dictionary, news items from HealthDay News, Reuters Health, the Food and Drug Administration, the Centers for Disease Control, and many other federal agencies with responsibility for addressing health issues. *MedlinePlus* also contains interactive health tutorials, with video and sound, produced by the Patient Education Institute. By using animated graphics, each tutorial explains a procedure or condition in plain language.

Information can be found on *MedlinePlus* by searching or browsing. The site currently contains over 750 health topics in English and over 700 in Spanish. Topics are organized by physiological system, disease, diagnosis and therapy, demographic groups, and health and wellness. Many of the *Health Topics* pages contain links to documents that have been labeled as easy to read by the agency that produced the information.

In 2007 more than 120 million unique visitors went to *MedlinePlus* for authoritative medical and health care information, resulting in about 900,000 Web page views on the website that year.

MARYLAND HEALTH → GO LOCAL

The NLM partners with libraries and library consortia to provide national coverage of health services by including *Go Local* links on *MedlinePlus* health topic pages.

Staff at the HS/HSL gathered and organized information on programs and services for *Maryland Health → Go Local* from city, county, and state health departments, and from social service agencies, community-based organizations, hospitals, and more.

Maryland Health → Go Local is a database that covers local health-related services and programs for specific health conditions and links to information about the conditions in *MedlinePlus*. Consumers read about a health condition in *MedlinePlus* and link to local programs and services in their community through *Maryland Health → Go Local*. There are links to information for hospitals, nursing homes, support groups, adult day care centers, hospice care, substance abuse treatment centers, health screening providers, and more.

A map of Maryland allows the user to click on a county to search for services in a community or search for all programs of that type in the state. These links take users to health services in their local community and direct users of the state or region's *Go Local* site to *MedlinePlus* health topics. Health consumers in Maryland can link directly from each *MedlinePlus* health topic to services offered in Maryland that are related to that particular topic. For example, choosing "Maryland" from the *Go Local* regions on the *MedlinePlus* Breast Cancer page links a user to local services such as cancer clinics, oncologists, and support groups in the state. *Maryland Health → Go Local*'s address is http://medlineplus.gov/Maryland. Including Maryland, there are twenty-four *Go Local* participants. NLM's goal is to have national coverage.

TRAINING

The project librarian's main task was to develop comprehensive training materials for the team. This included creating a demonstration using PowerPoint slides, class scripts for the trainers, exercise questions, and support handouts. The project team worked together to create evaluation forms and a Frequently Asked Questions document and to arrange training sessions in English and Spanish for audiences of various ages. We created a checklist of things to do prior to an outreach event, such as confirm that the Flash application was loaded on the site computers and to make certain that relevant services provided by organizations involved in the training were indexed in *Go Local*.

Backup presentations were created for instances when we might not have Internet access to perform live demonstrations of the websites. The project librarian created a presentation template focusing on resources for alcoholism within *Go Local*, assuming that social work professionals, one of the main target audiences for training, would have a need to access information on that topic. However, the SWCOS staff thought that using "alcoholism" to demonstrate searching could potentially send the wrong message to some of the individuals we train and could affect building rapport with a particular community if we approached them using "alcoholism" as a first example. The SWCOS staff suggested creating a presentation about a medical issue like asthma or diabetes. The project librarian and an SWCOS intern created a PowerPoint presentation about asthma. They also created separate training templates based on the audience (general public versus health care providers). The presentations were translated into Spanish by an SWCOS intern.

During the course of the project, *MedlinePlus* underwent a redesign of navigation features, though content remained consistent. To reflect the changes, we redesigned the presentations and updated some of our handouts. This was a minor setback, especially since the team was thrilled with the changes to *MedlinePlus.*

We presented live training sessions or canned demonstrations to groups of people using a computer, projector, and screen or wall. We also demonstrated searching *Go Local* at exhibits, where most of the training was with individuals or very small groups. The ideal training situations were those where each student had his or her own computer and we were able to project the website live onto a screen. Unfortunately, this was not always possible.

Some community groups would fit us into their already busy meeting agendas but could only give us a short amount of time for a presentation. Though this was better than nothing, to be able to cover the materials thoroughly the ideal conditions were when we had from thirty minutes to an hour for the training sessions and our audience had use of computers.

The project librarian was often the main presenter when the target audience consisted of health care or social work professionals. The SWCOS staff did the majority of off-campus training. The project librarian was the primary support contact for the trainers and was available to provide refresher training as needed. The project librarian attended train-the-trainer sessions when other NLM products were incorporated into the trainings, and she addressed questions about NLM products and services. Time constraints limited us to training participants to search *Go Local* and *Medline Plus* only; instructional materials for other products (e.g., NIH *SeniorHealth. gov*) were distributed as appropriate.

We initially had some challenges deciding how to share information beyond just meeting and emailing. Members of the team were working in separate locations and needed a way to work on the same documents at the same time. A shared network folder was set up by the library's IT department, but it proved too cumbersome to access across divisions. The librarians looked at various project management software options to streamline collaboration, but the software was too costly for such a small project.

A wiki was established by the project librarian as a communication tool for the project team. The wiki was created using PBwiki software, which is free, password protected, and hosted on the Internet so that it is accessible from anywhere that there is Internet access. Using a wiki as means for collaboration was not part of the original proposal, so the team piloted its use, and in the end it proved to be very helpful. Our wiki was used solely for project management, material creation, and tracking; all communication and documents lived in one place for easy organization and reporting. As with other relatively new tools, various members of the project team had different comfort levels using the wiki. Because some on the project team used the wiki and others did not, the SWCOS training scheduler kept track of training sessions manually and entered them into the wiki calendar for the project team.

To encourage community leaders to train others and to continue training once the project was complete, we made all of our presentations and support materials accessible online to the general public. The *Maryland Health → Go Local* website was enhanced to add an "Instructional Materials for the SWCOS Project" link (http://www.hshsl.umaryland.edu/golocal/teaching.html). We plan to maintain the link by keeping the information up to date and by adding new materials when needed. We had a total of 159 hits on the instructional materials site from March through December 2007 and will continue keeping track of usage as long as the site is available.

PUBLICITY

Most promotion for the training sessions was done using flyers and handouts. Announcements were made at community meetings where attendees were encouraged to participate in *Go Local* training sessions. The project team created a flyer for broad distribution that was designed to promote general awareness of *Go Local*. An additional flyer was created as an invitation to a training session and was designed for the time and place to be added as the sessions were scheduled. The flyer templates were mounted on the project training materials website for access by the project team and the trainers. At festivals we used a large banner to promote awareness of *Maryland Health → Go Local*. An effective strategy was to schedule further training with trainees and their colleagues during a session.

A member of the SWCOS staff participating in the project has an extensive background in television production. He worked with the University of Maryland, Baltimore Public Relations Liaison to the School of Social Work to get announcements into local newspapers as well as into campus publications. Members of the project team were interviewed by the campus Office of External Affairs for an article that is to be published in the campus newspaper and distributed widely to other print and online news outlets. The project was highlighted in SWCOS' and HS/ HSL's annual reports; both reports were distributed to the campus and Baltimore community members. Information about *Go Local* was added to SWCOS' "Baltimore Area Resource Manual," a print resource available to individuals and service providers. The latest edition was available in the fall of 2007 and has been widely circulated to service providers in Baltimore City public schools. A poster about the project was presented at the annual meeting of the Mid-Atlantic Chapter of the Medical Library Association. Another poster was shown at the annual meeting of the Medical Library Association in May 2008.

STATISTICS

The following is a summary of training events and participants:

Total number of sessions conducted as part of the project: 40

Total number of sessions in which half or more than half of participants were from minority populations: 28

Total number of participants in the project's sessions: 927

Breakdown of participants:

Health care or service provider, with a subtotal for public health personnel: 438/80

Health sciences library staff member: 3

Public/other library staff member: 3

Member of the general public: 387

Monthly Page views for *Maryland Health → Go Local* during 2007

January	11,445	July	9,105
February	12,525	August	7,242
March	10,034	September	8,980
April	9,415	October	9,120
May	10,555	November	6,845
June	11,491	December	5,879

EVALUATION

A two-month preparation time frame resulted in our having to wait to begin training sessions until early spring, reducing the number of training sessions we could offer. We had intended to train more of the community leaders than we were able to. Instead, some of the training was done directly with community members. Now that the project is complete we hope that community leaders will continue to demonstrate *Go Local* and *MedlinePlus* to their community members.

The training team met periodically during the year to assess progress and to make appropriate changes to the project. Participants shared suggestions for improvement, resulting in changes such as translating the evaluation form into Spanish.

Evaluation sheets in English or Spanish were distributed at the end of most of the training sessions. Overall, the training sessions were well received. Attendees were enthusiastic about *Maryland Health → Go Local* and *MedlinePlus* and said they would recommend the class to a friend.

There was a request for a subject heading for free or low-cost medical services, which was added to the *Go Local* sites as "Health Insurance." Another suggestion was for *Go Local* to indicate when a service provider focuses on Spanish-speaking people. It was requested that *MedlinePlus en Espanol* be linked to *Go Local* and that an option to link back to *Go Local* from *MedlinePlus en Espanol*. Someone requested that maps and directions on *Go Local* be made printer ready. We passed these comments along to the NLM.

We conducted an interview session with community leaders from the area: a social worker/department head from a campus community psychiatry department, a social work intern at a local community center, and two Head Start coordinators. Many search *Go Local* and/or *MedlinePlus* at least once a day; some indicated they search the resources several times a week. They share the information with friends and family as well as community members and clients. However, the responses to the question "How has *Maryland Health → Go Local* helped you answer a question?" indicated that the attendees were confusing *Go Local* and *MedlinePlus.* We explained the differences between the two, but the attendees insisted that they freely navigate from one to the other and don't think of them as separate resources.

Included in the response to the question "What do you like most about *Maryland Health → Go Local?*" were comments such as "The information is easy to understand and the website is easy to train others to use." All attendees expressed appreciation for the quality of the online training resources for *Go Local* and *MedlinePlus.*

We attempted to schedule a second interview group consisting of students on campus who had been trained during the past year. However, because of end-of-semester commitments and final exams, we were unable to locate participants.

The academic calendar made it difficult to schedule training and follow-up sessions during August and December, when students, staff, and faculty typically take time off. We discovered that it is best to plan follow-up sessions for trainees well in advance.

Some participants were unfamiliar with using the Internet. To help with this, one of the SWCOS interns developed a step-by-step written guide, with screenshots, for their use. Some participants did not speak English. Another intern made presentations in Spanish and translated the project evaluation form into Spanish. There is a need to have a Spanish language version of *Go Local*. We have learned that Spanish-speaking immigrants often lack access to health care. Having a language barrier makes the challenge of meeting their health needs even more difficult.

The wireless Internet connection that we used was a great resource. When a connection failed, trainers relied on a PowerPoint presentation, written material, and verbal instruction.

It is most efficient to concentrate training efforts on groups of health and social services providers, rather than the general public, who are interested in the information but do not need it on a daily basis. Because such organizations have much to accomplish with limited resources, we should consider offering some sort of incentive to these groups.

The HS/HSL staff provided their service as an in-kind contribution. Given the number of hours they devoted to the project, it would have been appropriate to include a salary for the staff at the library.

Consider reducing the number of individuals working on the project and giving each individual additional responsibility. This would improve communication within the group and might improve follow-up efforts. The same project could probably be handled with one or two library staff members and three SWCOS staff members, including a student intern, for a total of five people on the team over an eighteen-month time frame.

CONCLUSION

This project provided a positive experience for SWCOS staff, who enjoyed doing the training and working with HS/HSL staff. Working with social workers allowed library staff the opportunity to go into communities where relationships had already been established, so that we were not seen as total strangers.

The SWCOS interns were afforded excellent opportunities for outreach to the community, public speaking, training, team work, and project planning, implementation, and evaluation. The SWCOS interns intend to continue demonstrating and using *Maryland Health → Go Local* now that the project is complete.

We were successful in reaching the medically underserved populations identified in our proposal, including the homeless. The community leaders we have talked with have expressed their intention to continue using and showing others how to use the resources. We have asked them to add links to *MedlinePlus* and *Maryland Health → Go Local* on their websites. The library's visibility within the city and surrounding areas has been increased, and we have a better sense of who is likely to use *Maryland Health → Go Local* and how to market it. Statistics indicate a slight increase in usage, but it is obvious that we will have to demonstrate the value of *Go Local* continuously to increase its visibility and usage in any significant way. By receiving input from the community, we were able to work with the NLM to make *Go Local* a better product.

Note: This project has been funded in whole or in part with federal funds from the National Library of Medicine, National Institutes of Health, under Contract No NO1-LM-6-3502.

REFERENCES

Brookings Institution Center on Urban and Metropolitan Policy. *Living Cities: The National Community Development Initiative. Baltimore in Focus: A Profile from Census 2000.* Washington, D.C.: The Brookings Institute, 2003. http://www.brookings.edu/es/urban/livingcities/baltimore2.pdf (accessed March 10, 2008).

City of Baltimore—Census 2000. http://www.ci.baltimore.md.us/government/planning/census/index.php (accessed March 10, 2008).

ADDITIONAL READINGS

Cook, D., A. F. Bond, P. Jones, and G. L. Greif, "The Social Work Outreach Service within a School of Social Work: A New Model for Collaboration with the Community." *Journal of Community Practice* 10, no. 1 (2002): 17–31.

Gore, S. "All Health is Local: Go Local Massachusetts Helps Consumers Locate Health Care Services Close to Home." *Journal of Consumer Health on the Internet* 10, no. 4 (2006): 1–14.

Richwine, P., E. Skopelja, and L. Rider. "Better than Yellow Pages: Go Local for Health Services Where You Live." *Journal of Consumer Health on the Internet* 10, no. 4 (2006): 15–26.

Workman, T. E. and J. M. Stoddart. "Building Online Health Resources Using Freely Available Tools: The goLocalUtah Experience." *Journal of Consumer Health on the Internet* 11, no. 1 (2007): 15–31.

20

REDEFINING OUTREACH FROM INSIDE THE ACADEMY: LAW SCHOOL LIBRARIES AND THEIR COMMUNITIES

Paula Seeger

How are academic law libraries serving the legal information needs of the larger community—and should they be? As more and more people go to court or try legal options without the benefit of an attorney's assistance, academic law libraries have been asked to help fill the gap in providing legal information and, in some cases, facilitating referrals for legal assistance. Law librarians often find the line between offering legal information and offering legal advice hard to draw, sometimes erring too far on one side or the other. Through collaboration with other libraries, legal service programs, and their law schools, academic law libraries can provide a useful service to community residents; however, much of a library's success relies on its image, role, and mission within the university setting and within the larger community. This chapter discusses these issues and highlights outreach strategies that are currently in place at academic law libraries, gleaned from two polls of academic law librarians the author conducted.

THE SERVICE MISSION IN HIGHER EDUCATION

Within the literature on university outreach to the community, the theme of service emerges clearly when examining the reasons for establishing outreach programming. Outreach is viewed as an extension of the "town-gown" relationship, a term used to denote the interaction between the local community and the academic world located within its boundaries. Over the years, this relationship has seen conflict and tension, but also cooperation and respect as the reality of the interaction plays out in the local economy, government, and infrastructure. This relationship is at the forefront of university outreach offices as they look to develop or advance innovative community partnerships. A similar relationship exists between local communities, specifically the local courts, legal organizations, law firms, and the university's law school. The local legal community and courthouse serve as training grounds for law school students involved with law school clinics, outreach programs, or internships. Community members rely on these programs for legal assistance that is low-cost or free, often meeting with law students at the courthouse or law school. By extension, academic law libraries that serve law school programs are in an opportune situation to reach community members and offer services to lay users of legal resources. "Outreach programs increase the visibility of the library and the university in the community," and help to make the institution seem more accessible (Jesudason 1993, 31).

Outreach is also viewed as an opportunity for clearly establishing authority in the civic engagement of citizens within democratic culture. Under the mission of service, universities use talents within their institutions to partner with community agencies to educate and respond to perceived or stated needs of local citizens. This service mission is especially evident at land grant institutions that were developed with the education of the local citizens in mind. In addition to providing services based on user need and demand, academic law libraries use these roles of outreach to establish positive services to their local communities, both inside and outside university boundaries.

DEFINING OUTREACH IN ACADEMIC LAW LIBRARIES

Before distinguishing between the different types of outreach that law libraries use to engage their users, it is helpful to define "outreach services" as demonstrated by universities. One definition of outreach is that it "involves the generation, transmission, application or preservation of knowledge in manners consistent with university and unit views of [the teaching, research, and service missions] ... these activities are carried out to directly benefit audiences external to the university—and are to be defined by these diverse community groups, in concert with universities" (Lerner and Simon 1998, 14). Despite the insistence found in most definitions that outreach be directed to external groups, there persists the concept and demonstration of active "internal" outreach, especially in academic law libraries. This internal outreach is directed at providing and promoting information and services to the law school or university community to which the library belongs. Examples include internal document delivery or book retrieval services, teaching and research support services for faculty, workshops or specialized research support for law school students or organizations, or special borrowing privileges for alumni of the law school. These services may be coordinated by a specific department or staff person, such as a "faculty services librarian" or "outreach and reference librarian." Internal outreach services often encompass a significant part, if not all, of the outreach services provided by an academic law library.

In contrast, "external" outreach is directed at providing information and services to the community outside the law school or university. Members of this community include other librarians, legal service providers, corporations, community organizations, as well as the general public. Most academic law libraries do not have extensive external outreach services, despite the fact that many academic law libraries are publicly financed and otherwise open for public use. It is unknown if this is because academic libraries consider their services less vital as community resources than those of public libraries, or if it is because they are more focused on providing services to their primary users within their campus communities. According to the literature, "Academic libraries determine their interaction with their communities based on three factors: whether a need is expressed from outside the academy, whether they see their mission as an invitation to pursue an action on their own accord, or whether they construct a form of outreach in response to a specific problem or crisis" (Schneider 2003, 199). Academic law libraries base decisions about their interactions and levels of involvement on similar criteria. Some factors a library might consider include its traditional role within the university, whether the university is privately or publicly funded, and whether the law library is open to the public. The library also might consider whether other area resources are available for public use, such as county or court law libraries. In a time of competition for public tax funding, duplication of efforts is often viewed as a waste of time and money, especially in medium to small cities. In large urban areas the demand for legal information services is so great that there is usually no duplication of resources between multiple service providers in keeping up with population growth.

OUTREACH AS CIVIC ENGAGEMENT

The literature is clear that "…our society must think of innovative and productive ways to make the wealth of higher educational resources more useful to the broader society" (Maurrasse 2001, 187). In that vein, the time is right for law librarians to step up and take the lead with regard to educating or reeducating the public about American government and its resources and publications, which are at the core of basic legal research, whether at the federal, state, or local/municipal level. In an era of decreasing civics education in American schools, increasing numbers of citizens arriving from other countries without basic knowledge of American government or laws, and increasing levels of misinformation being pushed out by media sources or special interest groups, basic skills with finding and using government or legal resources is an actual need that must be addressed in a democratic society. Law librarians, familiar with legal and government publications and research, are primed to become leaders in establishing and conducting programs of civic engagement and education. "As community leaders turn to libraries for help in solving social problems, we are in a unique position to share the depth and breadth of our knowledge base and training" (McKinstry and Garrison 2001, 165).

Academic law librarians are perhaps most contextually suited to lead programs of this type because they can more easily rely on institutional support while using their academic networks to connect with those organizations that can reach the most citizens. For example, partnering with areas of the schools of education, public policy, or government, a law library can reach young people still in primary or high school, perhaps with educational opportunities or unique events such as a "civics bee" or "government information bowl."

Partnering with public libraries or service organizations, the law library can provide outreach programs such as topical research classes or basic legal research programs, using both print and online resources. Partnering with law school departments, the law library can provide online tutorials, in-house print displays and study guides, and special forum events, such as town hall meetings or presentations with members of the government or legal community. The law library can also work to produce or provide access to local government or community legal resources, such as local court decisions or legal briefs or filings, as well as government reports or other local civic information.

An advantage academic law libraries have over many other smaller law libraries is their government depository status, especially with legal resources or United Nations or state documents. Though these libraries usually offer limited, if any, circulation of print resources to the public, and the United States Government Printing Office (GPO) has committed to digitizing the "entire collection of legacy materials that have been disseminated through the Federal Depository Library Program" (United States Government Printing Office 2008), state and United Nations documents continue to be collected in larger academic law libraries in print, microform, and electronic format. Despite GPO documents being available freely online, community members engaged in legal research will find an advantage to using a depository collection, especially because academic law libraries are more likely to have a librarian who specializes in government publications and can more readily assist in the location and use of these documents, no matter their format. By increasing access to these resources, law libraries provide a valuable service to the community engaged in legal research and civic engagement while saving valuable collection budget money and space.

OUTREACH STRATEGIC DECISIONS

Once an academic law library determines that it is committed to making outreach services a priority, either through the mission, strategic planning, or other administrative decision, and the commitment is supported with funding, staffing, and institutional resources, there are several decision items that will lead to an effective outreach services strategy. As library staff members prepare outreach service programs, they need to decide what level of involvement they are willing to provide and commit to: a partnership; a solo venture; a supportive sponsorship of another library, department or agency; or tangential involvement with no direct role, perhaps as consultant. Who will make decisions regarding involvement: an outreach committee, outreach services staff, or the library director, and how will this decision be made and implemented? Library staff must clearly see the need that is being filled by the library's involvement, from both the point of view of the service mission of the institution as well as from that of the community or special population that the outreach service targets. When the latter becomes too vague or not clearly defined, the library may want to step back and evaluate its involvement to make sure that only positive outcomes will result, rather than disorganized or frustrating experiences.

Because academic law libraries are often large, with numerous employees and varied funding and institutional resources, it may be possible to establish outreach services programs without a partner. The literature indicates that the success of striking out on a solo outreach mission depends on administrative or institutional support. Those academic law libraries that have made outreach a part of their strategic planning or visioning process to meet the goal of living their mission will have an easier time with this support, which includes a commitment of resources, staffing and development or implementation time.

However, libraries also face outreach implementation challenges. Funding can be a deciding factor when planning or implementing outreach services: "Equitable access [through outreach services] needs to be a real part of library service, fully funded in the annual budget and not just supported by grants or other 'soft money' that can disappear at any time" (Meadows 2004, 2) Other common challenges include lack of or limited support staff. These challenges often lead many libraries to reconsider their involvement level or to give programs lower priority in long-term planning, despite many librarians insisting that outreach is important for survival among competing legal information or service providers.

From the poll responses, it seems evident that a key to success besides institutional support is the active participation of library staff who believe in the necessity of outreach programs, or a successful collaborative relationship that evolves when faced with challenges or changing user needs. This is borne out in the literature: "The library's operating principles must reflect its outreach objectives. That means its services are planned and evaluated with partners in the community, outreach to the community is part of everyone's job description, and outreach skills and abilities are a measure of staff performance" (Cuesta 2004, 112–113). One of the factors that encourage university staff to want to participate and succeed in outreach services is the opportunity for recognition, especially if recognition is counted as professional service in consideration of tenure or tenure-equivalent appointments. Outreach involvement should be considered as important as research, publication, or teaching by those universities that rely on the traditional prongs of research, teaching, and service as part of the model mission of higher education. Outreach lends itself to more than the "service" prong of this model by leading to research and teaching opportunities: "… outreach … is a dynamic process from which both community and university benefit. Not only does outreach push knowledge into the community to address problems, it serves as a conduit for information to return back to campus to stimulate more research and improve teaching methods" (Wilson 2004).

After solidifying institutional and staff commitment, one of the questions that academic law libraries ponder is to what extent they need to market their services—not just to the public community but to their own faculty, staff, students, law school organizations, or alumni. This type of internal outreach indirectly affects the public community because the services that the library provides to support organizations, such as law school clinics, have direct access and offer services to the public. Internal outreach is more likely to be found in academic law libraries than external outreach to the public. This leads partly to the imbalance in services between the university or law school community and the public. By expanding public outreach, academic law libraries gain credibility as useful community resources for legal information needs. Public universities, especially, seek to gain this image as lawmakers and taxpayers decide budgets, keeping tabs on those services and institutions serving the most constituents in the most helpful and cost-efficient ways without duplicating efforts by other agencies. It's a tight line with complex factors to consider, but the rewards of a better library image and greater support are worth the effort.

Much of the success of the academic law library's outreach activities depends on its role and image in the public community. Has the community embraced the law school and university as a place the public is welcome, or has the community viewed the university or law school as not particularly inviting? There are a multitude of answers to this question. Some factors that influence the results include university financing (private versus public), the university's accessibility, and how well the university's mission is communicated. Outreach to the community plays a very strong role in the development and maintenance of the university, law school, and academic law library's image and support: "... a strong outreach program can meet the needs of library users while raising the profile of the library system and changing its image in the city" (Sumerford 2004, 40–41).

The law library has many ways to gather information about its image in the community, including surveys, interviews, focus groups, blogs, or other Web forums. One way to find out if the community is engaged and encouraged to use the academic law library's resources is to simply ask appropriate questions of those currently using the library. Some of these questions include the basic "Why do you use the library?" or "What could the library do to make it easier for you to find the information you need?" More complex questions provoke more thoughtful answers and could solicit suggestions for service or facilities improvements that only a community member's perspective can provide. Using feedback from community members can help guide outreach planning by identifying legal information needs that are not being adequately fulfilled by other legal information service providers in the community. Even if the academic law library does not use the feedback for its own outreach services, sharing the results of community perspectives with other area law libraries or legal organizations that serve the public maintains the helpful, collaborative image that law librarians value from their peers.

Using feedback from library users is helpful in forming an outreach agenda. However, there is still the dilemma of gaining the perspective of potential library users who have not relied on library services or collections in the past. This is an area where academic law libraries can learn from public libraries. How do area public libraries reach those in the community who are not taking advantage of library services or resources? By consulting with public library outreach librarians and staff, a potential partnership opens up, and law library staff can gain valuable insight into the information-seeking behavior of local community members.

If an academic law library decides to pursue a solo outreach venture, community feedback will be a vital step in shaping outreach programming and permanent library services. Several libraries have transformed outreach initiatives into successful library services based on user feedback. Many of these transformed services have included the use of technology to provide resources, such as legal information blogs, wikis, or specially designed websites or Web tutorials about community legal research needs. Other law libraries have installed interactive exhibits, displays, or multimedia kiosks. Exhibits are mentioned in the literature as a model outreach initiative: "When collaboratively developed and professionally executed, a library exhibit is a memorable, tangible, and easily documented outreach vehicle," whereas "... multimedia kiosks present a new modality for library instruction" (Fabian, D'Aniello, et al. 2003, 42, 52).

Schmid Law Library at the University of Nebraska College of Law in Lincoln, Nebraska, provides targeted outreach services to Lincoln-area landlords. Although tenants have used the library in the past, the library decided that landlords, owners, and land manager associations should also take advantage of the library's resources and services. Using the American Library Association's (ALA) "@ your library" campaign, Schmid Law Library promoted their collection, Web resources, and programming tailored to specific legal research needs of a special group in the community. Library staff committed to evaluating the services so that budget, staff time, and resources were used most efficiently (Dority Baker 2008).

Other considerations can also determine outreach success and bring additional decisions and questions into play. Will the program require special staffing or the use of volunteers? What if the program becomes "too" successful and overwhelms staff time or resources to the point of compromising services to law school or university users? Should there be a minimum evaluation period to determine success? If institutional support for the service changes in the future, how can the library change its level of involvement without negatively affecting the program's users who have begun to rely on its services? These are only a few of the difficult factors an outreach services unit may consider to become or remain a success.

Academic law libraries without a commitment to outreach services still manage some local community involvement if they allow the public access to their facilities, collections, or reference staffs. Many law libraries have government depository status, which incurs certain public access obligations; however, for many academic law libraries, this access is the only service they provide to the public. Public access represents minimal service; surely an academic law library can make more effort without compromising service to its primary university or law school users. For example, academic law libraries that decide to circulate materials to external users often develop lending policies as a way to ensure that services to external users does not negatively affect services to university or law school users. Larger academic law libraries in metro areas also take security of their facilities into consideration when extending access to the public, ensuring that the security of their buildings and collections are not compromised by those intending to do harm.

PARTNERING RELATIONSHIPS

The Association of College and Research Libraries (ACRL) Research Committee (2008, 5) identified collaboration, partly in the area of public engagement, as an emergent issue for the profession: "There will be broader collaboration between academic, public, special, and school librarians on topics of common concern, e.g., public engagement, media literacy." Communities, in turn, are increasingly interested in partnering with local service agencies, including universities and libraries: "The civic library movement attempts to build on the vital public information commons that already exists in libraries across the U.S., using the Internet as a way to deepen libraries' public functions" (Friedland and Boyte 2000, 7). Never was this more evident than during recent natural and infrastructure crises. Libraries distributed vital information to community members after such disasters as Hurricane Katrina, the California wildfires, and the Minneapolis bridge collapse, ensuring timely and accurate distribution of valuable public resources. Examples of the services provided in these situations included Internet links to community services, contact information for emergencies, as well as an update on the latest information provided by government officials.

Despite their unique access to resources, funding, or staff, some academic law libraries may hesitate to take on an active role in community outreach on their own, opting to enter into partnerships instead. Partnerships are most likely to be successful when providing services to meet a perceived, stated need. Outreach services often meet certain needs by reminding people of the availability of library services or with one-time events that officially introduce new library services, physical features (such as a library remodel or furniture upgrade), or collections.

One of the best partnership relationships an academic law library can establish is with other departments or programs within its own law school, and by partnering with them, law libraries are able to discover perceived and stated needs of special populations with ties to the law school community (Beaning 1998, v). By working together with the alumni or development office, libraries can make sure that law school or university alumni groups become refamiliarized with library services open to them. Law schools also are including libraries in community legal services. People's Law School at the University of Texas is partnering with area lawyers in the Austin Bar Association to present legal classes on various topics to community members. Each class includes a tour of Tarlton Law Library at the university (Hodnicki 2008).

Collaboration is increasingly important between the various stakeholders in reaching library users and ensuring that the library remains a vital and relevant research facility within the law school. Just as libraries "partner with faculty to create content to support students' development of information literacy skills" (Reyes 2006, 302), law librarians need to forge alliances with legal writing instructors and other law faculty to support the development of legal research skills, especially in classes other than the ones taught by librarians. Using library resources to support classroom instruction is not a novel idea, but collaborating with librarians to supplement assignments and the development of legal writing and research skills deserves special attention within the law school curriculum. There is growing interest in state bar examinations requiring a legal research component, and law firms increasingly expect first- or second-year associates to demonstrate their legal research and writing competency immediately upon hire. Both situations impact the relationship between library research and legal writing skills and instruction.

Law school clinics should be invited to consult the library about the informational needs of clinic clients. In response, the library could develop legal information programs as an extension of the clinical services. Perhaps the clinic could then use library outreach programming as a prerequisite to certain services they offer. If clients meet at the law school, library services will be available in-house as needed. The clinic and library need to work together to promote educational services and resources. A successful clinic-law library internal partnership is in place at Stanford Law School Library. They provide a "Reference-on-the-Road" program to serve their law school clinical programs. "Stanford's law librarians felt [they] could best serve [the clinical] community through working closely with the individual clinicians and providing in-class training to the students" (Wilko 2006, 3). The program provides specialized training and resources for the needs of the clinical faculty and students who directly serve the local community.

Together with local legal organizations or law firms, libraries can plan and offer programs and services to both librarians and community members about such topics as voting, legal rights and services, or other government information. Potential partners include the local courts, legal aid services, law firms, or organizations such as the League of Women Voters or the Urban League. "Working through a community partner enhances the presentation of resources to the community by working with this already established trust that the partner has built up and maintains" (Crowther and Trott 2004, 15). Examples of successful partnerships include a library-attorney partnership that has pro bono attorneys using library space each year for an income tax preparation service for the public; the University of New Mexico School of Law Library collaborates with the New Mexico Supreme Court Library to provide the "New Mexico Collaborative Law Library Outreach Program." Before collaborating, each library tried to present its own outreach services, but by combining resources, all were able to create a "stronger unified effort" (Cohen and Robledo 2006, 2). The collaborative provides programs about legal resources and referral to public and college librarians around the state.

One of the obvious opportunities for partnership is for academic law libraries to join with other types of libraries to produce resources or events. Academic law libraries partnering with other law libraries set up prime opportunities to create definitive studies, such as the state of public access to legal information or assistance within a particular area. Law school libraries often partner with public law libraries, if any are located nearby, by joining established programs or by generating new programs based on other current or past outreach services. Public law libraries, which may include county or court law libraries, have a direct impact on and relationship with the community since public citizens are the main user group. However, many smaller public law libraries have difficulty establishing outreach service programs due to lack of staffing, funding, or support. It is especially with these struggling law libraries that academic law libraries should explore partnerships first.

Academic law libraries may also create relationships with general public libraries or local special libraries that are open to the public, such as those in public corporations, organizations, or museums. As mentioned above, partnering with a public library is especially useful in gaining insight into the information-seeking behavior of local community members, as well as furthering good will among librarian colleagues.

Non-law librarians, that is, librarians who do not specialize in law, are a particular segment of librarians that deserve consideration. Again, though law libraries should consider partnering with non-law libraries to provide outreach services to the public, law librarians should also consider their assistance to colleagues who provide direct services to the public. Law librarians can provide refresher workshops on how to use the legal resources found in non-law libraries, as well as teaching the recognition of legal information questions versus legal advice and at what point to refer patrons to legal service providers, law libraries, or other agencies. Getting this message out to non-law librarians goes a long way to encourage collegiality and respect, as well as keeping the helpful image of law libraries entrenched among professional associates. Some academic law libraries work with other local libraries to present events, such as a legal research course to first-year pre-law students at a community college. The "Circuit Riders Outreach Program," based out of the Coleman Karesh Law Library at the University of South Carolina School of Law, teaches public and academic librarians with a "Legal Research for Non-Law Librarians" class. The class presentations and schedule are available on the Circuit Riders' website: http://law.sc.edu/library/research_aids/circuit_riders/. Academic law libraries in other states have developed similar programs.

Another special segment of the community that warrants unique outreach consideration is the local legal community of lawyers, judges, paralegals, and other legal service providers. Although libraries may partner with them to provide outreach services to the community, libraries can provide events, classes, or other services to the legal professionals themselves as well. According to the American Bar Association (2008), forty-three states require lawyers to complete continuing legal education (CLE) to keep their professional licensure current. Academic law libraries can provide these types of education events on a recurring basis while familiarizing the bench and bar with the ongoing services and resources that they can provide. One consideration, however, is whether a law school receives funding by offering CLE events, and whether law school administration has come to expect this revenue source in the future. This may determine the library's involvement because the relationship between the event organizers, the library, and law school administration is an especially important one to nurture and develop for future good will and partnership. One simple strategy several libraries have used is to lend their space for training events for local attorneys, often taught by Westlaw or Lexis representatives, which also fosters a collaborative attitude between the representatives and library staff. Some of these courses for local attorneys are taught by librarians on topics such as Internet or public records research.

Courts without their own libraries may want occasional updates on recent legal technology products, resources, or tools needed for legal research. Academic law libraries may consider legal research "house calls" to court staff and judges or establish an online service, such as a blog, that can reach these professionals. Enjoying a cooperative relationship with the courts not only ensures that litigants, especially those without representation, are being referred to useful resources for legal information, but it also improves the image of local law libraries and the university in the minds of the local legal community.

Academic law libraries have typically shied away from providing outreach services to jail or prison populations, often relying on the services of court offices or public law libraries to meet these legal information needs. However, if a local jail or prison has no public law library to meet their needs or an inadequate response from courts that are understaffed and careful about providing what they may consider unfairly "favorable" services, the academic law library could provide a valuable and needed service. Inmates are a forgotten group in many communities, but outreach to them ensures that they receive accurate legal information, discouraging uninformed or frivolous litigation from being pursued.

One of the important considerations law librarians must remember while providing research or informational assistance to members of the public, and especially to jail or prison inmates, is recognizing the difference between legal information and legal advice. Giving legal advice is considered to be the unauthorized practice of law or practicing law without a license (Rostain 2006, 1407 n.53) and is included in the definition of "Practice of Law" by *Black's Law Dictionary*: "The professional work of a duly licensed lawyer, encompassing a broad range of services such as ... advising clients on legal questions" (Garner 2004, 1210). Even though many academic law librarians may have law degrees, they are usually not practicing attorneys, and if they are, need to differentiate their roles as librarians from their roles as attorneys while working with the public. Sometimes librarians take this admonishment too far and do a disservice to the public by erring too much on the safe side, refusing to answer certain questions without explaining why or adjusting their answers to provide the information that is allowed. For example, if a patron asks: "Can you recommend a specific form for pursuing a legal case?" the answer should not be just "No, that's giving legal advice," but rather, "I can't recommend a specific form, but here is a formbook with the various forms and explanations of when they are used."

CONCLUSIONS

Librarians have a strong ethic toward advocacy. To be a strong presence in the community and to make a clear difference in the life of the local region, former ALA President Sarah Ann Long (2000, ix) encourages library staff to "be part of the decision-making process in those communities. We have to be at the table with other organizations and government agencies. We have to be involved in giving and getting assets for the common good of the community." Academic law libraries can make a difference in their local communities by partnering with other agencies and libraries or with solo outreach efforts. Using their advantages with strong staff commitments to planning, institutional support, and funding, academic law libraries are primed to become leaders in the reengagement of civic education in a democratic society.

Academic law libraries have multiple communities they can choose to support and serve. The future of "outreach services" is perhaps best explained in terms of the promising movement by libraries away from creating services *for* community members to partnering *with* and enabling communities to create and mobilize knowledge for meeting community needs. These types of social experiments comprise the field of community informatics and promise to enrich the traditional concept of outreach services by engaging community members in civic participation, providing opportunities for authentic dialogue and offering a public space for fostering democratic discourse and renewal (Bishop and Kranich 2008). By redefining outreach from inside the academy, law school librarians can find support through a network of individuals and service agencies to continue the mission of higher education and engage community members with a commitment to service.

REFERENCES

American Bar Association. *Summary of MCLE State Requirements.* 2008. http://www. abanet.org/cle/mcleview.html (accessed February 8, 2008).

Association of College and Research Libraries (ACRL) Research Committee. *Environmental Scan 2007.* Chicago: ACRL, 2008. http://www.acrl.org/ala/acrl/acrlpubs/whitepapers/ Environmental_Scan_2.pdf (accessed February 1, 2008).

Beaning, D. *Law School Involvement in Community Development: A Study of Current Initiatives and Approaches.* Washington, D.C.: Department of Housing and Urban Development, 1998. http://www.oup.org/files/pubs/LawSchoolInvolvement.pdf (accessed February 1, 2008).

Bishop, A. P. and N. Kranich. "People Watching With a Purpose: Meeting Needs Before They Need It." *Soaring to Excellence 2008*. Glen Ellyn, Ill.: College of DuPage Press, 2008. [Teleconference handouts and teleconference] http://www.dupagepress.com/ library-learning-network/soaring-to-excellence-2008/people-watching-with-a-purpose/ (accessed February 8, 2008).

Cohen, E. and A. Robledo. "New Mexico Collaborative Law Library Outreach." *RIPS Law Librarian: A Special Interest Section of the American Association of Law Libraries* 29, no. 1 (2006): 2, 17. http://www.aallnet.org/sis/ripssis/Fall2006.pdf (accessed February 4, 2008).

Crowther, J. L. and B. Trott. *Partnering with Purpose: A Guide to Strategic Partnership Development for Libraries and Other Organizations*. Westport, Conn.: Libraries Unlimited, 2004.

Cuesta, Y. J. "Developing Outreach Skills in Library Staff." In *From Outreach to Equity: Innovative Models of Library Policy and Practice*, ed. R. Osborne. Chicago: American Library Association, 2004, pp. 112–113.

Dority Baker, M. L. "Leading Landlords to the Law Library: How to Use ALA's @ Your Library Campaign as an Outreach Tool to Local Communities." *AALL Spectrum* 12, no. 4 (2008): 14–15, 22–23.

Fabian, C. A., C. D'Aniello, C. Tysick, and M. Morin. "Multiple Models for Library Outreach Initiatives." *The Reference Librarian* 39, no. 82 (2003): 39–55.

Friedland, L. and H. Boyte. "The New Information Commons Community Information Partnerships and Civic Change." University of Minnesota Hubert Humphrey Institute, Center for Democracy and Citizenship, 2000. http://www.publicwork.org/pdf/work ingpapers/New%20information%20commons.pdf (accessed February 1, 2008).

Garner, B., ed. "Practice of Law." In: *Black's Law Dictionary*. St. Paul: Thomson/West, 2004, pp. 1210.

Hodnicki, Joe. "Free Legal Classes at People's Law School Set Example for Law Schools, Law Libraries and Local Bar Associations to Follow." [weblog entry] *Law Librarian Blog*, February 22, 2008. http://lawprofessors.typepad.com/law_librarian_blog/ 2008/02/free-legal-clas.html (accessed February 27, 2008).

Jesudason, M. "Academic Libraries and Outreach Services through Precollege Programs: A Proactive Collaboration." *RSR Reference Services Review* 21, no. 4 (1993): 29–36, 96.

Lerner, R. M. and L. A. K. Simon. "The New American Outreach University: Challenges and Options." In *University-Community Collaborations for the Twenty-First Century: Outreach Scholarship for Youth and Families*, ed. R. M. Lerner and L. A. K. Simon. New York: Garland Pub., 1998, pp. 3–24.

Long, S. A. "Foreword." In: *A Place at the Table: Participating in Community Building*, Kathleen de la Pena McCook. Chicago; London: American Library Association, 2000, pp. vii–ix.

Maurrasse, D. J. *Beyond the Campus: How Colleges and Universities Form Partnerships with their Communities*. New York; London: Routledge, 2001.

McKinstry, J. and A. Garrison. "Building Communities @ Your Library." *College and Research Libraries News* 62, no. 2 (2001): 165–167, 186.

Meadows, J. "Services outside Library Walls." In: *From Outreach to Equity: Innovative Models of Library Policy and Practice*, ed. R. Osborne. Chicago: American Library Association, 2004, pp. 1–6.

Reyes, V. "The Future Role of the Academic Librarians in Higher Education." *Portal: Libraries and the Academy* 6, no. 3 (2006): 301–309.

Rostain, T. "The Emergence of "Law Consultants." *Fordham L. Rev.* 75 (2006): 1397–1428.

Schneider, T. "Outreach: Why, How and Who? Academic Libraries and Their Involvement in the Community." *The Reference Librarian* 39, no. 82 (2003): 199–213.

Sumerford, S. "Libraries as Community Builders: The Greensboro Experience." In: *From Outreach to Equity: Innovative Models of Library Policy and Practice*, ed. R. Osborne. Chicago: American Library Association, 2004, pp. 39–41.

United States Government Printing Office (GPO). *Synopsis of D-RFI for Mass Digitization Opportunities*. Washington, D.C.: GPO, 2008. http://www.fbo.gov/spg/GPO/ PSPSD/WashingtonDC/GPORFI08001/SynopsisR.html (accessed February 27, 2008).

Wilko, K. "Stories from a Fledgling Outreach Program." *RIPS Law Librarian: A Special Interest Section of the American Association of Law Libraries* 29, no. 1 (2006): 3, 17. http://www.aallnet.org/sis/ripssis/Fall2006.pdf (accessed February 4, 2008).

Wilson, D. "Conclusion." *Perspectives on Outreach*. Auburn, Ala.: Auburn University, 2004. http://www.auburn.edu/outreach/events/publications/perspectives2004.pdf (accessed February 1, 2008).

21

GRAND ROUNDS: MEDICAL LIBRARY OUTREACH

Becky McKay Johnson

Academic medical libraries have had an organized form of extramural outreach since 1965. The program, sponsored and funded by the National Network of Libraries of Medicine (NN/LM), a network of health libraries headed by the National Library of Medicine (NLM), is the primary focus of this chapter. Medical library outreach and education programs enable NLM and NN/LM members (more than 5,000 mainly academic medical and hospital libraries) to extend their services and expertise beyond traditional local constituencies. The NLM, located in Bethesda, Maryland, and part of the National Institutes of Health (NIH), the primary federal agency for conducting and supporting medical research, produces several important Internet-based information products for a range of audiences. These include: PubMed, the world's largest electronic life science journal index; PubMed Central, an open access digital archive with free full text covering more than 400 biomedical journal titles; MedlinePlus, a source of authoritative consumer health information; and several other health information resources about specialized topics such as toxicology, chemistry, and genetics. Outreach librarians teach and promote these resources in addition to their own library services with the ultimate aim of improving access to biomedical information for health care professionals and consumers, especially the underserved. Outreach is essential to the mission of medical libraries, so much so that "Trusted Information Services that Promote Health Literacy and the Reduction of Health Disparities Worldwide" is the second of four goals in NLM's Long Range Plan 2006–2016 (National Library of Medicine, 2006a).

The Regional Medical Library Program, NLM's involvement with other libraries and thus medical library outreach, was born in 1965 with the passage by Congress of the Medical Library Assistance Act. Although funding for medical research and education was abundant in the period after World War II, funding for libraries did not keep pace. This lack of support was evidenced by the "lamentable condition of the nation's health science libraries" (Bunting 1987). Academic medical libraries were unable to meet the increased demand for information services created by the exponential growth of the medical literature, the expansion of multidisciplinary research, and the need for speed in information retrieval and dissemination (Bloomquist 1963). Two influential reports in the mid-1960s advocated that NLM lead the effort to strengthen the nation's medical library system: the 1963 NLM-commissioned study by Harold Bloomquist of the Harvard University Schools of Medicine and Public Health and the report of President Lyndon Johnson's Commission on Heart Disease, Cancer, and Stroke, chaired by Michael E. DeBakey, a prominent heart surgeon (Bunting 1987). NLM drafted legislation using information from these reports, and the Medical Library Assistance Act passed expeditiously in 1965 due to strong support from the library and medical communities. The bill enormously increased NLM's budget (Cogdill 2006) and authorized NLM to provide extramural funding in several areas, including renovation, expansion, or construction of library facilities; training of medical librarians; research in medical library science and related fields; acquisition of materials such as books and journals; and the development of a national network of medical libraries known then as the Regional Medical Library Program (Bunting 1987).

This arrangement evolved over time and received a boost in 1989 in response to *Improving Health Professionals' Access to Information: Report of the Board of Regents*, a report by Dr. DeBakey, longtime library supporter and NLM board member, calling for an expanded staff, an increased outreach role by network personnel and member libraries, and a new name. The program is known today as the NN/LM, which Cogdill credits, along with Medline, as being one of the key developments in the field of health sciences librarianship in the last thirty years. NLM coordinates the program and sits atop a nationwide networked hierarchy of health science libraries. The mission of NN/LM is "to advance the progress of medicine and improve the public health by providing all U.S. health professionals with equal access to biomedical information and improving the public's access to information to enable them to make informed decisions about their health" (National Library of Medicine 2002a). Special priority is given to reaching underserved constituencies including various ethnic and racial groups and inner city and rural health professionals unaffiliated with an institution maintaining a health sciences library.

Five-year contracts are granted competitively to eight large, prestigious academic medical libraries appointing them to serve as Regional Medical Libraries (RMLs) over eight fixed geographic regions and to house the NN/LM office and staff. Presently, nearly 5,000 institutions belong to the network. More than 150 academic medical libraries at larger schools of the health sciences comprise the network membership at the Resource Library level and the smaller, local libraries (often hospital libraries) belong at the Public Access Library (PAL) level (Bunting 1987). In addition to serving as regional hubs for outreach and outreach funding, NN/LM offices also coordinate resource sharing with DOCLINE, NLM's Web-based interlibrary loan system for medical libraries; SERHOLD, a serials holdings database available to DOCLINE users; document delivery via Loansome Doc; linking PubMed with electronic journal subscriptions with LinkOut; and the promotion of electronic interlibrary loan payments via the EFTS (Electronic Fund Transfer System).

The 2006–2011 Regional Medical Libraries are:
[http://www.nlm.nih.gov/pubs/factsheets/nnlm.html]

Middle Atlantic Region
Region 1
Frederick L. Ehrman Medical Library
New York, NY
States Served: Delaware, New Jersey, New York, and Pennsylvania
New York University

Southeastern/Atlantic Region
Region 2
University of Maryland, Baltimore
Health Sciences and Human Services Library
Baltimore, MD
States Served: Alabama, Florida, Georgia, Maryland, Mississippi, North Carolina, South Carolina, Tennessee, Virginia, West Virginia, the District of Columbia, Puerto Rico, and the U.S. Virgin Islands

Greater Midwest Region
Region 3
The University of Illinois at Chicago
Library of the Health Sciences
Chicago, IL
States Served: Iowa, Illinois, Indiana, Kentucky, Michigan, Minnesota, North Dakota, Ohio, South Dakota, and Wisconsin

Midcontinental Region
Region 4
University of Utah
Spencer S. Eccles Health Sciences Library
Salt Lake City, UT
States Served: Colorado, Kansas, Missouri, Nebraska, Utah, and Wyoming

South Central Region
Region 5
Houston Academy of Medicine
Texas Medical Center Library
Houston, TX
States Served: Arkansas, Louisiana, New Mexico, Oklahoma, and Texas

Pacific Northwest Region
Region 6
University of Washington
Health Sciences Libraries and Information Center
Seattle, WA
States Served: Alaska, Idaho, Montana, Oregon, and Washington

Pacific Southwest Region
Region 7
University of California, Los Angeles
Louise M. Darling Biomedical Library
Los Angeles, CA
States Served: Arizona, California, Hawaii, Nevada, and
U.S. Territories in the Pacific Basin

New England Region
Region 8
University of Massachusetts Medical School
The Lamar Soutter Library
Worcester, MA
States Served: Connecticut, Massachusetts, Maine, New Hampshire, Rhode Island,
and Vermont

Staff members at NL/LM offices conduct outreach themselves in the form of free, two- to eight-hour classes about topics related to health information resources and services offered at their locations or at libraries in their regions. Attendees are often librarians (public, academic, and medical) who are taking the classes so that they can train end users. Other target audiences include health care providers, public health workers, and the general public. A full list of subjects taught is available at http://nnlm.gov/training/classes.html, and includes PubMed and other NLM products, evaluating the reliability of health information, providing consumer health information to a variety of consumers in both English and Spanish, grant writing, and how to use DOCLINE and LinkOut.

NN/LM offices administer funding programs to support outreach efforts of network members and other medical library functions. NN/LM offices are contractors to NLM and thus funds take the form of awards and subcontracts, not "grants." Awards support smaller, brief projects, and subcontracts support larger projects lasting a year or more. The outreach awards are relatively small (ranging from a few hundred to around fifty thousand dollars), usually require a competitive proposal in response to a Request for Proposal, have a fixed performance period, and require reports back to NN/LM. Generally, the awardee performs the work, the awardee's institution covers the cost and sends an invoice, and then the NN/LM office writes a reimbursement check. Each NN/LM regional office has its own roster of outreach-oriented funding opportunities, which may vary over time and budgetary fluctuations, although common themes emerge. A review of all the NN/LM outreach Web pages shows that funding is available to hold a symposium on a hot topic in health information (health literacy, health disparities, or library space); to develop a course online or in person; to purchase or upgrade technology for both library staff or end users; for Go Local projects (creating websites that provide the MedlinePlus user access to information about local health care resources and providers); to promote health information and NLM products by exhibiting at local, regional, and national conferences; for providing health information and technology training especially to underserved or difficult to reach populations, either health professionals or consumers; and to conduct assessment. These items generally define the activities considered "outreach" by medical librarians.

The meat and potatoes of medical library outreach involves promoting awareness of and providing training on NLM Internet-based information products, all of which are available to everyone free of charge. All of NLM's information resources can be found at the NLM website (http://www.nlm.nih.gov/). Medical librarians performing outreach promote NLM information products by conducting demonstrations or hands-on teaching anywhere a person or group is willing to learn—at hospitals, clinics, libraries, schools, community-based organizations, health care organizations, public health sites, etc.

PubMed is NLM's flagship information resource for health care professionals. It is a free, Web-based interface for Medline, the world's premier biomedical bibliographic database containing over seventeen million citations and abstracts to published literature in the life sciences, including mainly clinical medicine, but also nursing, dentistry, veterinary, public health, allied health, health administration and policy, complementary medicine, and basic biological sciences. More than five thousand journals are indexed, most of which are scholarly with content such as reports of original research; original clinical observations; analysis of philosophical, ethical, or social aspects of the health professions or biomedical sciences; critical reviews; statistical compilations; descriptions of evaluation of methods or procedures; and case reports with discussions (National Library of Medicine 1988). PubMed and Medline's primary audience is health care professionals, but they may also be of use to well-educated and motivated consumers. More than three million searches worldwide are performed using PubMed every day (Library of Medicine 2006b).

Loansome Doc, NLM's Internet document delivery program, works with PubMed and is aimed at getting health care providers (usually those unaffiliated with an institution maintaining a health science library) access to the full text of journal articles. Loansome Doc users must first establish an agreement with a participating library, usually a Resource Library, and then register online at the Loansome Doc site (https://docline.gov/loansome/login.cfm). Placing a request through Loansome Doc is simple. It involves selecting article citations online within PubMed and then sending the selections electronically to the lending library. Registration and use of the software are free of charge, but fees for the delivery of articles vary from library to library, approximately ten to thirty dollars per article.

The NIH instituted a requirement that, beginning in April 2008, all NIH-funded research reports be available to the public via PubMed Central, NLM's open access repository, within one year of publication. As the volume of open access biomedical literature available to anyone free of charge expands at an accelerated rate, health sciences libraries may play a role in assisting researchers with submitting their material to PubMed Central and teaching users to access this important information.

In the late 1990s NLM began providing quality health information targeted specifically to the general public. Nearly one-third of PubMed searches were being done by consumers looking for the names of diseases and probably expecting to find full-text medical information (Miller, Lacroix, and Backus 2000). Trustworthy health information on the Web was and continues to be notoriously difficult to find by surfing the Web. Therefore, with its mandate to serve health care consumers, NLM made several consumer-oriented resources freely available online. MedlinePlus (http://medlineplus.gov) is NLM's primary outlet for consumer health information. It is a meta-site with links to NIH health information, other government agencies, and authoritative health organizations. MedlinePlus covers more than 750 health topics. NLM thoroughly vets the sites for authority and accuracy, keeps the links current, permits no advertising nor offers any endorsements, and presents information at appropriate literacy levels in English and Spanish with one click to switch between languages. MedlinePlus provides extensive drug information (prescription, over-the-counter, and supplements); a medical encyclopedia and dictionary; interactive patient tutorials; list of online health care directories; the latest health news; and video recordings of a variety of surgical procedures.

There is a link on the MedlinePlus home page to ClinicalTrials.gov, an NIH registry of federally and privately funded studies in the United States and abroad of new drugs and treatments for a wide range of conditions. The site provides information about the purpose of the study, location, eligibility criteria for participation, and if new subjects are being recruited. Also linked is NIH Senior Health, a website designed in conjunction with the National Institute on Aging. This website focuses on topics of particular interest to older persons and offers navigation aids to improve access, such as options to change text size and color contrast, use keyboard shortcuts, and enable an audio feature that reads the content to the user.

MedlinePlus also helps the health care consumer find local health care resources for specific geographic areas through its Go Local program (http://www.nlm.nih.gov/medlineplus/golocal/index.html). More than 150 types of services are covered, including hospitals, various physician specialties, clinics, nursing homes, assisted living facilities, day care services, a variety of social services, and complementary medicine providers. Go Local works with MedlinePlus, linking health topics of interest to the consumer with local providers relevant to that topic. NLM partners with libraries or library consortia to develop and maintain Go Local projects for states and portions of states and offers a maximum $25,000 subcontract to gather, index, and maintain the data. To date, twenty-five Go Local projects are complete, with ten more in progress and nationwide coverage in mind. A portion of locally awarded funds is expected to go toward promoting the Go Local site, a form of outreach done by medical librarians.

NLM has several online resources aimed at both health care consumers and professionals concerning how the environment affects human health and development. These are available through NLM's Special Information Services Division's Environmental and Toxicology portal. For the public, students, and educators, Tox Town is an interactive guide to potentially toxic substances in everyday places such as at home, on the farm, and in the workplace. Also for the public, the Household Products Database can be searched for over six thousand household substances (cleaning, automotive, personal care, lawn and pool care, pet care, office, arts and crafts, and home maintenance) and their possible health effects and safe handling.

More extensive resources exist for clinicians and researchers. Toxnet, the Toxicology Data Network, enables the user to search one or more specialized databases there for the toxicological, occupational, and teratogenic effects of drugs and other chemicals. WISER, a PDA and Windows wireless information system, provides a wide range of information for first responders to hazardous materials incidents. WISER helps in the identification of more than four hundred substances and gives guidance on actions to be taken to save lives and reduce environmental impact in the event of a spill. Outreach projects have been aimed at first responders such as firemen, emergency medical technicians, and paramedics, providing these personnel PDAs and WISER training.

In addition to instruction and demonstrations, exhibits are an effective outreach method for increasing the awareness of NLM resources and local library services. Librarians, often with computers and Internet access on-site, staff display booths right alongside vendors promoting their products and trying to increase sales. Exhibits can take place in a variety of venues, including physician specialty meetings, nurses' association meetings, public health conferences, state library association meetings, local health fairs, even county and state fairs. Exhibit costs, logistics, and sophistication vary with the type of event, location, and audience. Exhibits provide the opportunity to focus on a targeted, specialized, and captive audience and to highlight the most appropriate products and services. For example, PubMed and Loansome Doc would be appropriate services to promote at physician-oriented meetings, MedlinePlus and Tox Town at local health fairs. NN/LM has funded several hundred exhibits in the last few years, with the average award of approximately $1,300, ranging from $125 to $2,600. NN/LM offers these small awards specifically for exhibits, but exhibit funds can also be included in larger awards for more comprehensive outreach projects.

The NN/LM Projects Database (http://nnlm.gov/funding/database.html) lists in excess of one thousand library projects funded since the year 2000; the database is freely available on the Web. NLM also directly funds large outreach efforts. There are many reports of outreach projects in the health sciences library literature. The following describes a few projects that are representative of medical library outreach to the usual audiences—doctors, public health workers, and the public—and provides an idea of what can be accomplished with the right combination of people, ideas, and money. An additional cutting-edge project regarding a health science library outreach effort in cyberspace is also illustrated. Issues encountered in the projects are noted, reflecting the challenges in performing effective outreach.

OUTREACH EXAMPLES AND ISSUES

VALUABLES Project

Few of the small hospital facilities and clinics in east Tennessee have library facilities or any access to libraries. The VALUABLES project (Value Added Library Users Access to the Biomedical Literature via Electronic Systems), a collaborative effort by the East Tennessee State University James H. Quillen College of Medicine Library, the local Area Health Information Center (AHEC), and the hospitals and clinics in seventeen surrounding counties, aimed to address the problem of information access. This ambitious project had several facets: to provide document delivery via Loansome Doc, on-site training to users, mediated searching, computers with Internet access, purchase of a proprietary evidence-based medicine product, and Ariel software to facilitate electronic delivery of information. The project librarian visited sites regularly to market the services to clinicians, provide training in the databases, and collect reference requests. The program began in 1996, received a large award for 2001 to 2003, and continued afterward with twenty-eight clinics and seven hospitals paying modest fees to maintain library service from the medical school library (Stephenson et al. 2004).

Successful outreach requires persistence. News about the availability of library service to those who had never received it in rural east Tennessee was met with apathy. The project director found a way to overcome the indifference of the target audience by identifying opinion leaders at the institutions and convincing these peer leaders of the value of the service. The opinion leaders participated in the training, used the service, and served as a model for others to emulate (Stephenson et al. 2004). Enlisting opinion leaders is a fundamental tenet of the diffusion of innovations theory, one often used as a theoretical model for outreach provision. Providing information access is not enough; persuading and marketing relentlessly, addressing motivational and education issues, and conquering technical difficulties are required to make outreach work.

Public Health

In 2001 NLM indentified the public health sector as a likely outreach target to help fulfill its mission to reduce health disparities (i.e., differences in health and health care across racial, ethnic, and socioeconomic groups). NN/LM outreach coordinators were tasked with encouraging and improving outreach to public health personnel, a group relatively poor in funds and library access, yet in need of quality information to promote the health of the nation. Outreach librarians at Louisiana State University Health Sciences Center in Shreveport received a $25,000 NN/LM award in 2004 to build a portable nine-laptop computer lab to transport to the public health offices in twenty-nine north Louisiana parishes. Recognizing that public health personnel lacked computer labs, had limited staff and limited funds for travel, and were geographically dispersed, the Shreveport librarians brought needed information training to public health workers (Watson et al. 2006).

This project faced its share of difficulties. Ensuring that nine laptop computers work wirelessly at various locations with different network specifications required the presence of a systems librarian and precise logistical planning in advance. Even so, they still encountered some connectivity issues. Flexibility regarding class size, location, and scheduling on the part of the librarians was necessary to accommodate staffing and location limitations. The only suitable table at one location was a stovetop island. However, the greatest challenges they faced involved meeting the complex and varied information needs of multiple public health constituencies (epidemiologists, a variety of nurses, and sanitarians) while not overwhelming attendees with information overload. A needs assessment was performed prior to the project, but it had not yielded helpful results, a common problem in trying to ascertain the information needs of the public health work force. The classes were refined over time, and the librarians developed strategies to address unanticipated problems (Watson et al. 2006).

Social Networking

The library world is all abuzz about ways to participate in social networking and Web 2.0, the second wave of Internet use that features creativity, sharing, and collaboration. NN/LM has funded three projects since 2007 totaling $87,000 through the Alliance Library System in Peoria, Illinois, to explore the provision of health-related library services in the virtual environment of Second Life, a social networking site. Second Life (http://www.secondlife.com) is a three-dimensional virtual world created and owned by its residents. Since opening to the public in 2003, it has grown explosively to a population of thirteen million members (one million of whom have used the system in the past month) who can do just about anything that people do in "real life." Members create avatars, a virtual representation of the self; they can make friends, marry, buy property, build buildings, pay taxes, shop, own a business, take a class, explore, and enjoy entertainment and culture. Alliance Library System is the leader of the Second Life Library Project where libraries from all over the world participate. As of 2007 more than five thousand people per day visit what is known as the Alliance Information Archipelago (Hurst-Wahl 2007). Health Info Island is a part of that archipelago, is funded by NN/LM, and provides access to consumer health information resources, programs, and events; one-on-one support; and outreach to virtual residents and medical communities. A second project concerns virtual world and game accessibility and assistive technology. Health Info Island will offer exhibits, programs, and activities related to the use of gaming and virtual worlds for underserved users, including those with learning disabilities, mobility or dexterity challenges, visual impairment or blindness, or deafness or hearing impairment (NN/LM 2008). A future project proposes to offer customized orientation and information services to people with disabilities and chronic diseases who join the virtual world of Second Life. These projects are cutting-edge efforts to reach people where they are, including the millions of people in cyberspace.

HI HO

Locating reliable Spanish language consumer health information on the Web is exceedingly challenging. MedlinePlus is available in Spanish, with a click of a button to switch back and forth from English. Health Information Hispanic Outreach (known as HI HO), described by Bowden et al. (2006), was a two-year project to find ways of collaborating with other organizations and to test methods for reaching the Hispanic community in the Lower Rio Grande Valley region, four counties along the border of Mexico in south Texas. Needs assessment in the form of interviews and focus groups led the group to concentrate their efforts on promoting the use of both the English and Spanish versions of MedlinePlus. Targeted sites included two health clinics, one rural and one urban; Med High, the South Texas High School for the Health Professions; and a community resource center in a *colonia*, which is defined by the Texas Secretary of State's office (http://www.sos.state.tx.us/border/colonias/what_colonia.shtml) as a "residential area along the Texas-Mexico border that may lack some of the most basic living necessities, such as potable water and sewer systems, electricity, paved roads, and safe and sanitary housing."

The goal of the two clinic projects was to increase patient use of MedlinePlus *en español*, the Spanish version, among the primarily Spanish-speaking patient population. Project staff placed computers with Internet access in patient waiting rooms, trained staff on how to use the resources and how to encourage patients to use the workstations, and spent a few hours per week on-site instructing patients. Postpilot evaluation showed that the clinic-based projects were the least successful of the projects. Low-income patients are often very ill by the time they are willing to spend sparse resources traveling to and paying for a clinic visit. This may have made some patients less inclined to learn to use a computer to find information. Some patients were illiterate, and many patients and staff were unfamiliar with and uncomfortable using the technology. Staff members were busy with a high volume of patients and were not paid to train patients on using the information workstations (Bowden et al. 2006).

On the other hand, the Med High and *colonia* projects are extremely successful and have achieved national awards and received additional funding. The Med High project (Warner et al. 2005) aimed to increase the use of MedlinePlus by partnering with a health professions public high school. Four peer tutors were carefully selected to teach other students about MedlinePlus. This model had been successfully used before by Med High librarians, trusted members of the community and crucial to the program's success. The peer tutors were academically successful, skilled in computer and Internet use, bilingual, effective public speakers, and regarded as leaders among their peers. More than two thousand people were exposed to MedlinePlus at Med High through classes for students, open houses for students and family, training sessions for teachers and administrators, and Health Occupations Students of America events during the one-year period of the pilot project. Outcome evaluation showed increased use of MedlinePlus for schoolwork and outside of school to help family members find health information about a loved one's condition.

The community resource center at the Cameron Park *colonia* in Brownsville, Texas, has many programs for the residents, most of whom are low-income Mexican immigrants with little formal education. Programs include English, GED, and parenting classes, in addition to referrals to public assistance programs. The center uses the services of paid *promotoras* (promoters), community leaders, and lay outreach workers to inform their neighbors about educational, government, and social programs. Project librarians trained the *promotoras* in the use of MedlinePlus *en español*, who in turned used it to find health information for fellow residents (Bowden et al. 2006).

Bowden et al. (2006) identify several factors to account for the success of the Med High and *colonia* projects. People are interested in health information when they have an immediate need for it. A convenient, accurate, and personalizable source of information was needed at the school of health sciences and by the *promotoras* who served as information providers in their community. MedlinePlus fulfilled that need. Educational settings are better than clinical settings for providing Internet-based health information. Both successful sites had paid staff members who understood the potential application of MedlinePlus and promoted it enthusiastically. Peer training is an effective way to share information—high school students and *colonia* residents both showed a preference for learning from a peer over learning from an unfamiliar librarian. Finally, assessment and evaluation were crucial to the success of the projects. According to Warner et al. (2005), the following elements were vital: community assessment or researching the needs of the target group, using a theory-based model to guide the outreach methods and evaluate the results, and flexibility on the part of outreach planners.

NLM has learned the importance of assessment and evaluation in taking on the important but tough challenge of outreach. In an effort to encourage planning and assessment, NLM in collaboration with the Pacific Northwest Regional Medical Library (also home to the Outreach Evaluation Resource Center [OERC]), published a manual, *Measuring the Difference: Guide to Planning and Evaluating Health Information Outreach*. The guide encapsulates the importance of evaluation: "Overall, evaluation helps programs refine and sharpen their focus; provide accountability to funders, managers, or administrators; improve quality so that effectiveness is maximized; and better understand what is achieved and how outreach has made a difference. Limited attention to evaluation can result in continuation of outreach activities that are ineffective and/or inefficient; failure to set priorities; or an inability to demonstrate to funding agencies that the outreach activities are of high quality" (Burroughs and Wood 2000).

Despite NLM's guidance in evaluation, the availability of evaluation training and resources from OERC, and the general nudging from NN/LM offices, a survey of forty libraries engaged in outreach showed that 36 percent of projects reported no formal evaluation method (Fama et al. 2005). Clearly, outreach librarians in health sciences libraries are struggling to understand and apply evaluation methods.

In conducting their survey, Fama et al. learned that the term "outreach" is used in multiple ways in health sciences libraries. It can refer to externally funded projects to unaffiliated users as described above. Outreach can also refer to liaison type activities, where medical librarians serve as library representatives to a particular college or department on campus, a service model frequently used in general academic libraries. Several academic medical libraries offer "house calls," a form of outreach whereby librarians go to faculty or staff offices to provide individual or small group training and assistance in using the plethora of electronic information products that can overwhelm new or infrequent users. Outreach can also refer to clinical librarian programs where librarians rapidly supply clinicians with research-based information to support patient care and may accompany providers on rounds. Supported clinicians can be treating humans or animals; Texas A&M University Medical Sciences Library has a veterinary clinical librarian program (Olmstadt et al. 2001). Medical librarians may describe marketing effort or Web-based projects as outreach. Because outreach is a necessarily flexible concept, agreement by stakeholders on the definition and goals of outreach and how those align with the missions of the library and institution are prerequisites to planning and creating a successful outreach program (Fama et al. 2005).

Academic medical libraries and outreach librarians across the country exert great effort to reach beyond the campus walls. The ubiquity and longevity of medical library outreach are the result of several factors. First, the aims are noble and important. For both health care providers and consumers, having access to information can mean the difference between sickness and health or even life and death. The NLM, the top of the health sciences library hierarchy, creates important information tools and encourages their promotion by supporting outreach financially and structurally through the NN/LM. The regional NN/LM offices cultivate close relationships with member libraries, administer programs, and disperse the funds on a local level. For every federal dollar spent, health sciences libraries doing the outreach contribute several in-kind dollars (Bunting 1987). Effective health information outreach needs many ingredients: sufficient time, money, and personnel; persistence; flexibility; collaboration with partners; knowing and addressing the needs of the targeted population; technological and cultural know-how; and a sense of humor. It is a difficult task that is worth taking on because, ultimately, having access to and using good information can improve a provider's ability to treat patients, help patients make good decisions, reduce health disparities, and assist the public health community to promote the health of the population.

REFERENCES

Bloomquist, Harold. "The Status and Needs of Medical School Libraries in the United States." *Journal of Medical Education* 38, no. 3 (March 1963): 145–163.

Bowden, Virginia M., Frederick B. Wood, Debra G. Warner, Cynthia A. Olney, Evelyn R. Olivier, and Elliot R. Siegel. "Health Information Hispanic Outreach in the Texas Lower Rio Grande Valley." *Journal of the Medical Library Association* 94, no. 2 (April 2006): 180–189. http://www.pubmedcentral.nih.gov/articlerender.fcgi?tool=pubmed& pubmedid=16636711 (accessed March 15, 2008).

Bunting, Alison. "The Nation's Health Information Network: History of the Regional Medical Library Program, 1965–1985." *Bulletin of the Medical Library Association* 75, no. 3 supplement (July 1987): 1–62. http://www.pubmedcentral.nih.gov/articlerender. fcgi? tool=pubmed&pubmedid=3315058 (accessed March 15, 2008).

Burroughs, Catherine M. and Fred B. Wood. *Measuring the Difference: Guide to Planning and Evaluating Health Information Outreach.* Bethesda, Md.: National Library of Medicine, 2000.

Cogdill, Keith. "Progress in Health Sciences Librarianship: 1970–2005." *Advances in Librarianship* 30 (2006): 145–177. http://www.sciencedirect.com/science?_ob=Article URL&_udi=B7J0F-4MTDBJN-6&_user=952835&_coverDate=12%2F31%2F2006&_ rdoc=6&_fmt=full&_orig=browse&_srch=doc-info(%23toc%2321325%232006%239996999 99%23641806%23FLA%23display%23Volume)&_cdi=21325&_sort=d&_docanchor=&_ct= 15&_acct=C000049198&_version=1&_urlVersion=0&_userid=952835&md5=db6bfe8644 dc1bc15910cae6b8ad56be (accessed March 15, 2008).

DeBakey, Michael E. *Improving Health Professionals' Access to Information: Report of The Board of Regents.* Bethesda, Md.: National Library of Medicine, 1989.

Fama, Jane, Donna Berryman, Nancy Harger, Paul Julian, Nancy Peterson, Margaret Spinner, and Jennifer Varney. "Inside Outreach: A Challenge for Health Sciences Librarians." *Journal of the Medical Library Association* 93, no. 3 (July 2005): 327–337. http://www.pubmedcentral.nih.gov/articlerender.fcgi?tool=pubmed&pubmedid=16059422 (accessed March 15, 2008).

Hurst-Wahl, Jill. "Librarians and Second Life." *Information Outlook* 11, no. 6 (June 2007): 44–45, 47, 49–50, 53.

Miller, Naomi, Eve-Marie Lacroix, and Joyce E. B. Backus. "MedlinePlus: Building and Maintaining the National Library of Medicine's Consumer Health Web Service." *Bulletin of the Medical Library Association* 88, no. 1 (January 2000): 11–17. http:// www.pubmedcentral.nih.gov/articlerender.fcgi?tool=pubmed&pubmedid=10658959 (accessed March 15, 2008).

National Library of Medicine. "Charting the Course for the 21st Century: NLM's Long Range Plan 2006–2016." September 19, 2006a. http://www.nlm.nih.gov/pubs/ plan/lrp06/report/default.html (accessed March 15, 2008).

National Library of Medicine. "Factsheet: MEDLINE Journal Selection." January 1, 1988. http://www.nlm.nih.gov/pubs/factsheets/jsel.html (accessed March 15, 2008).

National Library of Medicine. "Factsheet: National Network of Libraries of Medicine." October 8, 2002a. http://www.nlm.nih.gov/pubs/factsheets/nnlm.html (accessed March 15, 2008).

National Library of Medicine. "National Network of Libraries of Medicine (2006–2011)." December 10, 2002b. http://www.nlm.nih.gov/nno/nnlmlist2.html (accessed March 15, 2008).

National Library of Medicine. "PubMed Celebrates its 10th Anniversary," *NLM Technical Bulletin*, October 5, 2006b. http://www.nlm.nih.gov/pubs/techbull/so06/so06_pm_10.html (accessed March 15, 2008).

National Network of Libraries of Medicine South Central Region. "Guide for NN/LM SCR Awardees." http://nnlm.gov/scr/outreach/subcontractorsguide.html (accessed March 15, 2008).

Olmstadt, William, Christine L. Foster, Nancy G. Burford, Norma F. Funkhouser, and Joe Jaros. "Clinical veterinary librarianship—the Texas A&M University experience." *Bulletin of the Medical Library Association* 89, no. 4 (October 2001): 395–397. http://www.pubmedcentral.nih.gov/articlerender.fcgi?tool=pubmed&pubmedid=11837262 (accessed March 15, 2008).

Second Life Library. "About SL Library 2.0." http://infoisland.org/ (accessed March 15, 2008).

Stephenson, Priscilla L., Brenda F. Green, Richard L. Wallace, Martha F. Earl, Jan T. Orick, and Mary Virginia Taylor. "Community Partnerships for Health Information Training: Medical Librarians Working with Health-care Professionals and Consumers in Tennessee." *Health Information and Libraries Journal* 21, supplement 1 (June 2004): 20–26. http://www.blackwell-synergy.com/links/doi/10.1111/j.1740-3324.2004.00498.x (accessed March 15, 2008).

Warner, Debra G., Cynthia A. Olney, Fred B. Wood, Lucille Hansen, and Virginia Bowden. "High School Peer Tutors Teach MedlinePlus: A Model for Hispanic Outreach." *Journal of the Medical Library Association* 93, no. 2 (April 2005): 243–252. http://www.pubmedcentral.nih.gov/articlerender.fcgi?tool=pubmed&pubmedid=15858628 (accessed March 15, 2008).

Watson, Michael M., Donna F. Timm, Dawn M. Parker, Mararia Adams, Angela D. Anderson, Dennis A. Pernotto, and Marianne Comegys. "Using a Portable Wireless Computer Lab to Provide Outreach Training to Public Health Workers." *Medical Reference Services Quarterly* 25, no. 4 (Winter 2006): 1–9. http://www.haworthpress.com/store/E-Text/View_EText.asp?sid=0F7TXSVAR5WB8K1VWQLJ7CE32752C771&a=3&s=J115&v=25&i=4&fn=J115v25n04%5F01 (accessed March 15, 2008).

22

ENGAGING IN ECONOMIC DEVELOPMENT: PURDUE UNIVERSITY'S MANAGEMENT & ECONOMICS LIBRARY

Hal Kirkwood and Tomalee Doan

Purdue University's Management & Economics Library (MEL) is embarking on a significant engagement initiative to meet the goals and objectives of the Purdue Libraries' Strategic Plan 2006–2011. Contributions to the engagement mission of the university arise from the libraries' strength in support of learning and discovery and a commitment to help meet the information needs of the residents of Indiana. In 1999 the Kellogg Commission on the Future of State and Land Grant Institutions set out to define the future direction of public universities and to recommend a course of action. One of the reports to come out of this commission was "Returning to Our Roots: The Engaged Institution, Third Report," which focused on the importance of public universities increasing their connection with their communities. The commission recommended moving beyond "outreach" toward "engagement"; more specifically, they "refer to institutions that have redesigned their teaching, research, and extension and service functions to become even more sympathetically and productively involved with their communities, however community may be defined." In support of the commission recommendation, the Purdue University Strategic Plan emphasizes this concept of "engagement" by addressing the needs of society. Key characteristics include effective partnerships with public and private agencies and organizations as well as among disciplines within the university community to respond to a variety of social, environmental, and economic development needs. This is a vital role for the university in strengthening Indiana's economy and improving the qualifications of the state's workforce. The Purdue University Libraries have also built into their strategic plan a key section on "engagement." The libraries' strategic redesign seeks to:

- Provide focused collection and information resources to support the university's learning and discovery goals.

- Preserve the intellectual and cultural record through collections and archives.
- Meet the changing needs of students and faculty through access to information resources characterized by an effective balance of collections held locally, cooperation with resource-sharing partners, and availability of electronic resources.
- Actively seek opportunities to collaborate with organizations that reach the greater community.

Our vision focuses on the significant value that business information can bring to a community for greater economic development and individual enrichment. MEL is uniquely placed to provide resources, deliver training, and to facilitate communication between varied constituents. We strive to leverage these assets to support the greater community while fulfilling the land grant role of the university. MEL's focus on participation in educational outreach, collaboration with libraries across the state, and participation in sponsored economic-outreach activities required putting energy and resources into developing engagement initiatives to support small businesses and entrepreneurial development within the state of Indiana. Two MEL collaborative state outreach projects currently underway are:

- *Indiana Cooperative Library Services Authority* (INCOLSA) to promote the state-funded consortium databases available through the INSPIRE portal (http://www.inspire.net/); the Libraries Mean Business Initiative.
- *Entrepreneurship Business Information Network* (e-Bin), a partnership with Purdue Extension, Indiana Wired, and the Indiana Small Business Development Centers to pilot a project providing access to resources at the extension offices to support small businesses and entrepreneurial growth in 14 surrounding counties (http://sharepoint.agriculture.purdue.edu/ebin).

WHAT'S INVOLVED IN SUPPORTING ENGAGEMENT ENDEAVORS

Before involving MEL in these collaborative partnerships, there was a need to review several managerial objectives to lead the organization properly and ensure alignment with library strategic efforts. Some of the objectives included analyzing organizational support, project management strategies, internal and external communication methods, assessment and overall impact of the project, and determining what constitutes a successful outcome. The primary purpose is to promote economic development and advance information literacy throughout our community and state. In any engagement effort, the use of library resources, including access to electronic databases, not only increases the usage of our resources but also demonstrates added value to a broader range of users. Promoting library value through information literacy outreach initiatives and informing our community of users about business information resources through our instructional training opportunities serves to meet a critical role in broadening our overall information literacy objective for enhancing lifelong learning throughout our community. To make these resources available requires a considerable demand for effective communication between database vendors, institutional and library IT departments, and those individuals involved in licensing at the institution. Negotiation among the various partners comes into play if additional costs are incurred to provide access beyond the campus environment. It is not unrealistic to envision creative partnerships as engagement efforts strengthen and grow. Grant money to acquire additional resources and personnel may be required.

From an administrative perspective, leadership must focus on having adequate staff to support excellent service to both the library's primary users in addition to the new "engaged" constituents. Certain customer service standards must already be in place within the library organization before embarking on any external outreach and engagement initiative. Using project management software at this time can be very effective in examining your library projects and all critical timelines. If the engagement opportunity is assessed as a high priority, it may be time to determine what projects or work processes do not move forward and communicate that information to library staff. It is better not to take on an engagement activity if you cannot deliver on your service promises to your primary and new external constituencies. The message here is *focus on your customers and their desired outcome*, which requires excellent communication, often times among several groups both internally and externally.

Library managers must also consider how initiatives are conceived, how professional librarian specialists pursue opportunities, who the key players are in the engagement initiative, and how best the library can serve the needs of the community. Understanding these components will assist in assessing the impact of the total outreach effort for the project. From a marketing perspective, librarians all need to be sharing, communicating, and sending the same messages about the library's resources and its value so the engagement partners do not mistake what deliverable can be expected. Taking great care about the library's reputation and deliverables will build value and create recognition for further engagement opportunities.

This happened with our Entrepreneurial Business Information Network engagement effort; an additional follow-up project resulted because of our involvement with the agricultural extension community working with small business entrepreneurs. Therefore, listen to your staff and their suggestions regarding strategies in creating the implementation plan for any engagement effort. Their insight and expertise is extremely useful information in determining effective support, important buy-in about the project, and determining assessment for success. You must build trust so you will have bench strength in your professional staffing for your organization to be able to carry out a sustained engagement plan. Once the project has been assessed, expectations of the library's role has been determined, the deliverables agreed upon, such as level of staffing, how transfer of knowledge will take place through instructional training sessions, resources used, and technology platforms determined, it is important for the manager to turn over the project to the appropriate staff to do the work and build in check-in mechanisms to track the progress of the project. Let others manage and lead.

As the process for the engagement plan continues, it is also important to convey the library's effort through appropriate channels of communication and marketing. Providing accurate information about the initiative with appropriate marketing channels helps strengthen the overall branding and strategic efforts of the library. This sounds so simple but, in reality, as a profession we don't necessarily do this final step well.

INFLUENCE OF STRATEGIC PLANNING

MEL's initiatives are driven by the strategic plans of Purdue University and of the Purdue Libraries. The mission of the university is "to serve the citizens of Indiana, the United States, and the world through discovery that expands the realm of knowledge, learning through dissemination and preservation of knowledge, and engagement through exchange of knowledge." The mission of the Purdue Libraries is "to foster a dynamic information environment that advances learning, discovery, and engagement." The key term within these two mission statements is "engagement," for this is the externally focused concept in each statement.

The university strategic plan consists of several goals; one goal focuses specifically on external engagements.

Engagement: Effectively address the needs of society through engagement. Key characteristics include:

- Effective partnerships with public and private agencies and organizations as well as among disciplines within the university community to respond to a variety of social, environmental, and economic development needs.
- A vital role for the university in strengthening Indiana's economy and improving the qualifications of the state's workforce.

The Purdue Libraries" strategic plan also contains a goal on engagement: Engagement: Enhanced quality of life.

- Apply specialized knowledge and information resources to collaboratively address challenges and to enhance the intellectual, economic, and cultural life of individuals and communities at the local, state, and national levels and internationally.

It is within the context of these strategic plan goals that MEL moved forward on the INCOLSA Libraries Mean Business and Purdue Extension eBin initiatives.

PRIOR ACTIVITY

The Purdue Libraries embarked on an outreach project in the late 1990s as part of a grant with the Purdue Employees Federal Credit Union. The grant emphasized providing services to the local community in conjunction with the local public libraries. A workshop series was created and taught by Purdue Librarians as a service to the community. The workshops were marketed by the West Lafayette Public Library and the Tippecanoe County Public Library to their constituents. The topics of the workshops were Online Investing, Online Drug Information, and Searching the Internet. These topics were identified as the most relevant for the greater community. The workshop series was a success, running during the summer for three years. A new library administration determined that new endeavors were desirable, and the workshop series came to an end. The workshop series effectively laid the foundation for further engagement opportunities. It demonstrated the ability of the Purdue Libraries, and especially the MEL, to develop successful programs external to Purdue University. The series also demonstrated the need within the surrounding community for greater exposure to business information.

CURRENT INITIATIVES

Libraries Mean Business

A consultant hired by the Indiana Cooperative Library Services Authority (INCOLSA) approached the libraries seeking assistance with a planned statewide initiative, Libraries Mean Business. INCOLSA is a consortial body that facilitates resource sharing and database acquisition across the state. INCOLSA joins 768 member institutions and 2,200 physical libraries with the purpose of making consortial database acquisitions, sharing library catalogs, interlibrary loan, and continuing education opportunities. An INCOLSA portal called INSPIRE (http://www.inspire.net) provided access to a suite of EBSCOHost databases to all of the residents of the state of Indiana. The INSPIRE databases were one of the earliest statewide database arrangements providing access to every resident within a state. INCOLSA had identified that, although there was substantial use of the INSPIRE site at the K–12 level, there was less use by Indiana businesses. They saw an opportunity to market the business information within INSPIRE to support small business and economic development activities throughout the state.

The consultant's role was to schedule, market, and facilitate events at regional development centers and public libraries for the Libraries Mean Business Initiative. He would conduct the initial communication with the public library host; assist with marketing materials; and communicate with local newspapers and chambers of commerce to facilitate effective media exposure for the event. Librarians participated as the "experts" on the resources and databases within INSPIRE. Librarians from several academic libraries and the Indiana Chamber of Commerce all participated in the initial pilot of the Libraries Mean Business Initiative. Each event consisted of a training session for librarians and staff, followed by an open session for the public. The consultant introduced INCOLSA and the INSPIRE portal while the librarian then presented a series of questions on the topics of small business development, job hunting/career development, and nonprofit support.

MEL became involved very early on in the project, seeing an opportunity to participate in a statewide initiative to spread business information knowledge to a much broader audience and to support greater economic development within the state.

The early objectives of the Libraries Mean Business initiative were to:

- pilot the content and format of the presentations
- expose the resources and databases within a community and economic development setting
- develop a cadre of librarian "experts"
- assess the impact of the program for further development statewide

A longer term goal was to present a workshop in all ninety-two counties within the state. The content and format of the sessions mutated noticeably after the earliest sessions. Originally, the sessions consisted of three distinct workshops on career development, small business development, and nonprofit support. However, this format was problematic in regard to attendance and scheduling. The participation from MEL resulted in revising the questions in the three topical sections and in focusing the workshop into a single combined session. The combined session format produced a dramatic positive impact on attendance because participants were often deeply interested in one topic but curious about the other topics. Numerous sessions were presented throughout the state. A key issue in the early stages was the appropriate level of instruction within the workshops. The expectation was that the attendees would have a disparate level of technical ability, and this was found to be true throughout the sessions. Consideration was given to the primary objectives and how best to meet them. Thus the focus was on answering likely questions within each of the three topic areas: career development, small business development, and nonprofit prospect research. Answers were provided in handouts with a step-by-step list of actions taken to obtain the correct information. The handouts also served as effective tools for users to explore after the sessions. The questions focused on valuable content that was otherwise considered unavailable or prohibitively expensive to obtain.

The sessions successfully highlighted the value of the business databases and resources to key people within each community. Entrepreneurs, nonprofit representatives, career guidance counselors, and key financial officers from local banks were in attendance at many sessions. They were consistently unaware of the company profiles, business articles, funding opportunities, and career resources available through the INSPIRE portal. Many attendees saw the value of the information during the session when problems they were dealing with were quickly solved by the available resources. It also stoked greater demand for this type of information, providing an opportunity to seek additional funding and consortial arrangements for additional resources. An outcome from the Libraries Mean Business initiative was the recent statewide acquisition of the ReferenceUSA database. The Libraries Mean Business initiative provided effective exposure across the state. Because of a restructuring within the state, INCOLSA now reports to the Indiana State Library, and the Libraries Mean Business Initiative is currently on hiatus. However, a recent development is the rollout of a new INCOLSA business portal called Indiana Business Builder (http://www.indianabusinessbuilder.net/).

ENTREPRENEURSHIP BUSINESS INFORMATION NETWORK

In 2006 the Burton D. Morgan Center for Entrepreneurship developed a Certificate of Entrepreneurship for undergraduate students. The purpose of the certificate was to provide students from any discipline with a strong foundation in entrepreneurial skills. A committee was formed of faculty from across campus, including staff from the MEL, to provide interdisciplinary insight and discussion regarding the curricular development of the certificate. MEL's participation also included providing business information instruction in the core courses within the Entrepreneurship curriculum.

In the fall of 2007 the assistant program leader of the Purdue Extension Office and a senior associate from the Purdue Center for Regional Development were beginning to develop an idea based on the concept of economic gardening developed in Littleton, Colorado. Economic gardening focuses on growing the economy from within by assisting local businesses, supporting local and regional entrepreneurship activities, and by cultivating local expertise. Their idea was to create the Entrepreneurship Business Information Network (eBin). The director of the Certificate of Entrepreneurship program connected them with the MEL. A dialogue was started between the Purdue Extension Office and the Purdue Center for Regional Development and Tomalee Doan and Hal Kirkwood from the MEL. Their desire was to strengthen the economic development mission of the Purdue Extension Office to increase community vitality, build leadership capacity, enhance public decision making, and resolve public issues. The objective was to serve a selected group of MEL's resources out to the extension offices to support their role in increasing economic and small business development. Tomalee Doan, head of the MEL, recognized this as an opportunity to partner with a university organization that supports statewide economic development.

Specific business information needs were identified with the representatives from the Purdue Extension Office and the Purdue Center for Regional Development. Key areas included business periodicals, agricultural and demographic data, company information, tax/accounting information, and business start-up resources. These were all areas that MEL could provide to the extension offices. The resources, valued at over $100,000 annually, are served through the eBin portal https://sharepoint.agriculture.purdue.edu/ebin. The libraries' role is to provide a selection of databases and resources; work on the navigation and architecture of the portal; support the marketing; and provide training on resources to the extension office staff. A browser toolbar (http://mymelebin.mylibrarytoolbar.com/) was also created for installation at each workstation location with the objective of facilitating better access to the resources.

The network will initially consist of a pilot program within the fourteen surrounding counties to Purdue University. A workstation will be set up at each Purdue Extension office to provide access to the eBin portal. Each rollout of a workstation will consist of a training session on the portal and available databases. The long-term target for eBin is to connect to every Purdue Extension office in each of the ninety-two counties within the state of Indiana. Different entities provide support for the eBin project. Support for questions on the database content is provided by the MEL. Technical questions are handled by the School of Agriculture's Information Technology Department (AgIT). AgIT is also responsible for the hardware and network configuration for each workstation. AgIT coordinating the implementation guarantees that each will be a Purdue University workstation and provide the necessary access to the databases. Other organizations involved include Indiana WIRED and the Greater Lafayette Small Business Development Center; both focused on promoting business development and regional economic development within the state.

Clinton County, Indiana, was selected for the initial pilot in the late fall of 2007. The Small Business Development Specialist on-site at the Extension Office was trained on the resources and handled the marketing of the event. A ribbon-cutting event held at the Extension Office highlighted the launch of the eBin portal and on-site workstation. Several more offices were scheduled to have rolled out, but because of database access and hardware installation issues, the next set of offices will come online in October 2008. The expectation is that Fall 2008 will see the rollout across the remaining offices within the pilot group. An assessment will then be made to determine the most effective course of action for rolling out across the remaining counties. The MEL is using information-tracking software to record questions relating to entrepreneurship and small business queries that come into our information services unit via email, phone, and instant messaging. The library is also identifying inquiries directly related to the eBin when possible and will use that data to assess staff time and resources used to support the fourteen-county pilot. That information will then be provided to the Purdue Extension Office and the Purdue Center for Regional Development for consideration of extending the project beyond the pilot.

CONCLUSION

The Indiana Business Research Center at the Kelley School of Business-Indiana University surveyed public and academic libraries on their economic impact. The outcome was the Economic Impact of Libraries report (2007; http://www.ibrc. indiana.edu/studies/EconomicImpactOfLibraries_2007.pdf). The key findings identified academic libraries as providing significant value to the state and local communities. However, they were not always perceived as effectively supporting statewide economic development. Recommendations included:

- Implement a program to expand business and economic development focus
- Increase outreach to the business community

The university's and libraries' strategic plans target precisely these types of initiatives for exploration and development. In its own spirit of entrepreneurship, the MEL has extended substantive business information resources and information literacy initiatives beyond campus boundaries. The library has placed a significant value on forging creative partnerships with campus partners to support the goals of the university's strategic efforts. New business faculty librarians have been hired to support interdisciplinary research throughout campus and forge new campus partnerships. These outreach efforts with other campus units, schools, and colleges broaden the impact of shared university resources and leverages expertise in several areas, which better serves our statewide community. The engagement projects supported by the MEL have provided other useful information. The library has discovered several statewide organizations whose mission is to also serve small business and entrepreneurial efforts. Many of these organizations have significant overlap in service efforts and resources. The MEL envisions its future role as an effective partner with these statewide organizations in collectively coordinating and organizing their business information needs, which in turn will produce even greater economic development opportunities across the state.

REFERENCES

Indiana Business Research Center. *Economic Impact of Libraries Report*. Commissioned by the Indiana State Library, Bloomington, Ind., 2007. http://www.stats.indiana.edu/topic/libraries.asp (accessed May 1, 2008).

Kellogg Commission on the Future of State and Land-Grant Universities. *Returning to Our Roots: The Engaged Institution*. Third Report. Washington, D.C., 1999. http://www.nasulgc.org/NetCommunity/Page.aspx?pid=305&srcid=236 (accessed May 1, 2008).

SELECTED BIBLIOGRAPHY

Deidra N. Herring

This annotated bibliography provides resources and background information supporting significant academic library outreach and digital initiatives discussed in this book. Listed resources include helpful articles, websites, blogs, and books focusing on university library collaborations with P–12 schools, public libraries, and initiatives pertaining to special collections. Although "outreach beyond the campus walls" can be defined and interpreted in many ways, the selections capture a broad range of model programs and resources for a variety of librarians and educators.

To bridge the gap between P–12 schools and universities, much emphasis has been placed on establishing national standards and finding the appropriate resources to support these collaborations, both to prepare students for success in college and to support information literacy in general. Because public libraries are closely connected to communities and are educators of diverse populations, they too have worked to prepare students and the communities they serve for information literacy in the twenty-first century.

Several themes emerge throughout the readings. In addition to public and academic libraries, specialized readings include promoting special collections, digital projects, and medical library outreach. Successful outreach and programming includes establishing national standards, strategic planning, time, and financial support. Significant resources about grants are also included through articles, blogs, and websites that provide opportunities for grant seekers to apply for federal, state, or private funding for special projects. These readings focus on issues surrounding partnerships and explain the importance of educating and providing users with access to needed information.

Much has been published about many of the topics covered, but the compilation is selective. The readings were chosen to provide an overview of what was done in the past, what is currently being done, and recommendations for the future. The topics discussed are worth exploring to prepare users for lifelong learning.

P–12 AND INFORMATION LITERACY

American Association of School Librarians and the Association of College and Research Libraries Task Force on the Educational Role of Libraries. *ACRL/AASL Blueprint for Collaboration*. 2000. http://www.ala.org/ala/acrl/acrlpubs/whitepapers/acrlaaslblueprint.cfm (accessed March 25, 2008).

This document is repeatedly cited in the library literature. It provides information about the ACRL/AASL Joint Task Force on Educational Collaboration between K–12 and academic librarians. The outline includes guidelines created to define information literacy and competency standards for students. Four major recommended areas are addressed in the document: collaboration, joint association activities, continuing education for librarians, and outreach. The blueprint also provides a noncomprehensive list of examples of possible university and school partnerships.

Barefoot, Betsy. "Bridging the Chasm: First-Year Students and the Library." *Chronicle of Higher Education* 52, no. 20 (January 2006): B16.

As an extension to Cahoy's article (see below), Barefoot further identifies issues related to student anxiety by suggesting that librarians and teaching faculty share the responsibility of encouraging student confidence. Educators can help first-year college students adjust and become more confident in their research by sharing library contact information and actively assisting with projects. The author examines differences between students entering academia who are prepared for college-level research versus those who are not. First-year student attitudes and perceptions about academic libraries and benefits of peer support are discussed. Librarians and any educator working with college-bound students will benefit from the article.

Boff, Colleen. *Bowling Green State University Libraries' Pathways to Academic Libraries (PAL)*. 2007. http://www.bgsu.edu/colleges/library/infosrv/lue/pal (accessed March 20, 2008).

For students who experience library anxiety, the PAL website can be a useful tool. It is easy to use and helps high school students to use academic resources. The website answers general questions about Bowling Green's Library system. The user has a choice of reading text or watching a short video. Categories include Places and Spaces, The Big Information Picture, Online Searching, and Tips for Success.

Bowling Green State University Libraries. *Transitioning to College: Helping You Succeed*. http://www.transitioning2college.org (accessed March 20, 2008).

The website is similar to PAL and serves as an excellent introduction for first-year academic students to academic library resources.

Burhanna, Kenneth J. "Instructional Outreach to High Schools: Should You Be Doing It?" *Communications in Information Literacy* 1, no. 2 (Fall 2007): 74–88.

This article is an important contribution to the literature examining academic institutions involved with high school outreach. The article takes a practical approach in documenting key issues and questions that should be addressed before collaborating with schools. Kent State University has committed to supporting young adults entering college. They have found it to be a positive but challenging experience. The article suggests that institutions should ask hard questions, including whether or not establishing an outreach program is within their mission and if they have the personnel and other resources needed to establish and maintain a successful program. Communication, time, and class size are major concerns as well as the lack of research and assessment on how students benefit from instructional outreach.

Burhanna, Kenneth J. and Mary Lee Jensen. "Collaborations for Success: High School to College Transitions." *Reference Services Review* 34, no. 4 (2006): 509–519.

The authors identify the benefits of preparing students for higher education and provide key factors for establishing meaningful high school partnerships between academic librarians, high school library media specialists, and teachers. Burhanna, a First-Year Experience librarian, outlines his experiences at Kent State University. The authors examine grants supporting several successful programs including the College Transition Initiative and Informed Transitions: High School Outreach Program. Both programs focus on helping Ohio students successfully transition to college.

Cahoy, Ellysa Stern. "Put Some Feeling into It!: Integrating Affective Competencies into K-20 Information Literacy Standards." *Knowledge Quest* 32, no. 4 (March/April 2004): 25–28.

The article argues the need for establishing Affective Competency Skill standards as a part of the AASL and ACRL guidelines to support confidence building for students. Research clearly indicates that confident students are able to become more competent researchers over time and confident students feel more comfortable in seeking help to complete tasks successfully. However, those who struggle with "library anxiety" may fail to complete tasks. Until such affective competency skill standards are adopted, Cahoy encourages librarians to strive for new forms of academic programming to generate positive outcomes.

Carr, Jo Ann and Ilene F. Rockman. "Information Literacy Collaborations: A Shared Responsibility." *American Libraries* 34, no. 8 (2003): 52–54.

Carr and Rockman review the national trends on P–20 alliances for information literacy and provide background on the *ACRL/AASL Task Force on the Educational Role of Libraries*. A helpful chart shows the alignment of standards between academic and school librarians and how partnerships naturally make sense. Examples of institutional collaboration include five universities.

Kent State University Libraries' Library and Media Services. *ILILE: High School to College Transition Initiative*. http://www.library.kent.edu/page/10988 (accessed March 20, 2008).

The website provides background information about how these initiatives were developed by Kent State University Libraries and the Institute for Library and Information Literacy Education (ILILE). More information on Kent State University's ILILE Institute for Library and Information Literacy is available at http://www.ilile.org/index.html.

Manuel, Kate. "National History Day: An Opportunity for K–16 Collaboration." *Reference Services Review* 33, no. 4 (2005): 459–486.

Manuel discusses a unique program for National History Day partnering between K–12 schools, public libraries, academic libraries, and museums. She covers themes and shares background on how the program started. National History Day (NHD) is sponsored by the University of Maryland, Case Western University, the History Channel, Jostens, and ABC-Clio Schools. Its website is available at www.nationalhistoryday.org.

Miller, William and Rita M. Pellen, eds. *Libraries Beyond Their Institutions: Partnerships That Work*. New York: Haworth Information Press, 2005.

Both editors have served as administrators at the libraries for Florida Atlantic University. Dr. Miller has served as past president of the Association of College and Research Libraries and was awarded the Instruction Librarian of the Year in 2004. The editors have compiled a diverse group of articles written by notable authors that focus on how libraries partner and work with other units outside their institutions. The book is suitable for anyone looking for unique engagement opportunities within the community. The book has been published simultaneously as *Resource Sharing & Information Networks* 18, no. 1–2 (2005/2006).

Nichols, Janet W., Lothar Spang, and Kristy Padron. "Building a Foundation for Collaboration: K–20 Partnerships in Information Literacy." *Resource Sharing and Information Networks* 18, no. 1/2 (2005/2006): 5–12.

Nichols serves as a Coordinator of Instruction and Information Services and has served as co-chair of the AASL/ACRL Task Force. Spang and Padron are librarians for Instruction and Public Services. Nichols has contributed publications about information literacy and partnerships. Their article examines existing outreach opportunities and elaborates on pilot projects resulting in for-credit course workshops and in-service collaborations for teaching faculty, library media specialists, and administrators. Grant seeking is also covered as being a priority for collaborative programming. Background information on the AASL/ACRL Task Force and Standing Committee on Information Literacy is presented. The article has been published simultaneously in *Libraries Beyond Their Institutions: Partnerships That Work* (see Miller above.)

Smalley, Topsy N. "College Success: High School Librarians Make the Difference." *Journal of Academic Librarianship* 30, no. 3 (May 2004): 193–198.

The article supports the significance of teaching information literacy to high school students and outlines the ACRL and AASL literacy standards and competencies. The author examines a case study comparing schools with library programming to those without library media specialists. Results suggest that schools without libraries have a negative impact on student achievement not only for first-year college students but for research skills for lifelong learning.

Smith, Suzanne. "The Top 10 Things High School Seniors Need to Know About College Libraries." *The Book Report* 20, no. 5 (March/April 2002): 42.

Smith provides a succinct list for teens on suggested ways to approach academic research. The list can be used in any classroom situation for educators working with college-bound students.

FUNDING

Curry, Elizabeth A. "Play with the Slinky: Learning to Lead Collaboration Through a Statewide Training Project Aimed at Grants for Community Partnerships." *Resource Sharing & Information Networks* 18, no. 1/2 (2005/2006): 25–48.

As a trainer and consultant, the author shares her workshop experiences working with librarians to improve their leadership skills. She discusses building partnerships and how to initiate collaborations successfully. The article is important because training is often a key factor that is overlooked in starting new projects, mainly due to time and money. The author stresses the importance of providing professionals with essential skills needed to carry out the complex process of developing active relationships as well as obtaining grants for project support. Curry offers a refreshing approach encouraging participants to "think outside the box" during her sessions.

Fernandez, Donna. *School Grants for PK–12 Educators.* March 2008. http://k12grants.org/ (accessed March 20, 2008).

The author provides a helpful guide for PK–12 educators who are interested in writing grants. The purpose of the website is to help ease the tension of the process by including tips, sample proposals, workshops, government websites, and a listing of humorous postings as an added bonus. The "Let's Write a Grant" CD is optional and available for purchase.

Gerding, Stephanie and Pam MacKellar. *Library Grants* [blog]. http://www.librarygrants.
    blogspot.com/ (accessed March 20, 2008).

The authors maintain a current and comprehensive compilation of grant announcements.
The blog includes detailed descriptions on a variety of grants, website links for additional information, and deadlines. The authors have also posted reviews from their book, *Grants for
Libraries: A How-To-Do-It Manual*, published in 2006. According to Gerding and MacKellar, the blog is for "librarians interested in grant opportunities!"

Sullivan, Laura A."Grant Funding for Libraries." *The Bottom Line: Managing Library Finan-
    ces* 20, no. 4 (2007): 157–160.

Sullivan, a twenty-five-year library veteran, provides a concise and comprehensive overview of available funding resources provided by government and private organizations. She
provides additional resources that include useful blogs, professional websites, and information on major reference materials for university, public, and school libraries. Sullivan provides a good starting point for those seeking specific funding for programming or special
projects.

PUBLIC LIBRARY OUTREACH

American Library Association Rural, Native and Tribal Libraries of all Kinds Committee. *The
    Small but Powerful Guide to Winning Big Support for Your Rural Library.* Chicago:
    American Library Association, 2006. http://www.ala.org/ala/olos/oloscommittees/
    rnt/ruraltipsheet.pdf (accessed March 23, 2008).

The ALA Rural, Native and Tribal Libraries of All Kinds Committee provides an eight-
page, easy-to-use, downloadable booklet that supplies guidelines and tips for public librarians. Ideas include how to make the library more visible and strengthen community support
by establishing partnerships. Academic and other types of libraries, regardless of size, can also
benefit from the outline. The last page contains a useful list of Web resources including tools
and organization links for specific areas of interest.

DeCandido, GraceAnne A., ed., and the Office for Literacy and Outreach Services (OLOS).
    Literacy and Libraries: Learning from Case Studies. Chicago: Office for Literacy and
    Outreach Services, American Library Association, 2001.

This book provides a variety of case studies on adult learners and how literacy programs
across the country have made a significant difference in their lives. The author shares view-
points from librarians, educators, and administrators. The book helps readers understand
how public libraries provide adult education and technology in a diverse and multilingual society. The editor also discusses the "Literacy in Libraries Across America" initiative. The book
is a good example of how public libraries create opportunities within their communities and
implement programs to suit their users' needs.

Library Services to the Spanish-Speaking Committee, Reference and User Services Associa-
    tion, American Library Association. "Guidelines for the Development and Promotion
    of Multilingual Collections and Services." *Reference & User Services Quarterly* 47, no.
    2 (January 2007): 198–200.

Guidelines begin with a discussion of libraries on a national level and the lack of
adequately providing multicultural resources for an increasing immigrant population in the
United States. Readers are reminded that libraries are responsible for providing diverse and
appropriate services to support the needs of users. The prepared document is intended to be
a model for libraries to follow and use for evaluating programs and services.

National Endowment for the Arts and the Institute of Museum and Library Services. The Big Read. 2008. http://www.neabigread.org/ (accessed March 21, 2008).

The *Big Read* was created in 2006 as a pilot project and has continued to expand. This successful project has been a great way to promote reading and initiate open discussion. The website offers a national calendar of events and a list of featured books. The list contains a mixture of classic titles and popular authors. Information about guidelines is available for those seeking an opportunity to host an event.

Palmer, Liza and Elizabeth Peterson. "Grassroots Collaboration: Growing Community with the One Book, One Community Program." *Technical Services Quarterly* 24, no. 3 (2007): 51–65.

The One Book, One Community Program (OBOC) began in 1998 with The Washington Center for the Book at the Seattle Public Library. Its goal is to promote reading and initiate communication between library communities. Communities can include an array of groups such as schools and city, county, or state entities. The first event was *If Seattle Read the Same Book*, currently named *Seattle Reads*. The author talks about making creative connections not only for financial support but to develop new relationships. Over one hundred programs throughout the United States have adopted the *Seattle Reads* model. The article offers readers significant points to consider and a timeline for those seeking ways to develop similar programming.

The authors also emphasize the importance of collaborating with high schools. The National Endowment for the Humanities and National Endowment for the Arts grant segment has included a secondary school component for grant seekers. Research shows that there are great benefits for libraries when strong partnerships are formed.

The Center for the Book: Library of Congress provides the One Book Reading Promotion Projects site available at http://www.loc.gov/loc/cfbook/one-book.html. Past and present projects are listed by state.

Roy, Loriene. "Circle of Community." *American Libraries* 38, no. 10 (November 2007): 6.

The author addresses leadership and makes a strong point to remind library communities that there is still a desperate need to provide a variety of services to non-English-speaking users. Roy discusses services provided by the Minneapolis Public Library and its efforts to link its resources to a variety of languages for patrons. She addresses The American Library Association Office for Literacy and Outreach Services' efforts to provide minigrants to support information literacy. Roy also shares information about the International Children's Digital Library available at http://www.icdlbooks.org.

SPECIAL COLLECTIONS AND DIGITAL PROJECTS

Caplan, Priscilla. "Ten Years After." *Library Hi Tech* 25, no. 4 (2007): 449–453.

Caplan summarizes the past ten years on the progress of digital preservation efforts for cultural heritage institutions. She acknowledges a difference between the United States and Europe and programs to establish successful digital preservation. The collaborative and successful accomplishments of European efforts are due to a focus on training issues, research and publication, as well as creating a noncompetitive environment for funding. This is in contrast to the competitive model used in the United States. This article should be read in conjunction with De Stephano and Walters, who share data indicating a lack of collaboration between the archives and preservation departments in the ARL member libraries.

Carlson, Scott. "Few Libraries or Museums Digitize Collections." *Chronicle of Higher Education* 48, no. 47 (2002): A29.

This article summarizes several hundred institutions and discusses the area of digitization among academic libraries, museums, public libraries, and state library administrative agencies, a new development at the time the article was written. The survey shows lower participation in digital projects than expected. Policy and standards are recommended. Funding options are discussed, although some resources may be limited to ARL institutions. The ARL's Digital Initiatives Database is available at http://www.arl.org/did/ for registration.

Chute, Tamar G. "What's in a Name? Outreach vs. Basic Services: A Survey of College and University Archivists." *Journal of Archival Organization* 1, no. 2 (2002): 5–40.

This body of work shares information on what archivists consider to be outreach and what they practice in reality, as opposed to the definition created by the Society of American Archivists (SAA). Results of the survey show that basic reference services are considered to be a major part of outreach for archivists. Chute's work is an important contribution to the literature because it provides evidence that there are conflicting ideas about the definition of "outreach" and what it means among those professionals working with special collections. She recommends that the existing definition be updated to include specific examples for clarity and understanding. Change is needed as librarians strive to promote their collections in a nontraditional manner and promote other types of outreach initiatives.

De Stefano, Paula and Tyler O. Walters. "A Natural Collaboration: Preservation for Archival Collections in ARL Libraries." *Library Trends* 56, no. 1 (Summer 2007): 230–258.

One would assume that preservation and archives would be a natural partnership. However, De Stephano and Walters have found that during the past ten years low levels of collaborative efforts between archives and preservation within research libraries remain unchanged. Although the article does not specifically focus on outreach, it is an interesting take on the lack of cohesiveness between two very close entities. Compared to the Chute and Whittaker articles, similarities between preservation and archives are discussed. These issues are very relevant to how special collections, archives, and preservation view outreach and partnership. The disconnect between preservation and archives may have an impact on their future outreach initiatives.

Falk, Howard. "Developing Digital Libraries." *The Electronic Library* 21, no. 3 (2003): 258–261.

Falk provides an historical synopsis of the movement toward the creation of university digital repositories using DSpace technology and the use of rare and special collections. The importance of libraries as a physical space and place continues to diminish as digital resources grow in importance. The author also touches on the issue of consortial sharing of information and the need for reducing duplicate holdings.

Krishnamurthy, M. "Open Access, Open Source and Digital Libraries: A Current Trend in University Libraries Around the World." *Program: Electronic Library and Information Systems* 42, no. 1 (2008): 48–55.

The author addresses the global movement toward open access. The paper provides a brief history and definition of "digital libraries" created by the Digital Library Federation in 1998. An outline of major accomplishments provides detailed information about various technologies and software currently used to generate open access repositories. Scholars and researchers are increasingly benefiting from the struggle to gain free access to intellectual property through a growing number of repositories around the world. The following useful links are also included in the article.

• Bethesda Statement on Open Access Publishing. http://www.earlham.edu/~peters/fos/bethesda.htm.

- Berlin Declaration on Open Access to Knowledge in the Sciences and Humanities. October 2003. http://www.aepic.it/conf/index.php?cf=10.
- The Open Directory of Open Access Repositories- OpenDOAR, March 2008. University of Nottingham, UK. http://www.opendoar.org/.

Lavender, Kenneth, Scott Nicholson, and Jeffery Pomerantz. "Building Bridges for Collaborative Digital Reference Between Libraries and Museums Through an Examination of Reference in Special Collections." *Journal of Academic Librarianship* 31, no. 2 (2005): 106–118.

The authors discuss digital reference between libraries and museums becoming a common part of providing services as a collaborative effort to serve library patrons. However, museums may function differently from libraries and may not have comparable services. The authors describe the benefits and challenges to collaborative digital reference to serve both library and museum patrons.

Murray, Kathleen R. and Inga K. Hsieh. "Archiving Web-Published Materials: A Needs Assessment of Librarians, Researchers, and Content Providers." *Government Information Quarterly* 25, no. 1 (2008): 66–89.

The authors provide an in-depth study regarding a major digital preservation project called the "Web-at-Risk." The three-year collaboration between several universities is supported by the Library of Congress and is a part of the National Digital Information Infrastructure and Preservation Program. Participants include academic librarians, curators, archivists, researchers, and content providers. The study identifies materials to be archived for continuous access and to examine overall needs to make the project successful. Key concepts are defined and a list of valuable Web resources is included in the lengthy study.

Parry, Julie. "Librarians Do Fly: Strategies for Staying Aloft." *Library Management* 29, no. 1/2 (2008): 41–50.

In the interest of the twenty-first century librarian, the author elaborates on job descriptions and the necessary skills needed to survive in the age of digital resources. Technology skills and Web design are highly desired, but recent graduates do not always have that training. Parry shares the findings from a group of British academic librarians who outline four major areas "cybrarians" need to concentrate on to stay viable in the digital age. Collaboration is among the four major areas addressed.

Priebe, Ted, Amy Welch, and Marian MacGilvray. "The U.S. Government Printing Office's Initiatives for the Federal Depository Library Program to Set the Stage for the 21st Century." *Government Information Quarterly* 25, no. 1 (2008): 48–56.

The authors report on the successful initiatives implemented by the Government Printing Office (GPO). Over the years, the GPO has shown a great commitment by working with the Federal Depository Libraries Program (FDLP) to improve free public access to U.S. government information. The Catalog of U.S. Government Publications provides a user-friendly interface for searching at http://catalog.gpo.gov/.

The article also shares information for librarians concerning the FDLP Desktop including a free email news service called "FDLP Express." The service is for librarians interested in receiving information on topics of interest at http://www.fdlp.gov/. Although librarians can subscribe to the source, access is not obviously displayed on the home page. Users should go to the "Help" drop-down menu to access the login. Information about additional partnerships is also included.

Traister, Daniel. "Public Services and Outreach in Rare Book, Manuscript, and Special Collections Libraries." *Library Trends* 52, no. 1 (Summer 2003): 87–108.

Traister, a significant contributor to library literature, discusses issues surrounding rare books and manuscripts. The author anticipates the need for libraries actively to increase the visibility of their special collections through public service and outreach. Even though outreach is not a new concept, now more than ever library units are seeking unconventional ways to promote collections. It has become the norm to provide a more attractive and social atmosphere to make users feel welcome and encourage them to use materials. Compared to the past, it is now imperative that libraries promote their collections to remain relevant. Traister's idea of "get it, catalog it, and promote it" has become a way of life in special collections.

Visser, Michelle. "Special Collections at ARL Libraries and K-12 Outreach: Current Trends." *Journal of Academic Librarianship* 32, no. 3 (May 2006): 313–319.

The author shares information regarding her literature review and the lack of publications addressing K–12 and academic libraries working with special collections. She mentions successful programs and references Traister's article (see above), especially in regard to elementary and secondary students. Concerns with exposing rare materials during outreach programs are understandable. However, Visser dispels old traditions by reporting on great experiences of the University of Colorado at Boulder's Special Collections Department during K–12 visits.

Whittaker, Beth M. "Using Circulation Systems for Special Collections: Tracking Usage, Promoting the Collection, and Addressing the Backlogs." *College & Research Libraries* 69, no. 1 (January 2008): 28–35.

Whittaker has compiled useful information about patron use of special collections through The Ohio State University integrated library system. Although the article does not specifically address digital initiatives, it addresses selection and the decision-making process needed to connect readers to inaccessible special collections materials.

Whittaker, Beth M. "'Get It, Catalog It, Promote It': New Challenges to Providing Access to Special Collections." *RBM: A Journal of Rare Books, Manuscripts, and Cultural Heritage* 7, no. 2 (Fall 2006): 121–133.

The article is an important extension of Daniel Traister's views on promoting special collections. Challenges discussed include cataloging backlogs that result in inaccessibility, language barriers, and complications in determining users' needs. Whittaker examines how the material is being used because scholarship is constantly changing. She makes distinctions between departments of acquisitions, special collections, curators, preservation, and archives and points out the fragmentation, separation of workflow, and communication within technical services departments. She questions how special collections professionals can work with other departments to improve access, especially if there is a lack of communication. Readers are challenged to think of new ways to use existing resources.

Her experience in using MARC records and special collections cataloging provides needed information for catalogers and special collections professionals to improve services. She encourages readers to open a forum for more collaboration among librarians and reminds readers that Google has been at the forefront of providing access to more materials than ever.

DISCIPLINE-SPECIFIC OUTREACH

Arant, Wendi and Pixey Anne Mosley, eds. *Library Outreach, Partnerships and Distance Education: Reference Librarians at the Gateway.* New York: Haworth Information Press, 2000.

The book is divided into four sections relating to technology and outreach, making special connections by creating partnerships. A variety of approaches to outreach services are explored in the compilation of articles focusing on specific user groups from academic institutions. It provides excellent examples of websites and lists of references. Articles include topics addressing university archives via the Web, liaison programming, and outreach to distance learners.

Casey, Anne Marie, ed. *Off-Campus Library Services*. New York: Haworth Information Press, 2001.

The editor and contributors provide a wide variety of valuable articles taken from the proceedings of the Ninth Off-Campus Library Services Conference held in Portland, Oregon, in 2000. Sponsors include Central Michigan University Libraries and Central Michigan University's College of Learning focusing on supporting distance education. Articles address marketing library services to distance users and strategies to promote emerging technologies. Reliable resources include practical information that can be used by librarians and educators interested in distance programming.

Cogdill, Keith W. "Public Health Information Outreach." *Journal of the Medical Library Association* 95, no. 3 (July 2007): 290–292.

The author provides an introduction to the next article mentioned and provides a historical overview of partnerships between libraries and the public health workforce to educate health care professionals. He examines the challenges libraries face while promoting awareness of existing resources and providing multidisciplinary content to a growing workforce. The paper cites a variety of past projects placing emphasis on health care disaster-related resources, including the 9/11 response. Specific initiatives and websites are listed throughout the paper.

Cogdill, Keith W., Angela B. Ruffin, and P. Zoë Stavri. "The National Network of Libraries of Medicine's Outreach to the Public Health Workforce: 2001–2006." *Journal of the Medical Library Association* 95, no. 3 (2007): 310–315.

The authors provide an extension of the previous article "Public Health Information Outreach." The five-year study shares the accomplishments, issues, and future objectives of the National Network of Libraries of Medicine (NN/LM) regarding its outreach efforts. Study results show that most emphasis was placed on educating general public health workers on basic ways to access needed information.

Hallyburton, Ann, Nancy Kolenbrander, and Carolyn Robertson. "College Health Professionals and Academic Librarians: Collaboration for Student Health." *Journal of American College Health* 56, no. 4 (2008): 395–400.

Librarians Hallyburton and Kolenbrander share their experience based on a partnership with their Student Health Center's Wellness Coordinator, Carolyn Robertson. The authors sought a partnership to improve services for students. This was a natural extension and support system between the library and university health center professionals.

The study identifies students' specific health information needs and their inability to evaluate and access appropriate information. The paper notes a lack of involvement by academic librarians in guiding student research. Clear and significant recommendations are made by both librarians and the university health center staff to students seeking health care information. Collaboration regarding the provision of resources and training were key success factors.

According to the ACHA-NCHA Believability of Health Information, students preferred to consult with parents, the Internet, and friends as primary resources for health care information. However, they recognized that consultation with medical staff, health educators, and parents was more reliable. The study provides credible resources for libraries.

Hinegardner, Patricia G. and Alexa Mayo. "Selected Bioterrorism Web Sites for the Health Care Community and Consumer." *Internet Reference Services Quarterly* 6, no. 3/4 (2002): 1–15.

In response to the September 11, 2001, attacks and past threats of bioterrorism within the United States, the authors found a need to inform the public by providing online information specifically targeting bioterrorism and other related disasters. The paper is well formatted and can serve as an at-a-glance resource useful for the public and health care professionals. According to the authors, the websites are taken from "government organizations, educational institutions, or professional organizations and have been evaluated based on sponsorship, currency, content, and audience." The article was also simultaneously published in *Bioterrorism and Political Violence: Web Resources,* edited by M. Sandra Wood, Haworth Information Press, 2002.

Kelsey, Paul and Sigrid Kelsey. *Outreach Services in Academic and Special Libraries.* Binghamton, New York: Haworth Information Press, 2003.

The authors have compiled case studies on a variety of successful outreach programs across communities developed by academic librarians. The case studies are compelling and discuss ideas that are rarely explored. A variety of specific models of outreach are examined. Topics include providing programming to unconventional user groups, such as African American churches focusing on health, and addressing the information needs of firefighters. The book was published simultaneously as the *Reference Librarian,* number 82, 2003.

Medical Library Association. *"Top 10" Most Useful Web Sites for Health Consumers.* http://www.mlanet.org/resources/medspeak/topten.html (accessed March 30, 2008).

This website provides access to ten important health-related areas that can be used by librarians, health care professionals, and consumers. Links include the National Library of Medicine's Medline Plus at http://www.medlineplus.gov. The site is easy to navigate and offers high-quality information and free access to public users. Additional sources for medical librarians such as conference dates can be found on the site.

McKay, Becky, Chris Foster, and Martha Bedard. "Electronic Document Delivery: What Users Want and How to Give It to Them." *Journal of Interlibrary Loan, Document Delivery and Electronic Reserve* 17, no. 3 (2007): 49–56.

The free ILLiad-based document delivery service was created by Virginia Polytechnic Institute interlibrary loan staff and is now owned by OCLC. The system is examined as a successful way to get users to use a variety of materials from the Texas A&M University Medical Sciences Library. Because Texas A&M University is "the only veterinary medical library in the state of Texas and collects veterinary materials comprehensively...it has a strong commitment to serving animal health practitioners throughout the state." This is a good example of providing outreach through the NN/LM, which also provides information for the general public at http://nnlm.gov/outreach/community/weblio.html.

INDEX

About the Editor and Contributors

Nancy Courtney is Coordinator of Outreach and Engagement at the Ohio State University Libraries and the editor of *Library 2.0 and Beyond: Innovative Technologies and Tomorrow's User* (Libraries Unlimited, 2007) and *Technology for the Rest of Us: A Primer on Computer Technologies for the Low-Tech Librarian* (Libraries Unlimited, 2005). She has a B.A. in Classics from Northwestern University and an M.S. in Library and Information Science from the University of Illinois.

Laurie M. Bridges is Assistant Professor and Business and Economics Librarian at Oregon State University. Her primary responsibilities include instruction and research consulting. Laurie received her Master of Library and Information Science from the University of Washington in 2006. She also holds an M.S. in College Student Services Administration from Oregon State University and a B.S.Ed. from the University of Nebraska-Lincoln.

Kenneth J. Burhanna is Assistant Professor in Libraries and Media Services at Kent State University, where he has served as First-Year Experience Librarian for the past three years. He is the coauthor of *A Practical Guide to Information Literacy Assessment for Academic Librarians* (2007). Among Mr. Burhanna's achievements has been the founding of *Informed Transitions*, a library outreach program that has seen over 450 local high school students visit Kent State annually to help prepare them for college. He also has made important contributions to the Transitioning to College project. He previously worked as Instructional Design Librarian at Cleveland State University. Mr. Burhanna holds a B.A. in English and Masters in Library and Information Science from Kent State University.

Matthew Burrell is a Public Services librarian and Manager of the Memory Collection at Gulf Coast Community College. He graduated from Florida State University with a Master's degree in Library and Information Science and continued at the University of West Florida where he recently completed his Educational Specialist Degree in Education. Matt is also involved in instructing teachers how to effectively use technology in the classroom. He lives on a small farm in North Florida and raises endangered domesticated animals.

Ellysa Stern Cahoy is an Associate Librarian and Assistant Head, Library Learning Services, in the Penn State University Libraries, University Park. A former children's and school librarian, her research interests include studying the instructional bridge between K–12 and public and academic libraries. Ms. Cahoy's article in the March/April 2002 issue of *Knowledge Quest*, "Will Your Students Be Ready for College? Connecting the K–12 and College Standards for Information Literacy," explores this issue. With Lesley Moyo, Ms. Cahoy cofounded the Central Pennsylvania K–16 Information Literacy Network in 2004, an active, local collaborative of school, public, and academic librarians. Ms. Cahoy has also published research on library services for users at a distance, library orientation, and library instruction, and she is the Editor of the ACRL Information Literacy website.

Kirsten J. Clark is the Government Information and Regional Depository Librarian at the University of Minnesota-Twin Cities. Before coming to Minnesota, she worked as Project Manager for the IMLS Grant "Government Information in the 21st Century" at the University of Colorado at Boulder. She is interested in finding new ways to promote government information, especially online education and training.

Gail Clement is a University Librarian at Florida International University, where she serves as Head of the Digital Collections Center and Project Director for the Everglades Digital Library. She has been working in the areas of science information services, electronic publishing, and Web/digital library development for more than fifteen years. Gail teaches and consults in the areas of digital library management and sustainability, copyright management, academic integrity, and electronic publishing. She received her Masters in Library and Information Science from the University of South Florida; Masters of Science in Geology from the University of Oregon; and a B.A. from Carleton College.

Tara L. Coleman is a science librarian at K-State Libraries in Manhattan, Kansas. She is the liaison to the departments of Kinesiology, Human Nutrition, and Statistics and is responsible for library instruction, reference, collection development, and information literacy initiatives. Tara also cocoordinates instruction and outreach initiatives for the K–12 community and contributes to the libraries' blogs. Her research interests include information literacy in Science & Engineering/Technology and online outreach. Tara received her Masters of Library & Information Science from the University of Oklahoma in 2004.

Tomalee Doan is an Associate Professor of Library Science and the Head of the Management & Economics Library in the Krannert School of Management, Purdue

University. She has been at Purdue University since May 2006. Her primary responsibilities include all aspects of managing the library, from staffing, budgeting, collections, information literacy and instruction, interdisciplinary research, and building partnerships with faculty. Her current focus is to transform the Management & Economic Library from a primarily print collection to an electronic delivery of resources in preparation for a major renovation that will enhance the student experience.

Prior to joining Purdue University Libraries, Tomalee was the Library Director at the Kresge Business Library, Stephen Ross School of Business, University of Michigan from 2000 to 2006. During that time, she worked on many initiatives that enhanced the library services to the Business School. In 2003 the Kresge Business Library was recognized for those efforts and received the SLA Business & Finance Centers of Excellence Award in the service category. Tomalee received a B.A. from Indiana University and a Master of Library Information Science degree from Wayne State University.

Annie Downey is the Instruction Unit Head at the University of North Texas Libraries. Previously she worked as the Outreach Librarian, which provided her opportunities to respond to her yearning to connect with students and the community. Her passion lies in developing innovative programming and classes that inspire and excite students about the possibility and wonder of libraries. Annie received her M.L.S. from the University of North Texas in 2005, and she is currently pursuing a Ph.D. in Higher Education.

Lena E. Etuk is an Extension Social Demographer for the Oregon State University Extension Family and Community Development Program and is a faculty member in the Department of Human Development and Family Sciences. Lena holds an M.S. in Sociology from the University of Wisconsin-Madison and a B.S. from Indiana University-Bloomington.

Eric P. Garcia is a Reference & Instructional Services Librarian at California State University, Northridge. Eric is an alumnus of Loyola Marymount University. After completing his Master in History from Pepperdine University and M.L.I.S. from San Jose State University, Eric began working at CSUN in July 2006. He has served as the Interim Outreach Coordinator and is currently the Psychology & Educational Psychology Librarian as well as the bibliographer in the area of law.

Julie A. Gedeon is Assistant Professor and Coordinator of Assessment, Libraries, and Media Services, Kent State University and a TRAILS (Tool for Real-Time Assessment of Information Literacy Skills) project member. She is a founding member of Project SAILS, Standardized Assessment of Information Literacy Skills, an assessment aimed at undergraduate students. Dr. Gedeon analyzes TRAILS data to help with item and assessment refinement and works with the TRAILS team on ongoing development of the tools. She coauthored (with Barbara Schloman) "Creating TRAILS: Tool for Real-Time Assessment of Information Literacy Skills" (*Knowledge Quest*, May/June 2007). Dr. Gedeon has a Ph.D. in evaluation and measurement and an M.L.S., both from Kent State University.

Jennifer Gerke is the Electronic Government Information Librarian at the University of Colorado at Boulder. In addition to her work with the Government Publications Collection, she is also the Co-Principal Investigator for the "Government Information in the 21st Century" grant. Jennifer's research interests are in the electronic arena of information and the impacts on libraries and their patrons.

Mary E. Graham is the Head Librarian at the Arizona State Museum Library, University of Arizona. She is formerly the Librarian of The Heard Museum in Phoenix and a past president of the Art Libraries Society of North America (ARLIS/NA). Her background is in anthropology and field archaeology. She received her M.L.S. from the University of Arizona in 1978.

Thembi Hadebe is a campus librarian at the University of Pretoria in South Africa. She holds a Master's degree in Information Studies from the University of Johannesburg. Her professional interests are information literacy, diversity at the workplace, collection development, and customer services.

Marlene (Marly) Helm is the Assistant Librarian at the Arizona State Museum and adjunct professor at the School of Information Resources and Library Science, University of Arizona. As librarian, she is the principal cataloger for the documentary collections at the museum. As adjunct professor, she teaches cataloging and metadata management. Previously she was a library director and software developer.

Deidra N. Herring is an Education Subject Specialist for Collections, Instruction, and Public Services at The Ohio State University Libraries. She began working at the university in 2005 as a Mary P. Key Resident in the Technical Services Division alongside the Head of the Monographs Department. Deidra received her Masters of Library Science at the University of Illinois at Urbana-Champaign through the LEEP Distance Education Program and a B.S. in Education from Central State University, Wilberforce, Ohio. Deidra's research interests include outreach with juvenile prison libraries in Ohio.

Starr Hoffman is Librarian for Digital Collections at the University of North Texas Libraries. She is responsible for maintaining UNT's Congressional Research Service (CRS) Reports Archive and the CyberCemetery, a NARA-affiliated archive of defunct government websites. Starr received her Master of Library Science and Master of Art History from the University of North Texas and is currently pursuing a Ph.D. in Higher Education. Her research interests include distance learning, digital collections, government documents, library marketing, and graphic novels. She is the author of the Geeky Artist Librarian blog.

Debra Hoffmann is Information Literacy Coordinator for Broome Library at California State University Channel Islands. Debra received a Master of Library and Information Science from UCLA and has been at CSUCI since 2004. Debra's research interests include innovative instruction, creative outreach, lifelong information literacy, and the notion of "library as place." When she's not at the beach or playing volleyball, Debra teaches Research Methods for the English program and puts together lots of cool programs and events for students and faculty.

Yolanda Hood is Assistant Professor and Youth Librarian for Rod Library's Youth Collection at the University of Northern Iowa. Her research areas include children's and young adult literature and library and community collaborations.

Mary Lee Jensen is Assistant Professor and Head of Instructional Services for Libraries and Media Services, Kent State University. She serves on the executive board for the Institute for Library and Information Literacy Education (ILILE) and has been the coordinator for the Transitioning to College project. Ms. Jensen has also been involved in ILILE efforts to incorporate information literacy training into the education curriculum for preservice teachers. She is one of the coauthors of the book, *A Practical Guide to Information Literacy Assessment for Academic Librarians.* Mary Lee has an M.S. in Library Science from Drexel University.

Becky McKay Johnson is Assistant Professor and Outreach Librarian at Texas A&M University Medical Sciences Library. She provides outreach and library services to unaffiliated health care providers in a twenty-two-county region of central Texas. She also coordinates two Go Local projects, linking users of the MedlinePlus consumer health website to local health care providers. Becky has been a hospital and academic medical librarian since she received her M.L.I.S from Louisiana State University in 1992.

Robin Kear is a Reference/Instruction Librarian at the University of Pittsburgh. She holds a Masters in Library and Information Science from San Jose State University and a B.A. in Global Policy Studies from Chatham College. Her professional interests and association activities center on international librarianship, information literacy, and leadership. In 2008 Ms. Kear was named a Mover & Shaker by *Library Journal* and an American Library Association Emerging Leader. She has interned with the United Nations in Nairobi, Kenya, and has conducted a workshop in Vietnam on Library 2.0 and Reference Services.

Hal Kirkwood is an Associate Professor of Library Science and the Associate Head of the Management & Economics Library in the Krannert School of Management, Purdue University. He has been at Purdue University since 1997. His primary responsibilities include coordinating instruction activities, implementing outreach initiatives, staff training, and reference support. His current focus is to assist in transforming the Management & Economics Library to better serve students and faculty.

He has been recipient of the 2003 John H. Moriarty Award for Excellence in Library Service and the 2004–2005 Class of 1922 Helping Students Learn Award. Hal served as chair of the Business & Finance Division of the Special Libraries Association in 2007. Hal received a B.A. from Indiana University and a Master of Library Information Science degree from the University of South Carolina.

Stephanie M. Mathson is Assistant Professor and Instruction/Reference Librarian at the Central Michigan University Charles V. Park Library. Stephanie was appointed to her position at CMU in January 2005, shortly after completing a Masters of Library & Information Science degree at Wayne State University. She earned a B.A. in English and a B.A. in Anthropology at Michigan State University and is currently working on an M.A. in English Language & Literature at CMU.

Alexa Mayo is the Associate Director for Services at the Health Sciences & Human Services Library at the University of Maryland, Baltimore, where she oversees the public services within the library. She received her Master's degree from Simmons College.

Jenny E. McCraw is the Instructional Design Librarian at K-State Libraries in Manhattan, Kansas. She develops online learning tools and resources, teaches library instruction sessions, cocoordinates instruction and outreach initiatives for the K–12 community, and collaborates with other technology units on campus. Jenny's research interests include the use of Web 2.0 technologies for library instruction and outreach, gaming in academic libraries, marketing, and usability. She received her M.S. in Library Science from the University of North Carolina at Chapel Hill in 2007.

Lesley Moyo is an Associate Professor and Director for Library Research and Instructional Services in the University Libraries at Virginia Tech. Her research interests include investigation into the changing roles of academic libraries in serving virtual communities. Ms. Moyo, with Ms. Cahoy, cofounded the Central Pennsylvania K–16 Information Literacy Network in 2004. She has published widely on various areas, including library services for users at a distance, virtual reference services, and impact of technology on library services. She is a member of the Editorial Advisory Board of *The Electronic Library.*

Paula G. Raimondo is the Head of Liaison and Outreach Services at the University of Maryland Health Sciences & Human Services Library in Baltimore. She manages the liaison work between the library and professional schools on campus, as well as the library's outreach efforts to groups and citizens of Maryland. She received her Master's degree in Library Services from Rutgers University.

Emily Rogers is Assistant Professor and Reference Librarian for Instruction at Odum Library, Valdosta State University. Her research interests include faculty collaboration, community reading programs, and higher education and the public sphere.

Robin M. Sabo is Assistant Professor and Reference Librarian/Health Sciences Bibliographer at the Central Michigan University Charles V. Park Library. Robin received a Masters of Library Science degree from Kent State University, an M.S. in Human Nutrition and Food Management from The Ohio State University, and a B.S. in Dietetics from Michigan State University. Before becoming an academic librarian, Robin was employed as corporate librarian in Columbus, Ohio.

Alyce Sadongei (Kiowa/Tohono O'odham) is the Assistant Curator for Native American Relations at the Arizona State Museum, University of Arizona. Previously she worked at the National Museum of the American Indian and the Office of Museum Programs, both at the Smithsonian Institution. She has extensive experience in developing training programs in museum practice and cultural programming for tribal communities.

Joyce Salisbury is the Public Support Specialist for the Reference Department at Park Library at Central Michigan University. Joyce received her Masters of Library and

Information Science in August 2008 from Wayne State University in Detroit, Michigan. She also holds a B.S. in Psychology and an M.A. in History, both from Central Michigan University in Mount Pleasant, Michigan.

Barbara F. Schloman is Professor and Associate Dean for Public Services, Libraries and Media Services, Kent State University, and Project Director for TRAILS, Tool for Real-Time Assessment of Information Literacy Skills. She has been involved with TRAILS development since the beginning (2004) and serves on the executive board for the Institute for Library and Information Literacy Education (ILILE). Dr. Schloman collaborated with a library media specialist on the use of TRAILS in a poster session at the AASL 2007 Annual Conference. She coauthored (with Julie Gedeon) "Creating TRAILS: Tool for Real-Time Assessment of Information Literacy Skills" (*Knowledge Quest*, May/June 2007) and continues to actively direct the ongoing development of TRAILS and work with practitioners to make the tool more useful. Dr. Schloman has a Ph.D. in Health Education from Kent State University and an M.L.S. from the University of Wisconsin, Madison.

Suzanne Sears is head of the Government Documents Department at the University of North Texas Willis Library. Her primary responsibility is to administer the Federal and State of Texas depository collections. Suzanne came to the University of North Texas Libraries after working 23 years for the Tulsa City-County Library. She is passionate about overcoming barriers to accessing government information. Suzanne received her Masters of Library Science from the University of Oklahoma and a B.S. from the University of Tulsa.

Paula Seeger is Circulation Librarian at the University of Minnesota Law Library, supervising the circulation and reserves department, including library outreach, facilities and security, and managing the LexLibris blog. She received her Master of Arts in Library and Information Studies degree from the University of Wisconsin—Madison, and a Master of Arts in Theology and the Arts degree from United Theological Seminary of the Twin Cities (New Brighton, MN). She is active in the Friends of the Library group at her public library, serving as book judge for the Minnesota Book Awards in 2007–2008.

Paula M. Smith is Assistant Librarian at Penn State Abington. She holds a B.S. in Business Administration from LaSalle University and Masters in Library and Information Science from Drexel University. Her professional interests include cultural competencies, the digital and information divide, information literacy, and international librarianship. Paula has served as a volunteer to develop libraries in South Africa and has facilitated a workshop on academic libraries for faculty and administrators in Bangladesh.

Lothar Spang is Librarian IV, Adamany Undergraduate Library, Wayne State University and is responsible for several community outreach initiatives. He also serves as an adjunct professor in the university's Library and Information Science Program, is a frequent contributor to professional journals, and frequently conducts workshops on Information Literacy and grant writing.

Anna Tatro is a Liaison and Outreach Librarian at the University of Maryland Health Sciences & Human Services Library in Baltimore. She works with the faculty, staff, and students of the UMB School of Social Work. Anna received her Master's degree in Library Science from Emporia State University in Kansas.

Toni Tucker is Assistant to the Dean of University Libraries at Illinois State University. Her primary responsibilities include public relations, outreach, development, and grant writing. Toni began working at Illinois State University in 1999; prior to that she was the director of a medical library and college of nursing library for eleven years.

Toni received a Master of Library and Information Science degree from Dominican University, River Forest, Illinois and a Master of Science degree in Education from Purdue University. She is a recent winner of the John Cotton Dana Award and the ACRL Best Practices in Marketing Award. Toni is the incoming chair of the ACRL Marketing Academic and Research Library Committee.

Florence M. Turcotte is Research Services Archivist and Assistant University Librarian in the Department of Special and Area Studies Collections at the George A. Smathers Libraries of the University of Florida. Her primary responsibilities include providing reference and instructional services for manuscript material in Special Collections. She also serves as Curator of Literary Manuscripts and coauthored with her colleague John Nemmers *SPEC Kit 296: Public Services in Special Collections,* published in November 2006 by the Association of Research Libraries. Florence received her Masters of Library and Information Science from the University of South Florida in 2005 and a Masters in Liberal Studies and her B.S. from Georgetown University.

Sandra G. Yee is Dean of the Wayne State University Library System, which includes five libraries and the Library and Information Science Program, an ALA-accredited Library Science master's degree program. She also serves as President of DALNET (Detroit Area Library Network), an eighteen-member multitype library network in Southeastern Michigan that includes the Detroit Public Library, several hospital libraries, the Detroit Institute of Arts Library, and academic libraries. She has been instrumental in the development of community partnerships, especially with cultural institutions and museums.